Future War Technique and Strategy

Future War Technique and Strategy

Capt. (Retd.) Prem Singh

PRASHANT PUBLISHING HOUSE
DELHI-110094

Published by :
PRASHANT PUBLISHING HOUSE
C-34, 28 Foota Road, Gali-3,
West Karwal Nagar, Delhi-110094
Phone : 011-22963970, Mob. : 9810396373, 8826258746
e-mail.: prashantpublishinghouse@gmail.com

Future War Technique and Strategy

First Published 2019

ISBN : 978-93-88526-23-4

PRINTED IN INDIA
Published by Mr. R.K. Jha M/s Prashant Publishing House and Published at H.S. Offset House Press, Delhi.

Preface

Advanced militaries are only just beginning to perceive some of the different factors that may, in time, come to shape the character of future wars. Despite their best efforts, no nation-state can ever be fully prepared for the character of the next war. As such, the potential military applications of emergent technology should not be viewed as a panacea for the chaos, friction, and chance that will continue to define war in the future.

The overt nuclearization in south Asia brought peace and closed the doors for any major conventional war between India and Pakistan. But the Indian military's doctrinal transformation after 1998 threatened the deterrence stability in south Asia. The idea of limited war under the nuclear umbrella which was also known as CSD or proactive military operations compelled Pakistan to develop nuclear tipped low yield battlefield nuclear weapons to deter shallow maneuvers by the Indian army. Later, the Indian military realized that the idea of limited war is risky and it may escalate into a major war. Then, the Indian military came up with sub-conventional warfare strategy in 2012 and later in the 2017 joint armed forces doctrine, India emphasized on the possibility of surgical strikes.

Drone Warfare is a comprehensive look at the growing menace of robotic warfare, with an extensive analysis of who is producing the drones, where they are being used, who 'pilots' these unmanned planes, who are the victims, and what are the legal and moral implications.

As we move forward in the first decade of the 21st century, uncertainty, anxiety and pressures characterise the global security environment. With the disappearance of traditional and easily identifiable security threats the anxieties and fears have increased. The world has come to be dominated by one super-power and the global security agenda tends to be defined in terms of the US interests and perceptions and there is little likelihood of the situation changing in the foreseeable future. The events post 11 September 2001 have created a new security environment in which there is a paradigm shift in defining the nature of conflicts and in understanding the concept of national security. The lines between peace and war have become blurred and a large number of challenges, both military and non-military have become vital national security concerns. International terrorism now occupies an important slot on the security agenda of all nations. All countries affected by this phenomenon, have had to reassess their security estimates in view of the new challenges, to formulate well thought out long-term security strategies. In the Indian context this phenomenon is accentuated by the lack of a national security strategy that can be interpreted by the military to design a well defined national military strategy. Currently both are conspicuous by their absence despite the additional security structures like the National Security Council and the Integrated Defence Staff.

The Indian Army is the third largest army in the world in terms of the sheer number of personnel. However, this description obfuscates the fact that it is not as powerful as one of the world's largest armies. Its capacity to undertake military operations optimally in the multi-domain, technology-dominated battlefield of the future is questionable. The Indian Army essentially remains a force largely organised, equipped and trained to fight wars of the past. Having said that, it is not as if the Army cannot carry out its role and tasks successfully if it is provided the requisite means to do so. And so, it seems almost imperative that the Army be modernised expeditiously if it has to be prepared to take on the security challenges of the future.

This is a reference book. All the matter is just compiled and edited in nature, taken from the various sources which are in public domain.

The book takes us into the emerging arenas of war, including space and cyberspace. It evaluates the impact of technology and shows how dwindling resources and the scourge of global warming can precipitate conflict in the future.

—Editor

Contents

1

Introduction

When the US military prepares to fight its next major war, it won't be planning to fight the insurgents it has faced over the last fifteen years. As China and Russia begin to aggressively project their military might and revisionist ideas, the Pentagon must develop operational concepts aimed at outpacing technologically sophisticated nation-states.

In fact, the alarming reality is that the US military may operate at a local disadvantage in future conflicts. America can no longer assume the military advantage over its enemies on land or at sea—once the bread and butter of US power. China, Russia, and other potential enemies now boast an arsenal of advanced area denial capabilities, electronic warfare tools to disrupt communications, and precision-guided munitions that could stop American aircraft carriers or fighter jets from disabling high-value assets and enabling ground troops to enter the fray. American troops will also face massed precision fires that will threaten US assets in a future war.

The Army has advanced the multi-domain battle concept to respond to this environment, aiming to overcome local threats with small units instead of exposing major assets to anti-access/area denial (A2/AD) systems. Army leaders need to be prepared to rapidly improvise on the battlefield, operating in a world where many recent US advantages, including quickly communicating shifting orders or commands and relaying large amounts of information, are no longer available.

Swarming soldiers may offer the way to open the battlefield against an enemy focused on denying access, scrambling communications, and precisely targeting US forces. The multi-domain concept has generated buzz through its application to networked drones, such as the demonstration DoD's Strategic Capabilities Office conducted on CBS's 60 Minutes this spring, with over one hundred such drones that were able to communicate collectively. Paul Scharre has described UAVs' potential to swarm the enemy. Adapting the concept for infantry tactics will allow US ground forces to dominate in an increasingly contested environment, adding to the doctrinal development of an important niche in multi-domain battle.

NETWORKED SWARMING

John Arquilla and David Ronfeldt define swarming as "engaging an adversary from all directions simultaneously, either with fire or in force." While swarming has the potential to be an effective form of maneuver, it is also the most information-intensive. Sean Edwards built on their theory by dividing swarming into four stages: locate, converge, attack, and disperse. He assessed that swarms require elusiveness and superior situational awareness to evade long-range weapons.

The type of networked swarming Arquilla, Ronfeldt, and Edwards describe has significant advantages over more traditional, linear tactics. Swarming units attack from multiple directions, paralyzing the enemy's ability to decide, respond, and concentrate their efforts. This allows small units to disrupt and potentially destroy larger formations.

SWARMING FOR THE INFANTRY

On its own, information-intensive networked swarming can't work without assured communications. Synthesizing Arquilla and Edward's work with concepts inspired by biology, however, creates an image of a command structure useful in today's fluid information environment. The US military can use rules-based decision making and stigmergy—the use of environmental cues to communicate—to generate self-organizing swarms that function without electronic communications.

Rules-based decision making replaces hierarchical command structures with a pre-determined set of responses to specific situations. Junior leaders' ability to quickly apply these rules instead of relying on their command structure for guidance allows small units to act independently and speed up decision-making cycles. But while rules-based decision making creates troops that do not need direction from their higher headquarters, they still can't organize into swarms or replace electronic communications by themselves. Stigmergy fills that role.

Stigmergy relies on coordinating indirectly through the environment. It can allow swarming units to communicate without using the network. Self-organizing systems in biology rely on proximity to other organisms, pheromone placement, or terrain clues for cues to interact. The same patterns exist in simulated swarms in artificial intelligence. Similarly, small units can use auditory and visual signs to indicate the distance, direction, and concentration of other forces massed on the battlefield. Visual signals like star clusters or fluorescent panels can serve as a more direct form of communication.

Stigmergy-based rules allow units to deduce when to attack, retreat, and how much distance to maintain with other detachments based on the surrounding environment. Relatively simple sets of rules, properly vetted and trained, can allow junior leaders to rapidly self-organize with little to no electronic communication signature to complete a mission.

The Floating Box Ambush, seen in Figure 1, demonstrates the effects of stigmergy and rules-based decision making. The soldiers conducting the ambush are given a simple set of instructions: engage approaching units, retreat when shot at, and return and engage again.

The first soldier begins the ambush by engaging an advancing enemy unit. That typically leads the enemy to respond by firing on that soldier and advancing, prompting the soldier to retreat. As the enemy advances, they move in front of the second soldier, prompting him to engage. At this point, most units under ambush will reorient themselves toward the second shooter. With the enemy unit distracted by the second solider, the first soldier can then reengage, allowing the second shooter to retreat. Neither of those troops need to communicate to pull this off.

Wash, rinse, repeat. The ambushed unit typically switches its attention between both attacking soldiers, taking a significant amount of time to reorient, decide, and act during each recurrence. The unit's confusion will grow if it takes casualties or its vehicles are immobilized. The Army has tried this tactic in training with dizzying effects. One of the authors has seen training units facing this technique quickly become bogged down and disoriented. Two soldiers can often temporarily or permanently divert an entire platoon from their mission, and sometimes inflict a significant number of casualties.

SWARMING AGENTS IN MULTI-DOMAIN BATTLE

Stigmergy for multi-domain battle will expand on this example with more sophisticated rules and environmental cues and more diverse teams. As an example, soldiers can carry small arms, and prioritize attacking dismounted light infantry and soft-skin vehicles. Others may be equipped with anti-tank weapons to attack armored vehicles or strongpoints. Still other units could target A2/AD capabilities and other critical assets such as air defense systems. In line with multi-domain battle's vision, these small units could be the first on the ground to enable follow-on capabilities once an A2/AD network is disabled.

Rules-based decision making and stigmergy are not new ideas. Airborne units during World War II spawned Little Groups of Paratroopers, whose decentralization and initiative allowed them to have an outsized effect on German forces. Soldiers already use less robust versions of this type of decision making. Battle drills prescribe best responses to likely scenarios, including how to react to contact, attack a trench, or enter a building and clear a room.

But swarming uses rules-based decision making and stigmergy in new ways. Rather than serving as a replacement for traditionally structured units, which struggle in communications-denied environments, swarming units can fill a niche in multi-domain battle. Specialized swarming units can operate forward to destroy or disrupt adversaries' electronic warfare capabilities or air and coastal defense systems, creating opportunities for traditionally structured units to exploit with their heavier combined arms punch. This allows swarming units to enable traditional units, while still capitalizing on traditional units' firepower, mobility, and sustainment capabilities.

SWARMING COMMAND STRUCTURES LEVERAGE PROFESSIONALISM

Swarming also capitalizes on the US military's greatest competitive advantage: well-trained and experienced junior leaders. Rigidly clinging to a command structure limits rapid decision making and initiative at lower ranks. Rules-based decision making reverses that tendency and creates an advantage when US forces can't rely on communications. Fortunately, warfare revolves around competitive adaptation, and swarming is about changing military behavior, not technology. It is easier, cheaper, and faster to adapt small-unit tactics, or swarming rules, than it is to adapt technology.

RECOMMENDATIONS

We recommend the military begin experimenting with swarming command structures to assess its viability and determine possible rules. Simulations can allow units to cheaply test different sets of rules, cues, and agent types against soldiers using avatars in real time. Once experimenters have developed sets of rules and a mix of agent types in simulation, they can move to testing swarming units' capabilities in the real world. The Multi-Domain Task Force is designed to experiment with multi-domain concepts, and can evaluate swarming.

The use of swarming at a tactical level is not a new idea. Paratroopers, opposition forces used to train teams, and other small units have used similar techniques for decades. It could potentially, however, become even more valuable as the US Army aims to advance the multi-domain battle concept, specifically taking out high-value assets with denied communications. Technological solutions to assured communications are necessary for larger units to be able to communicate with higher commands and will require constant improvements and investment. However, for specific missions, those systems will be too risky or uncertain to rely on or they may not be worth the risk of signature exposure. The United States should turn to arguably its biggest advantage: junior leaders trained to readily adapt and show initiative in a dynamic environment. Using simple rules-based paradigms, small units can quickly swarm the ground and carry out specific missions without significant risk of detection. By doing so, these forces will enable the joint force to operate in a more contested, more lethal, and more complex world.

MERGING LEVELS OF WAR

The American public's lack of stamina to endure a protracted conflict and their abhorrence of battlefield casualties requires quick, decisive, strategic results. It is the warfighter's quest for immediate strategic results that will force the restructure of the three levels of war. With the help of information technology, joint commanders of the Twenty-first century will be able to efficiently command and control geometrically greater battle spaces at a far greater tempo and confidence level. The amount of uncertainty will be less. The virtually seamless flow of information from the lowest echelons--conceivably individual battalions, ships or aircraft--gives joint commanders a significantly increased knowledge base from which to coordinate, synchronize, and employ forces. This knowledge will be shared nearly simultaneous throughout the chain of command. The force multiplying effect of shared information will be to achieve a greater coherence and unity of effort with significantly fewer casualties. Consequently, actions at every level will instantaneously effect the other and will have the affect of reducing the time between decisions. Furthermore, the trend toward more powerful weapon systems will give rise to tactical elements being employed more often in direct support of strategic objectives. Situational awareness will permit the conduct of simultaneous offensive operations allowing the capability to convert tactical success immediately into decisive strategic results.

In the pursuit of more decisive operations, a great shift in the power to make operational and tactical decisions at one echelon will occur. The desirability of this shift will depend on how senior leaders adapt to the greater responsibility. A goal of joint digitization is to provide a greater assimilation of more information into the warfighting process. This implementation goal will ultimately expand the strategic level's span of control with the streamlining of the operational chain of command. Today, military organizations are generally sized by how much one commander can effectively control. By design, each echelon's commander is better informed to make appropriate decisions concerning his responsibilities. During the late 1980's and early 1990's, an evolution in business management led by the integration of information systems caused an increase in the span of control for a typical senior manager; this subsequently resulted in a flattening of the management structure. Likewise, digitization will provide more senior leaders the information that will permit them to feel comfortable making more judgments that were traditionally left to operational and tactical commanders. As in business, digitization will cause an increase in the span of control at the strategic level and a subsequent greater centralization of command. In the future, digital technology may render our current structure obsolete.

A flatter structure may not be always beneficial. The disadvantage of centralization is the magnitude that each decision potentially has. Mistakes in simple judgment can lead to greater, longer lasting consequences. Since the influence of a strong commander permeates throughout, there may be cases where trusting a single individual's perceptions may be, in the end, very costly in terms of resources, lives, and continued public support.

Another important reason for the merging levels of war is that communication between all echelons is expected to shift dissemination and collection of intelligence, targeting, and other data from hierarchical to a non-hierarchical command structure.

Hierarchial Structure Non-Hierarchial Structure

This internetted command structure undesirably leads to an "diffused command authority." Even today there are indications of just how future technology can alter command approaches within the military. Electronic mail (E-mail) has created a formal, as well as, informal dissemination structure within the Department of Defense. The ease at which an individual can send a courtesy copy or a message to anyone, regardless of position, has placed unusual demands upon an organization's hierarchy. It is easy to interpolate how the future and its promise for "smarter" systems, which are better able to assimilate and display information, can change the traditional needs for hierarchical levels. What is not clear is the effect that these informal lines of communications will have on a command structure during times of conflict.

As technology increases the strategic echelon's span of control, there will be a predictable gravitation to coordinate tactical weapons at the highest possible level; thus, more pressure to flatten or merge the levels of war. Improved war-fighting capabilities which have increased the mobility, dispersion, lethality, and tempo will drive control measures at least to a joint theatre level. Centralized control is needed for synchronization of combat power in order to conserve assets, and prevent fratricide and civilian collateral damage. Weapon systems could be enabled or disabled remotely whether they are on a ship, land or aircraft. It will be possible to control tactical fires and the maneuvers of combat elements to optimize the direct obtainment of the strategic goal. These combat elements will be armed with far more sophisticated direct and indirect munitions with ranges that exceed line of sight. Military professionals saw just a glimpse of technology during Desert Storm. By Twenty-first century standards, Desert Storm will look antiquated, but it illustrates just how complex and how important synchronizing forces are in order to prevent friendly casualties and to insure decisive strategic results.

The significance for future military organizations is that traditional tactical and operational levels will have the same information and same battle space concerns. The need for separation based upon capability to command and control will likely cease to exist in the Twenty-first century. The overall disadvantages of this merging has yet to form. How the senior leadership adapts and structures the resulting organizations will determine the magnitude of the drawbacks.

Diminished Command Prerogatives

Like many problems, the solutions often have undesirable consequences. It is quite possible that digitization upon Twenty-first century military organization will be detrimental to the concept of execution at the lowest level and could lead to over control. With the shared vision resulting from digitization, every one within the chain of command could have access to the same situational information. Theoretically, everyone from the White House, the Joint Staff and CINC Staffs, down to the tactical levels could have access to the same facts. Potentially it could become normal for some operational and tactical level decisions to come from the White House or the Joint Staff. The United States military requires leaders that possess boldness and initiative to act on one's own judgment. These traits within our leaders make the U.S. military a formidable force. Digitization may unintentionally affect the relationship between echelons by limiting the organization's initiative, ingenuity, and inventiveness through constant monitoring by superiors.

No one likes to have someone looking over their shoulder as they work. Increased theatre awareness and the ability to automatically transfer databases will result in the expansion and availability of on-line information. This may very likely result in a great deal of second guessing by senior commanders and staff. Invariably during a crisis, a subordinate commander who is closer to the action will select a different course of action than that of the senior commander. Should the superior commander second guess and redirect the effort or sit on his hands and wait it out? The challenge for senior leaders in the future will be curtailing their inclinations and allowing subordinate leaders their prerogatives. When a commander thinks he has all the facts, allowing a subordinate his prerogatives by not interfering goes against the "zero defects" culture that permeates the military today; unfortunately, there is no evidence that the future culture will be any different.

Information technology will also find it hard to digitize what is in the commander's head and what he feels--the kind of intangible awareness that comes from being close and near the area of operation. Our forces will fight the way they train. There is a danger that factors that cannot be quantified will be disregarded and our commanders not near the action will be "partly conditioned" by the technical tools available to them. For example, during a peacetime exercise, based on intuition or other undigitizable information, a commander may want to deviate from a plan during its execution. How many times will a commander accept corrections or challenges, by a "all-knowing" higher commander or superior's staff. Echelons above may believe they understand and have the "correct" bigger picture and demand adherence to previously coordinated plans or only minor tweaks to an existing plan.

There are very few commanders, believing they have the right situational information, that can allow a subordinate to act contrary or independently to their expectations without at least making an inquiry. Sure, the subordinate commander could explain and defend his actions and even prevail; however, a sense of autonomy, pride and creativeness is predictably lost by a subordinate each time it occurs. It doesn't take many real-time corrections or constant challenges by a boss to stifle boldness and initiative. It might be hard for today's leaders to appreciate the loss of initiative and boldness caused by digitization, since they have had these traits nurtured into them throughout their careers. The concern should be about the generation of leaders who grow up with extensive and perhaps constant oversight and monitoring.

The Marines "Warfighting" manual, FMFM 1, has recognized this concern and has succinctly stated, "Equipment that permits over control of units in battle is in conflict with the Marine Corps's philosophy of command and is not justifiable." The digitization technology of the Twenty-first century, by obtaining massive situational awareness, may have the unintended consequence of permitting commanders too much control. The military services could be entering into a new era of electronic micro-management.

The pressure to micro-manage, to ask questions, and to second guess field commander's decisions will be very high. Consider a CINC or a Joint

Task Force commander, with the military and civilian leadership in Washington D.C. and the media doggedly pursuing in "real time" their individual stories, demanding to know status and planned intentions. The pressures will be enormous for information. With instantaneous civilian global information networks, such as CNN and broadcast network news, our civilian population has become more addicted to war news. For the future, the "CNN war leads public and leaders to define political events in terms of the video clips and sound bites that compose TV news images." A causal effect of this coverage is that the available reaction time to events for civilian policy makers is going to decrease because of amplified public interest. The American people are going to demand more information from their senior civilian and military leaders. Accordingly, policy makers are going to want to know more and want to know it sooner.

The pressure upon senior military leaders to supply only the most accurate information and not to publicly embarrass themselves, as well as their civilian leaders, will be immense. The future joint leader and corresponding staff are going to be forced to make larger number of inquiries to satisfy the media and public. Situational awareness through digital technology will be the enabling technology for maintaining public support for the military, as well as keeping the political leadership from embarrassment.

A good counter argument might be that unintrusive electronic queries will be extensively used and the distraction will be very minor. This argument holds well, if the question is strictly qualitative in nature, is an acceptable answer, or doesn't require explanations. Unfortunately, it is more likely that one answer will precipitate several more questions that may or may not be available unobtrusively through an electronic data base. Digitization might inadvertently and unanticipatedly increase outside distractions through the answering of endless questions up the chain of command. On the positive side, it is easy to see how this kind of uncontrolled eavesdropping by a higher level staff can lead to better situational awareness and better serve a joint commander. Sadly, it is hard to imagine how unencumbered, direct access to planning and execution information by a superior and his staff, without the subordinate's personal spin, could have a positive effect on the hard-charging, self-motivated commander.

One could argue that the higher echelons will not be interested in information that is specific and in detail. It is more likely that the smaller Twenty-first century force structure will limit the options available to our senior leaders. Consequently, leaders will require more specific information in order to make decisions. For example, the Joint Staff is currently in the process of developing and fielding the first phase of the Global Command

and Control System (GCCS). ADM Owens, Vice Chairman, Joint Chief of Staff was given a demonstration of the Global Status of Resources and Training System (GSORTS). While being impressed with its capability to easily understand air base and other readiness ratings, he indicated it would be nice to also receive the aircraft availability by individual weapon's load, including Precision Guided Munitions (PGMs), and by sensors in a particular area of responsibility. What is significant is not that the Admiral wanted to know this information, but how the information going to be used at the strategic level. What if the information is not as expected or quantifiably correct? Very few leaders like to be surprised, and with the relatively smaller force structure, specifics are becoming very important.

Another concern is whether our warfighters will be prepared for the avalanche of questions. It cannot be discounted that routine questions from higher echelons tend to increase exponentially in importance the farther down the chain of command they propagate. So the lower echeloned, smaller staffed, war-fighting organizations are less prepared to handle queries and are distracted disproportionately.

Often in discussions about digitization and automation, it is surmised that staff sizes will decrease in numbers. It is quite possible that staff sizes may need to increase--not decrease. The requirement for information is compounded by the problem that during peace there is a tendency to become over organized and more bureaucratic in structure. This tendency can be summarized as the "need-to-know everything" syndrome. The propensity to explain and track data is gradually taking up more of the commander's and staff's time. As our services become more complex, more records and information are required to be processed and the demand for support staff increases. Large bureaucratic staffs do not normally foster and facilitate initiative and boldness in subordinate organizations.

The military has already experienced the unintended consequences of automation when it comes to bureaucratic staffwork. Consider how the word processor has streamlined typing and the electronic mailing of documents and messages. As stated before, automated offices are able to effortlessly and with efficiency send documents and E-mail via Local Area Networks and, through MILNET, between organizations. These tools obviously save time through simplifying distribution, increasing information transfers between organizations, thereby decreasing the number of secretaries and military clerks. However, the demand for more usable information by senior decision makers has also increased, requiring staff officers to spend greater portions of their time typing questions and answers.

With the increase in productivity, automation has fostered an increase in reporting and information generation. It is true that reports and briefs are now written easily on computers, but organizations tend now to spend more time reworking letters and briefing charts to achieve limited gains in redrafts and minor formatting. The reworking does not necessarily result in better content but only ensures cosmetically perfect documents. The labor saving and time saving office computer has the unintended consequence of creating more work. Computers have increased the military staffs work load and have unintentionally required more staff, not less.

Increased Fragility

General Sullivan, Chief of Staff, Army, states technology driven battle space awareness "can provide us with lighter, more effective and more lethal weapon systems to offset our smaller force structure." But, one also must consider that as these force multiplying systems are effected by attritions of war, their corresponding impact upon the force is an equally multiplying loss. Digital technologies provide a tremendous capability, however, they must be weighted cautiously against their vulnerabilities.

The use of digital technology has consequences that are paradoxical in nature. While it is true that the implementation of more advanced sensor-to-weapon systems will give better situational awareness, help minimize fratricide and better focus combat power, they can also be our Achilles heel. There is the concern whether the new electronic systems will have the resilience to absorb shocks and withstand perturbations associated with the realities of modern war. The more advanced the equipment the more complex it becomes. Generally, the more complex the system, the less reliable, and the harder or longer it takes to repair.

A possible solution to the attrition issue is the use of redundancy in the digital architecture. Redundancy is not likely to protect the force as technology is being looked upon by our senior leaders to help mitigate the smaller force structure. It is a reality that the U. S. military will always be dependent upon finite amounts of specialized electronic equipment that will invariably not be easily replaced nor repaired.

There are other compounding effects of attrition, such as the digital technologies dependence upon reliable communication architectures. It is the dependence and reliance of electronically synthesized data from widely dispersed systems that makes communications the most vulnerable segment. The greatest threat to the entire digitization architecture is the lack of robust, redundant communications paths. For example, Desert Storm validated the notion that a CONUS based force projection strategy, with its anticipated tempo is dependent upon assured satellite communications for both inter- and intra-theatre communications irrespective of use on land or sea. Above the tactical level of war, it is anticipated for the Twenty-first century that medium data rates for the military, as well as civilian satellite systems, will be vulnerable to jamming by today's low cost technology. Since digital communications demands are going to be predictably greater than their capacity, there will be no redundancy nor unused capacity. Even today, it is doctrine not to normally keep communication equipment in reserve. Also, key communications equipment is subject to targeting through old-fashioned direct or indirect fires. An unsophisticated enemy sharp-shooter could easily fire a well placed bullet and take out the feed to a critical satellite or a microwave antenna. This would effectively disrupt the digital architecture with devastating consequences to the command and control process. Communications will be the weakest link for the future's dispersed digitized systems.

There is a trend growing within the U.S. military to use commercially available off-the shelf technology that is generally not designed to Military Standards nor for ease of trouble shooting. An unintentional result of using the less rugged commercial electronic equipment is it will require warfighting organizations to have near-by repairmen and large stocks within theatre of specialized electronic repair parts. Otherwise, replenishment could become a problem since strategic mobility will always be at a premium during a crisis.

Repair parts may not always be available. A CONUS based support structure assumes that the tempo at which critical items are used and destroyed will not exceed the rate at which they are being replaced. If tradition holds, then the military will keep electronic equipment beyond normal commercial applications. CONUS depots will have to have on-hand the repair parts since industry does not normally keep the production lines of specialized nor dated electronic designs operating. Leaders will need to take into account and understand the perishability and limited availability of electronic equipment.

Lack of timely repair could contribute to the increased fragility of the force. The advanced equipment of the future, whether it be built to commercial or military standards, will require a greater level of maintenance expertise. The philosophy of using built-in diagnostic and automatic check-out equipment does design complexity away from the operator; however, repair responsibilities dramatically shift to maintenance personnel. Repairing systems in the forward areas will be more difficult and there will be a greater tendency to evacuate equipment for repairs to the depots; thus increasing the time to repair. Based on complexity, it can be anticipated that digital electronic systems are going to have a much longer logistics tail than we have today.

Our force structure will likely have a critical shortage of qualified electronic technicians. Consider the same scenario of equipment damaged by a "low-tech" sharpshooter. What if the shooter decides to wait around to kill the skilled operator or maintenance person conducting the repair? Skilled repairmen will not be replaced easily. Maintenance personnel of the future will require more extensive and sophisticated training than today's technicians, since the systems will be more intricate. As the armed forces continue to compete against educational institutions and private corporations for the limited number of qualified 17-24 year-olds, it is going to be a challenge to keep qualified personnel skilled in electronics. Even the reliance on dedicated and first-rate National Guard and Reserve units is optimistic. Units meant to augment during national emergencies may not be able to keep operator and repair personnel up to warfighting standards.

The implication--"there will be time for training after the troops are assembled--is virtually over." It is not quantitatively known whether the rate of replacement of critical specialty skills will be able to keep pace, but one has only to look at where we are, traditionally short of technical specialists today. As during Desert Storm, it will be common for the Services to depend upon civilian technicians in forward deployed areas for maintenance and repair, due to the maintenance complexity of electronic equipment and the lack of qualified military personnel. It is possible that demographics, and sociopolitical educational realities, might just be the limiting factors of the Twenty-first century digitized force. The demand for "high-tech" personnel is going to go up--not down.

Another concern for the future is that we will depend more upon our allies for support. As the United States modernizes its forces with the latest electronic gadgetry, will our allies be willing to invest in the same kinds of equipment, or will we be willing to sell or give it to them' By digitizing everything from Command and Control to weapons systems, they might make it impossible to be electronically interoperable within a theatre with our coalition partners.

2

Future Space Warfare

Space warfare is combat that takes place in outer space, i.e. outside the atmosphere. Space warfare therefore includes *ground-to-space warfare*, such as attacking satellites from the Earth, as well as *space-to-space warfare*, such as satellites attacking satellites. It does not include the use of satellites for espionage, surveillance, or military communications, however useful those activities might be. It does not technically include *space-to-ground warfare*, where orbital objects attack ground, sea or air targets directly, but the public and media frequently use the term to include any conflict which includes space as a theatre of operations, regardless of the intended target. For example, a rapid delivery system in which troops are deployed from orbit might be described as "space warfare," even though the military uses the term as described above.

A film was produced by the U.S. Military in the early 1960s called *Space and National Security* which depicted space warfare. From 1985 to 2002 there was a United States Space Command, which in 2002 merged with the United States Strategic Command. There is a Russian Space Force, which was established on August 10, 1992, and which became an independent section of the Russian military on June 1, 2001. Only a few incidents of space warfare have occurred in world history, and all were training missions, as opposed to actions against real opposing forces. In the mid-1980s a USAF pilot in an F-15 successfully shot down the P78-1, a communications satellite in a 345 mile (555 km) orbit.

In 2007 the People's Republic of China used a missile system to destroy one of its obsolete satellites, and in 2008 the United States similarly destroyed its malfunctioning satellite USA 193. To date, there have been no human casualties resulting from conflict in space, nor has any ground target been successfully neutralized from orbit. International treaties governing space limit or regulate conflicts in space and limit the installation of weapon systems, especially nuclear weapons.

History

Early efforts to conduct space warfare were directed at space-to-space warfare, as ground-to-space systems were considered to be too slow and too isolated by Earth's atmosphere and gravity to be effective. The history of active space warfare development goes back to the 1960s when the Soviet Union began the Almaz project, a project designed to give them the ability to do on-orbit inspections of satellites and destroy them if needed. Similar planning in the United States took the form of the Blue Gemini project, which consisted of modified Gemini capsules that would be able to deploy weapons and perform surveillance. One early test of electronic space warfare to ok place in 1963 when the United States exploded a ground-launched nuclear weapon in space to test the effects of an electromagnetic pulse. The result was a deactivation of many then-orbiting satellites, both American and Soviet. The deleterious and unfocused effects of the EMP test led to the banning of nuclear weapons in space in the Outer Space Treaty of 1968.

1970s–1980s

Through the 1970s, the Soviet Union continued their project and test-fired a cannon to test space station defence. This was considered too dangerous to do with a crew on board, however, so the test was conducted after the crew had returned to Earth. Space warfare strongly influenced the final design of the United States Space Shuttle. The distinctive delta wing shape was needed if the shuttle were to launch a military payload towards the Soviet Union and perform an immediate de-orbit after one rotation to avoid being shot down. Both the Soviets and the United States developed anti-satellite weaponry designed to shoot down satellites. While early efforts paralleled other space-to-space warfare concepts, the United States was able in the 1980s to develop ground-to-space laser anti-satellite weapons. None of these systems are known to be active today; however, a less powerful civilian version of the ground-to-space laser system is commonly used in the astronomical technique of adaptive optics.

2000s

China successfully tested a ballistic missile-launched anti-satellite weapon on January 11, 2007. This resulted in harsh criticism from the United States of America, Britain, and Japan.

Space warfare system

A space system has three segments, each of which, in principle, offers opportunities for attack to an enemy. The system comprises: (i) the satellite, perhaps the constellation of satellites in orbit; (ii) the up and down links to and from the orbiting vehicle, commands from the ground stations and information flow from the satellite; (iii) and the ground station that controls the behaviour of the satellite and distributes its information to the users."

MILITARY TECHNOLOGY IN SPACE WEAPONS

On Tuesday April 24 at 7pm Global Network (GN, Global Network against Weapons and Nuclear Power in Space) members and supporters gathered at the Continuing Education Building of the University of New Mexico to protest. Just a few days previously the campus paper had announced the award of a 'defence' grant to its Electrical and Computer Engineering department for work on a super laser weapon project.

Also, just a few blocks away at UNM's Institute for Space and Nuclear Studies, work is being carried out on nuclear power supplies for space vehicles and platforms. What have these two projects in common? The answer lies in the Space-Based Laser Integrated Flight Experiment, which forms what George Bush calls the "next generation weaponry" and is at the heart of our campaign against "weapons and nuclear power in space". Part of the 'experiment' is to build a Space-Based Laser Readiness Demonstrator - this is a scaled down version (at an estimated cost of $1. billion) of the proposed weapon system which would eventually be deployed for theater ballistic missile defense and as an anti-satellite weapon.

If the SBL IFX is successful, the US Department of Defense will decide whether to deploy a fully operational network of 20-30 laser battle stations giving global coverage. The first launch of an operational system could occur in 2020 and it could take several years to launch the full constellation of spacecraft around Earth. The Pentagon estimates that the total SBL program will cost $30 billion.

Why the nuclear connection? Any pace-based laser will require tremendous amounts of power and, as a study commissioned by the US Congress notes "nuclear reactors thus remain the only known long-lived, compact source able to supply military space forces with electric power"... nuclear reactors "could meet multimegawatt needs of space-based lasers, neutral particle beams, mass drivers, and railguns."

Also - New World Vistas: Air And Space Power For The 2lst Century, states: "In the next two decades, new technologies will allow the fielding of space-based weapons of devastating effectiveness... These advances will enable lasers with reasonable mass and cost to effect very many kills." But "power limitations... currently make large space-based radars and space-based weapons relatively unfeasible... A natural technology to enable high power is nuclear power in space." This is the reason why nuclear power is being developed for use in outer space. So - the development of a SBL is already well underway - and forms a major part of the US Space Command plans to "dominate" and "master" space. As international weapons expert John Pike has said:

> *"Whoever controls space has control of Earth... the United States is unable to resist it. If the U.S. is in a position to control Earth from outer space, there's nothing to stop us. Of course we're going to do it."*

In January this year US Defense Secretary Donald Rumsfeld spoke of a "space Pearl Harbor" and a commission he formerly headed unveiled a report calling for tighter security for American space systems. "The US... needs to take seriously the possibility of an attack on US space systems," said the report "... The US is more dependent on space than any other nation" and the report called for a 'technological push' to foil threats from foreign nations or terrorists.

However, as reported in the Spring 2001 GN Newsletter, the environmental assessment for the SBL refers to the possibility of a catastrophic explosion that could result in a sudden release of a large quantity of toxic materials and/or destruction of surrounding structures with additional environmental consequences - although no reason for such an assessment of risk is given. Just another reason why the SBL is nicknamed "Death Star". It is a frighteningly ambitious component of Star Wars to be used as a boost-phase missile interceptor and satellite destroyer

Boost-Phase Missile Interception

Lasers are very attractive to the military because they travel so fast - at the speed of light. Therefore they are being seriously considered for intercepting missiles during their boost-phase. Apart from the SBL, two other methods of achieving this with lasers are currently being funded - airborne and ground based High Energy Laser systems. Of course, one major difficulty with this approach (apart from the fact that it might be technically difficult - if not impossible - and extremely expensive) is that boost-phase defences would break the ABM Treaty (if it still exists at the time of this presentation!). However - as we know - a number of influential US generals and politicians believe that the laser weapon provides such a valuable defense that it is worth abrogating the treaty.

The stated advantages of a boost-phase system for Ballistic Missile Defence Systems are that it would:

- provide another tier of missile defence;
- remove the problem of debris falling over the target area (as occurs with "terminal intercept");
- prevent the deployment of multiple warheads;
- does not require the ability to differentiate between war-heads and decoys;
- would deter the use of payloads through threat of "country of origin impact of debris".

It also, of course, enhances the US first strike capability and its ability to knock out other nation's space hardware. The SBL can also be used for NMD as well as TMD - in fact strategic missiles would be more vulnerable to laser attack in boost phase than theatre missiles because of their longer boost times. They also have higher burn-out altitudes which reduces the atmospheric effects that would interfere with laser beam propagation from space.

An alternative space based system would incorporate fewer SBL platforms (perhaps 3) with a number of orbiting relay mirrors (perhaps 24) to direct the beams. A number of configurations are possible and this type of configuration is favoured by many military.

Military Lasers

The Air Force, Army and Navy all started working on lasers in the mid-1960s, and the idea of a SBL has been around since 1977. Initial tests involve a megawatt-class chemical laser with a large, multi-segmented mirror that unfurls and locks into place to create a 13-foot (4-meter) diameter reflecting surface. The entire spacecraft would weigh between 45,000 and 50,000 pounds (20,455 and 22,700 kilograms). The competing lasers are hydrogen fluoride (HF), deuterium fluoride (DF), and chemical oxygen iodine (COIL).

The HF laser uses atomic fluorine and molecular hydrogen to produce excited hydrogen fluorine molecules producing several simultaneous wavelengths in the range of 2. - 2. microns. At these wavelengths the beam is mostly absorbed by the earth's atmosphere and can only be used above the earth's atmosphere e.g. for the SBL. A HF laser has been test fired at the TRW San Juan Capistrano test facility in California.

The DF laser uses deuterium (an isotope of hydrogen) and atomic fluorine. Longer wavelength laser light than for HF lasers is produced (3. - 4 microns), giving better transmission through the atmosphere but requiring larger optical surfaces to shape and focus the beam. The Chemical Oxygen Iodine Laser (COIL) was developed at the Air Force Research Laboratory in Albuquerque in 1977. It is the basis of the $1. billion Air Force Airborne Laser Attack Aircraft - scheduled for anti-missile tests in 2003.

On October 1997 the Pentagon conducted a "laser dazzler" test against one of its satellites using the Army's MIRACL DF laser (Mid-Infrared Advanced Chemical Laser) based at White Sands Missile Range, N.M. In 1996 a MIRACL laser shot down a rocket at the same site.

A new, lightweight, "all gas" Iodine Laser, or AGIL has also been developed by the Air Force Research Lab. This laser uses nitrogen chloride and iodine which are mixed in a vacuum chamber. AGIL has a better atmospheric transmission, which is important for a laser weapon required to reach targets in the atmosphere or even near the surface of the Earth. A basic weapon-size AGIL laser will take at least until 2003 to develop, demonstrate and test.

The Army's Tactical High Energy Laser (THEL) system is designed by a team led by TRW Corp. After the war in Lebanon in April 1996, Israel was promised by the Clinton administration that the U.S. would help develop a laser-based anti-missile system capable of destroying incoming Katyusha rockets. The US Army and the Israeli Ministry of Defense paid weapons contractor TRW $200 million to build a HF laser to generate a powerful infrared beam that can pass through the atmosphere.

On 6 June 2000 the THEL intercepted and destroyed an armed Russian made Katyusha rocket at White Sands Missile Range, N.M. and on Aug. 28 and Sept 14 the demonstrator shot down two rockets launched in succession. The system detected the 10 foot long, 5 inch diameter rocket with its radar before shooting it down. THEL has a range of about 12 miles and costs about $3,000 per destroyed rocket to use.

The U.S. military's first high energy weapon is likely to be the Airborne Laser mounted on a Boeing 747, it is being designed to acquire, track, and destroy theatre ballistic missiles. The system is expected to be deployed in 10 years. The Air Force has proposed spending $11 billion to develop a fleet of seven airborne lasers that could be used for battlefield anti-missile defense at a cost of about $10,000 per shot, based on the price of the laser fuel.

Last month Raytheon Electronic Systems, a subcontractor to Lockheed Martin Space Systems, carried out a 'first light' test of the Track Illuminator Laser (TILL) at the High Energy Laser Centre in El Segundo in California. The TILL is part of the Beam Control/Fire Control system for the US Air Force's Airborne Laser (ABL) programme, which will aim and fire a high-energy laser at a target missile in its boost phase.

However, also last month Nathan Kopeika of Ben-Gurion University told a conference in Florida that he believes engineers working on the Airborne Laser (ABL) project have overlooked the effect of tiny dust particles in the atmosphere, called aerosols. These could scatter and weaken the laser beam, making it incapable of destroying incoming missiles. "We found that, after a propagation of 100 kilometres, aerosols can widen a laser beam up to a cross section one kilometre wide—several orders of magnitude worse than optical turbulence," he said.

The Space Based Laser represents the ultimate in current military thinking about space weaponry and demonstrates the extent to which the US Space Command is prepared to go to realize their vision of domination. We must continue to bring these issues to the attention of the citizens of the world - this is no way to spend our limited resources, no way to increase global security, no way to take our first steps outside our own planet. We must strive to keep space for peace.

On 21 December, 2000, the Stennis Space Center, Mississippi, was selected as the site of the SBL performance test facility. Local people will be holding a vigil at the site on 12 May and on 13 October there will be an action at Stennis as part of the GN International Day of Action.

BATTLE-SPACE AWARENESS

The potential of new military technologies to reduce the "fog or war" could change the way wars are fought. Sensors in satellites, manned aircraft, or unmanned aerial vehicles (UAVs) can now monitor virtually everything that is going on in a particular battle area, dramatically improving battlespace awareness resulting in complete "situational awareness" (information of own and enemy troops, terrain and weather characteristics) of commanders at various levels.

Improvements in the GPS satellite navigation network of the US, which now presumably have twenty-eight satellites, compared to sixteen during the 1991 Gulf War, have dramatically improved space-based sensor capabilities. Depending on the nature of the terrain, America's Joint Surveillance Target Attack Radar System (JSTARS), an airborne ground surveillance system, can display the position of vehicles in any weather within an area of two hundred square kilometers. JSTARS upgrades will enable these aircraft to locate, track, and identify vehicles even in mountainous terrain. For surveillance of the airspace, airborne warning and control system (AWACS) aircraft provide surveillance capabilities. The Indian Air Force (IAF) is reported to be acquiring the PHALCON system mounted on Russian IL-76 aircraft from Israel while Pakistan is reported to be acquiring the ERIEYE, airborne early warning and control system (AEW&C) system from Sweden. In view of the future threats and challenges India should also be examining an airborne ground surveillance system linked to a satellite navigation network of defence satellites.

Unarmed aerial vehicles (UAVs) for strategic roles are another area of development which promises to revolutionise surveillance capabilities. The US armed forces are also using them for combat role. Their mediumaltitude, long-endurance Predator UAV and the high-altitude Global Hawk UAV can loiter on station for twenty-four hours or more and provide specific imagery within a few minutes of the request. Both have been tried out in operations in Afghanistan and in Iraq. Indian armed forces are in a nascent stage in this context. They have acquired the Searcher and the Heron UAVs from Israel and have developed Nishant indigenously but these are designed purely for tactical surveillance. Induction of unarmed combat aerial vehicles (UCAVs) would become mandatory in the future for the variety of challenges that are likely to face India in the plains as well as and in the mountains. India also must learn to fight without necessarily putting boots on the ground on all occasions. Strategic and operational compulsions may dictate adoption of such methods.

Command and Control Architecture

The most significant technology in the current RMA is the one which increases battle-space awareness. Enhanced awareness can only be acquired by "digitising" the battlefield. That is to say, digital technology is built into aircraft, tanks, artillery, and individual soldier systems, with the intention of providing commanders with "situational awareness", an instantaneous and complete picture of the battlefield. The US army has already fielded it first digitised division, the Fourth Infantry Division (Mechanised) in Iraq. Enhancing battle-space awareness together with a command and control architecture to act on information received requires advanced command, control, communications, computers and intelligence processing (C4I) systems. Automation of command and control systems, have incrementally moved from C3I, to C4I, C4 ISR (SR stands for surveillance and reconnaissance) and now C4I2 (Intelligence and Interoperability) SR in order to meet the demand for real time, robust, reliable and efficient command and control systems. By reducing the information-decision-action loop to a matter of minutes, advanced command and control systems have the potential to allow a commander to control a battle from one moment to the next. This will also result in "information dominance" of the battlefield and confer battle-winning advantages.

A recent interview of the Director General Information Systems (DGIS) of the Indian Army, conducted by the author, and published in SP's Land Forces 4 of 2008, is revealing regarding our aspirations and the extent of progress in the army which is also somewhat indicative of the overall progress in this field. The DGIS states:

"Indian Army is in a phase of transition from conventional warfare to information enabled warfare i.e. from platform centric to network centric warfare. The full realisation of any such revolution is possible only with technological development, organisational adaptation, and most importantly a national will. An effective and technologically sound IT force along with robust communication networks has been created to facilitate real time sharing of information and quick decision making so as to achieve information superiority.

A road map has been formulated by which we can progress steadily towards being a potent IT force. We have identified the development of C4I 2 systems as a major thrust area for modernisation of our army. Development and fielding of automated operational and information systems for various levels of operations from Army Headquarters to Battalion headquarters to individual soldiers are in progress.

Command Information and Decision Support System (CIDSS), Artillery Command, Control and Computer System (ACCCS), Battlefield Support System (BSS), Air Defence Control and Reporting System, and Battle Management System (BMS) are the major projects under development. Integrated together with requisite communications, these systems will provide near real time "Sensor to Shooter" links to make army a network centric force.

Interoperability between the three Services is a problem facing not only the Indian Army but many other armies the world over. Since the systems were conceived and developed in stand alone modes, their integration into a system of systems in a seamless manner is a technological challenge. We are working in the direction finding appropriate solutions to that and a common network centric operations philosophy is being worked out. The integration at Headquarters Integrated Defence Staff level is ensuring the interoperability and synergy at the inter-services level." Progress in most projects mentioned above is very slow and the interoperability with other services is presently not on the horizon. Therefore time critical targets will inevitably suffer from delayed engagement. Limited technological comprehension at higher levels, short tenures of project managers due to career enhancement requirements of the armed forces, inadequate private industry participation and Army's natural conservatism in taking advice from non-government sources, are some of the drawbacks which are adversely affecting the entire process of transformation.

MILITARY SPACE TECHNOLOGY

One has to look to beyond forefront military space technologies in order to begin to map the future of space warfare. This is partly due to the fact that in recent years, research and development partnerships related to sensitive military space systems and dual-use commercial systems have grown broader and more inclusive. This trend has resulted in greater access for the United States to talented minds from all over the world and low-cost scientific contributions from university-based researchers and small commercial operations. It has also resulted in a greater probability for technologies developed in the U.S. to leak outside its borders. The realignment of the global economy stands to further shift the international balance of space power in the years to come. For nations that possess the relative wealth, infrastructure, and knowledge to develop space warfare technologies, their ability to become a leading military space power requires only the will to do so. The "brain drain" that hampered the space programs of many nations in decades past is weighing less on them today. The stagnancy of foreign economies that resulted in a flood of scientific minds to the U.S. is slowly ebbing, as many are now returning home to profitable jobs in booming defence and space industries.

This situation is compounded by increased competition in the launch services industry, which has resulted in reduced costs to place assets into orbit, as well as a decrease in the size and weight of satellites and space systems—developments that are conducive to space warfare. Consequently, access to space is no longer limited to nations with massive military budgets. In this rapidly changing environment, the greatest influence on the development of space warfare may rest on our ever-growing dependency upon satellites—for both military and commercial purposes—and their inherent vulnerabilities.

Furthermore, as we venture forward into a globalized security environment fueled by advances in technologies such as directed energy (DE) systems, artificial intelligence (AI), and nanomanufacturing, both the warfighter and the diplomat will be presented with new tools to respond to security crises.

Military space technologies currently in development are the precursor to a world where threats can be neutralized at the speed of light and conflicts may escalate at a rate too fast to curtail.

Accordingly, adjustments will soon have to be made across the entire spectrum of diplomatic and military affairs. If we fail to draft international treaties now that are in line with the pace of advancements in military space technology, a global technology free-for-all could result. This could contribute to a climate in which a spacefaring nation such as the U.S. would be bound to engage in a constant race against itself in order to maintain an effective defensive capability. The purpose of the following military space technology forecast and analysis is to provide new insights and specific recommendations that might protect peaceful cooperation in outer space. This forecast assumes that there are no binding constraints from international treaties. It depicts the current and future state of science related to military space systems, specifically systems that could lead to scenarios that could be precursors to or causes of warfare in space.

In the years leading up to 2020, tensions among military space powers have been mounting. This has been due, in part, to broad-spectrum advances that have materialized internationally in the "Five Ds" of counter-space operations: Deception, Disruption, Denial, Degradation, and Destruction. Even as nations flaunt their military space abilities as a means of intimidating and deterring space rivals, instances of space systems failures, though still uncommon, are slowly rising due to space-warfare systems testing and the increasing amount of space debris. Space systems failures in this new era are triggering accusations of systems disruption and sabotage between nations. The means to achieve an offensive and defensive military space capability in this heady space environment can be found in various force-multiplying arenas of technology.

2020

We enter 2020 to find that the disparities that existed in decades past regarding global space warfare capabilities have been fundamentally and irreversibly altered. Many leading nations are now operating on a near-level playing field. Complementary technologies are driving one another's progress; for example, as robotics concepts top out and undergo a momentary pause, they are soon catapulted ahead by explosive growth in the field of supercomputing.

The arrival and subsequent establishment of strong artificial intelligence is approaching. Key strategists of military space warfare systems are chasing full-spectrum, real-time, and seamless situational awareness of sea, ground, air, and space. The world's brightest minds are reaching new heights as human intelligence is fused with intelligent agents and neural networks. These are the systems that will deliver humanity to the next echelon as nations become increasingly reliant on AI systems and their ability to process a now humanly unmanageable stream of information–a torrent to which our military is now inextricably connected.

The five theaters of combat: Cyber, Space, Air, Land, and Sea, now resemble a unified battlesphere. The international space community is being led by drivers such as the still plummeting cost of computational power, the continued free exchange of knowledge, and the refinement of nanomaterials applications, which are resulting in stronger, lighter, faster and more responsive space systems. Featured most prominently in this transition process is the influence of the smaller commercial space systems companies and non-military R&D providers, such as universities.

The roles of large military and governmental-based, space-systems providers have been challenged effectively by the private space industry. This challenge was inspired in part by successes in the fields of launch services, satellite development, and niche emerging systems. During this era, the commercial launch industry in the United States is now spending as much as four times the total annual budget of NASA, with wide spread commercial space travel seeming more plausible than ever.

The threat spectrum for potential space-attack scenarios is no longer a distant hypothesis, nor does it seem an abstract possibility because the technology is unknown–in 2020 various advanced space-warfare technologies are openly displayed and touted as offensive attack systems. For many nations there is an ominous and increased probability of sustaining a space asset attack; running in parallel with such concerns are increasing fears of worst-case scenarios related to the accidental launch of nuclear forces. This is also due to measurable increases in space debris and the confusion that could arise should space systems be attacked or time-out for extended periods without explanation. As more countries than ever are now realizing their mounting reliance on space, and as tensions run higher, the range of possible deterrents and responses to a space systems attack are increasingly severe and include the possible use of nuclear weapons. Full-scale attacks on space systems can now deliver catastrophic effects upon economies, societal functions, and military operations that would take decades to recover from–even limited acts of space warfare could result in rapid conflict breakout and light-speed escalation scenarios. Intolerable demands have now been placed upon the government and military officials of the leading space powers, as the remaining human factors across the entire spectrum of military space operations must come to terms with the prospect that their continued presence might only serve as an impediment to the realized potential of computational efficiency.

CHANGING THE DECOR IN THE THEATER OF SPACE WARFARE

There are good lexicographic reasons not to use terms like "the military geography of space" or "the terrain of space warfare". In both case the words "geography" and "terrain" have their origins in the Greek and Latin terms for Earth. If space can be described as anything, it is definitely "not of the Earth." The term "space as a theater of war" is still not completely satisfactory, but for the moment it will have to do.

Cislunar space, give or take a few million kilometers, is for the next few decades the only place where space warfare is going happen. The most important fact about this area is that Earth has a deep gravity well and the Moon has one six times smaller. John Collins' 1989 study "Military Space Forces: The Next Fifty Years" divides it into four military regions: Earth and its atmosphere, circumterrestrial space, the Moon and its environs, and the outer envelope.

The vulnerabilities of Earth-based space installations are evident and need little emphasis here. Questions are still being raised, particularly on Capitol Hill, about the Air Force's efforts to exploit the upper atmosphere or what is called "near space". Circumterrestrial space, basically low Earth orbit (LEO) and geosynchronous orbit (GEO), is where almost all of today's military space activity takes place.

It is the last two regions, the Moon and beyond, as defined by Collins, that deserve a new look.

The Outer Space Treaty may prohibit certain types of military activity of the Moon, but that is not to going to stop the place from being used for all sorts of quasi-military roles. For example, what happens when lunar-produced hydrogen is used to fuel military spacecraft in LEO? Is the fuel manufacturing facility of the Moon a legitimate target? The treaty itself may not survive past the time when two or more nations have bases on or below its surface.

Proposals to use the surface of the Moon for a set of observatories that will both look outwards towards the rest of the solar system and inwards towards the Earth have a definite paramilitary aspect.

The size of the apertures that can be created on the Moon are huge and they could produce sets of detailed environmental data that would be extremely valuable for military purposes. Such observatories would be under civilian control, but the products of their observations would be controlled by the nation or nations that built them and thus available for military purposes, just like data from environmental satellites in LEO.

In the area Collins calls "the Moon and its environs", also sometimes referred to as "cislunar space", there are the Lagrange points. So far there has not been any serious known plan to use these for military purposes, but there has been speculation over the years that these could become bases for space surveillance systems or even for space control weapons. The stable L-4 and L-5 points might be especially useful for these roles, but, on the other hand, these locations are so well known that any military spacecraft or facility placed there would lack any camouflage whatsoever.

The nature of the new generation of US and foreign "non-kinetic" space weapons is already changing the nature of space warfare. There are basically three types of these weapons: jammers, such at the counter-communications device that the US currently has; disablers, such as medium- or high-powered lasers or high-powered microwaves (HPM) that can disable a target spacecraft; and electromagnetic pulse (EMP) weapons.

These last types of weapons are not strictly space weapons since they could also disable electronic systems over large swaths of the Earth as well as knocking out any satellites within range. Since EMP weapons are powered by nuclear explosions they can be classified as weapons of last resort. Any state that used them would have to expect a nuclear response.

It is the question of range that determines the new shape of the theater of space operations. Expensive and delicate surveillance satellites in LEO, such at the US KH-12 series, are vulnerable to laser or HPM attack, yet they need to fly relative low in order to get the best resolution for their optical systems. The same holds true for radar imaging satellites. Protecting these satellites from kinetic and non-kinetic attack is a difficult problem: it requires them to have plenty of propellant to maneuver out of the way of "normal" ASATs and to carry shielding of various kinds that will be effective against lasers and HPMs. Such defenses will inevitably degrade the performance of these spacecraft or, if ignored, will make them into strictly peacetime assets.

Navigation and communications satellites in higher orbits, including GEO, may be vulnerable to the same laser and HPM weapons, but obviously it will be more difficult for Earth-based beams to maintain their coherence at such ranges. If the beams were to come from laser- or HPM-equipped satellites then it will be more difficult to defend these craft, but the platforms for such weapons would themselves be targets.

In the future it may be that the US and other space powers will try to hide both operational and reserve satellites in cislunar space or beyond. Using complex orbits that depend on minute changes in the gravitational environment, such steathly satellites could remain undetected for many years. They would have to use nuclear power since solar arrays have an easily identified signature. They would also have to use "extremely low probability of intercept" communications. Another requirement is that they have a powerful "dash" capability to be able to change orbits quickly in response to a crisis.

Another new factor is the need for a new kind of space navigation system. GPS, and later Galileo, will not be all that useful in GEO orbit or beyond, and the current generation of star trackers, though obviously pretty good, represent what engineers call a "single point failure". One alternative is to find a way to use the sixteen or so powerful pulsars that are easily detectable from our solar system as a sort of natural space GPS.

In space warfare, it must be assumed that some satellites and spacecraft are going to be destroyed by the enemy. Therefore, it is simply prudent to have reserves in place. So far the GPS system is the only military asset with any significant on-orbit reserves. In the near future the US is going to have to start planning to hide some reserve satellites in cislunar space or even in the "outer envelope" of the Earth-Moon system. Reconstituting a satellite network after an attack will be a lot faster if there are spares already in orbit that can be moved into an operationally suitable position when needed. This may be one answer, among others, to the question of what are "Operationally Responsive" space activities.

FUTURE BALLISTIC SPACE WARFARE

In the late 1970s and through the 1980s the Soviet Union and the United States theorized, designed and in some cases even tested an astonishing variety of bizarre and exotic weaponry designed for warfare in outer space. Space warfare was seen primarily as an extension of nuclear warfare, and so many theoretical systems were based around the destruction or defence of ground and sea-based missiles. Space-based missiles were not a target due to the Outer Space Treaty, which banned the use, testing or storage of nuclear weapons outside the Earth's atmosphere.

Systems proposed ranged from measures as simple as ground and space-based anti-missiles to railguns, space based lasers, orbital mines and other such futuristic weaponry. Deployment of these systems was seriously considered in the mid-1980s under the banner of the Strategic Defence Initiative (popularly known as Star Wars). If the Cold War had continued, then many of these systems could have seen deployment: the United States got as far as developing working railguns, and a laser that could destroy missiles at range, though the power requirements of both were phenomenal, and the ranges and firing cycles utterly impractical.

Electronic warfare

With the end of the Cold War and continued development of satellite and electronics technology, attention was focused on space as a supporting theatre for conventional warfare. Currently, military operations in space primarily concern either the vast tactical advantages of satellite-based surveillance, communications, and positioning systems or mechanisms used to deprive an opponent of said tactical advantages.

Accordingly, most space-borne proposals which would traditionally be considered "weapons" (a communications or reconnaissance satellite may be useful in warfare but isn't generally classified as a weapon) are designed to jam, sabotage, and outright destroy enemy satellites, and conversely to protect friendly satellites against such attacks. To this end, the US (and presumably other countries) is researching groups of small, highly mobile satellites called "microsats" (about the size of a refrigerator) and "picosats" (approximately 1 cubic foot (H"27 litres) in volume) nimble enough to manoeuvre around and interact with other orbiting objects to repair, sabotage, hijack, or simply collide with them.

Kinetic bombardment

Another theorized use involves the extension of conventional weaponry into orbit for deployment against ground targets. Though international treaties bar the deployment of nuclear missiles outside the atmosphere, other categories of weapons are largely unregulated.

Traditional ground-based weapons are generally not useful in orbital environments, and few if any would survive re-entry even if they were, but as early as the 1950s, the United States has toyed with kinetic bombardment, i.e. orbiting magazines of non-explosive projectiles to be dropped onto hardened targets from low-earth orbit. Kinetic weapons have always been widespread in conventional warfare—bullets, arrows, swords, clubs, etc.—but the energy a projectile would gain while falling from orbit would make such a weapon rival all but the most powerful explosives.

A direct hit would presumably destroy all but the most hardened targets without the need for nuclear weapons. Such a system would involve a 'spotter' satellite, which would identify targets from orbit with high-power sensors, and a nearby 'magazine' satellite to de-orbit a long, needle-like tungsten dart onto it with a small rocket motor or just dropping a very big rock from orbit (such as an asteroid). This would be more useful against a larger but less hardened target (such as a city). Though a common device in science fiction, there is no publicly-available evidence that any such systems have actually been deployed by any nation.

Directed-Energy Weapons

Weapon systems that fall under this category include lasers, linear particle accelerators or particle-beam based weaponry, microwaves and plasma-based weaponry. Particle beams involve the acceleration of charged or neutral particles in a stream towards a target at extremely high velocities, the impact of which creates a reaction causing immense damage. Most of these weapons are theoretical or impractical to implement currently, aside from lasers which are starting to be used in terrestrial warfare. That said, directed-energy weapons are more practical and more effective in a vacuum (i.e. space) than in the

Earth's atmosphere, as in the atmosphere the particles of air interfere with and disperse the directed energy. Obviously, that problem would not occur in space.

Practical considerations

Space warfare is likely to be conducted at far greater distances and speeds than terrestrial combat. The vast distances involved pose difficult challenges for targeting and tracking, as even light requires a few seconds to traverse ranges measured in hundreds of thousands of kilometres. For example, if attempting to fire upon a target at the distance of the Moon from the Earth, the image one sees reflects the position of the target slightly more than a second earlier.

A projectile from a railgun recently tested by the US Navy would take over eighteen hours to cross that distance (making the simplifying and optimistic assumption that it will travel in a straight line at a constant velocity of 5.8 km/s along its entire trajectory). Even a laser will need approximately 1.28 seconds, meaning a laser-based weapon system would need to lead a target's apparent position by $1.28 \times 2 = 2.56$ seconds.

Three factors conspire to make engaging targets in space very difficult. First, the vast distances involved mean that an error of even a fraction of a degree in the firing solution could result in a miss by thousands of kilometres. Second, space travel involves tremendous speeds by terrestrial standards—a geostationary satellite moves at a speed of 3.07 km/s whereas objects in low earth orbit can move at up to 8 km/s.

Third, though distances are large, targets remain relatively small. The International Space Station, currently the largest artificial object in Earth orbit, measures slightly over 100m at its largest span. Other satellites can be orders of magnitude smaller, e.g. Quickbird measures a mere 3.04m. External ballistics for stationary terrestrial targets is enormously complicated—some of the earliest analog computers were used to calculate firing solutions for naval artillery, as the problems were already beyond manual solutions in any reasonable time—and the issues in targeting objects in space make a difficult problem even harder.

Additionally, though not a problem for orbital kinetic weapons, any directed energy weapon would require large amounts of electricity. So far the most practical batteries are lithium batteries, and the most practical method of generating electricity in space is through photovoltaic modules, which are currently only 5-18% efficient, and fuel cells, which have limited fuel. Current technology might not be practical for powering effective lasers, particle beams, and railguns in space.

Regardless of one's reasons for going to war, at present those reasons are not likely to suggest major targets located in space. Most of the main theories which attempt to explain human proclivity for warfare—psychological, sociological, demographic, economic, political, or otherwise—would not indicate space as a likely location of conflict until a significant population is engaged in large-scale activity there. Until then, space warfare is likely to take a supporting role to conventional, terrestrial warfare. Aside from applications such as communications, reconnaissance, GPS, and the like, which would be difficult or impossible without satellites, there do not appear to be any major advantages to basing weapons systems in space. The main reason is simply cost. Space warfare that involves humans being deployed in space to fight each other is not currently practical because of the difficulty and cost of sustaining human life in space, especially over long periods of time.

Additionally, there are few things that could be accomplished by space warfare that any nation wealthy enough to finance them cannot accomplish far more cheaply through conventional means. Raising any significant mass beyond Earth's gravity will always require a large amount of energy, and the cost increases with mass. For example, though kinetic bombardment potentially offers the ability to strike any target anywhere in the world within minutes, both the United States and Russia, possibly the only nations with the resources and facilities necessary to implement such a system, have sufficiently long-range supersonic bombers that the same target could already be deployed in a matter of hours at a mere fraction of the cost.

3

Information Warfare

The information technology explosion that's out there sweeping the world is an important matter, not just for the military services, but also for industry, the government, and our whole way of life. The history of the Second World War offers great examples of the military and civilian leadership manipulating information, even in a very crude fashion, to achieve rather spectacular results.

In those days, as we thought about dominating the information spectrum, we turned to the cryptographers who were on the leading edge of these efforts, the so-called "code breakers." These specialized folks focused intently upon breaking the Japanese and German codes. In Europe, the ULTRA project -- "ULTRA" for the "ULTRA secret" -- produced spectacular results. Our code breakers literally worked miracles.

After the Normandy invasion, the German 7th Army attempted a counterattack to drive the Allied forces from the rather tenuous beachhead that they held. But with the help of ULTRA's ability to read the German mail and message traffic, we knew precisely what they were doing as they began to gather their forces to make this attack. We were able to put the British Second Tactical Air Force and the United States Ninth Tactical Air Force immediately upon these armor formations just as they massed. ULTRA gave us the critical information that allowed us to defeat the German forces before they ever came in contact with our ground forces.

By comparison, if you think to December of 1944 and the Battle of the Bulge, we see an example of where the Germans were able to catch us by surprise. They used an alternative communications network, and the Allies did not realize that the Germans had made this switch. It was our lack of information that really fueled the initial German success in the Battle of the

Bulge. We had come to rely on ULTRA and had developed a little bit of self-delusion -- and the Germans took advantage of it very effectively.

Our ability to monitor the enemy's communications and use that information as an integral part of our operations is really nothing new. There is another example we should not forget. That's how we control the information that we allow the enemy to receive. Again, I am going back to the Second World War and talking about disinformation, particularly the disinformation campaign that centered on General Patton before and during the D-Day landings.

At that time, the Allies understood the other guy's ability to intercept our open signals, so we devised a rather elaborate plan that played to this emerging capability on the part of the Germans. The Allies set up a fake Army headquarters and generated false communications transmissions in England. As a result, the Nazis ended up with a significant number of troops placed in the wrong positions.

Even as they started to pick up indications that there was this great Allied armada that was going to invade Normandy, the Germans refused to believe that there could actually be an Allied invasion of Europe led by anyone but Patton. We played on that expectation in a way that kept Patton associated with his fake headquarters. Even as the Germans began to get higher and higher fidelity intelligence that indicated a real attack at Normandy, their leaders were frozen in indecision and, as a result, tied down considerable forces in France across from the shortest invasion route from England. For instance, the aircraft we will fly over this time frame are fundamentally the same kinds of aircraft we are flying today. Some will have more advanced avionics, more advanced stealth characteristics or other features; but in the main, aircraft will remain fundamentally aircraft as we know them today. Ships will remain fundamentally ships as we know them today. The same holds true for tanks and armored personnel carriers.

Information warfare is not the exclusive domain of the Air Force, or any other service. I think information warfare has different meanings to a soldier, sailor, Marine, or airman. For instance, the soldier's focus may be on what happens at the corps level and below. The sailor's and Marine's focus is on the maritime and littoral regions.

At the same time, an airman's focus is theater-wide, from the front lines to the adversary's capital. You begin to see how IW covers the entire battlefield. But, because of these divergent views and unique needs, I think it's critical that all services come to grips with and develop capabilities for their respective mediums of operations -- that is land, sea, and air. Then, it falls to the joint force commander, or the regional commander-in-chief, to integrate these capabilities to accomplish the mission.

The Air Force has put considerable effort into developing our concepts. In fact, over the past four months, we have had a team travel to every commander-in-chief (CINC) of a U.S. unified command and brief them on our efforts to incorporate IW into our doctrine and to integrate these concepts into our force employment. Most importantly, we want to be sure that what we are doing and how we approach the subject as an institution will be consistent with the way the CINCs intend to fight. And we want to make sure that what we are doing will meet their needs.

The information explosion discussed here today is going to make dramatic changes in how this nation fights wars in the future. Such technology will allow a commander's vision and view of the battlefield to be shared at the lowest level -- to the flight for the airman, to the company on the ground, and to the ship's bridge. Simultaneously, soldiers, Marines, sailors, and airmen on the front lines will be able to see and exploit opportunities as they occur. What this means is our joint forces may enjoy what some are calling "dominant battlefield awareness." We have some of this kind of capability today. We've made significant enhancements to our ability to leverage our forces with faster command and control and intelligence networks. Among other capabilities, these networks are dramatically reducing the time required to detect and destroy a target.

This process starts with how we gather data. Our intelligence, surveillance, and reconnaissance efforts have been significantly and dramatically improved since Desert Storm. If you are familiar with our TALON programs, you will appreciate what we are doing to reduce the sensor-to-shooter loop -- that is injecting what is detected by our space-based assets directly into the cockpit or a flight deck. We are making similar advances with the systems that operate within the earth's atmosphere. For example, our AWACS early warning aircraft have been greatly improved. Their current radar upgrade allows us to detect cruise missiles at twice the range that we could previously. The AWACS is being fitted with the Joint Tactical Information Distribution Systems, or JTIDS. We will start the initial JTIDS operational test this August. I expect that we will reach full operational capability before the end of the decade. JTIDS alone will give us some pretty significant capabilities. It is not restricted just to AWACS. It also gives our warfighters a secure and jam-resistant data link between Air Force, Navy, Army, and Marine units and future coalition partners -- on land, at sea, and in the air. What that really means is all the players will have a real-time picture and awareness of both what is happening on the ground and what is going on in the air above those forces. JTIDS will give us a tremendous capability to know, at a much higher fidelity, the location of both the enemy and our own forces.

We are also making similar improvements in how we plan and control air operations. Today, we are fielding CTAPS -- the Contingency Theater Automated Planning System. CTAPS will connect our command and control from the joint forces air component commander (JFACC) to the air wings and the base-level planning cells. It will allow us to generate, disseminate, and monitor the progress of the daily air tasking order much faster than we ever have been able to do before. CTAPS also will tie in with the Combat Intelligence System which will provide us the enemy's order of battle through imagery and integrated threat data.

What does this really mean to us? During Desert Storm, it took us about 48 hours to plan and disseminate the ATO. That doesn't mean that it took 48 hours to execute a request from the field. But, it means that the deliberative process that planners went through to service targets was a 36- to 48-hour process. And you had to have someone manually intervene with an immediate air request to get inside those planning cycles. What the CTAPS system will do for us is take this 48-hour cycle and compress it to 12 hours. This really isn't some pie-in-the-sky system that we're dreaming about or visualizing. This is something that is in full use in exercises today and will be operational across the force next year. We have a similar planning tool that has been operational with our global air mobility forces for about three years.

These are a couple of examples of the kinds of tools we are putting in place. They are going to do more than replace the grease pencil and butcher block paper that (retired Air Force General) Chuck Horner and his staff had to use to run the air war during Desert Storm. These systems are going to help us dominate the information spectrum. I am convinced that this capability will be critical the next time our forces are employed in combat. In the future, we will approach this objective by viewing our adversary's information activities as a system, and we will engage that system in a variety of ways. In fact, rather than put a precision guided munition into the central telephone exchange in Baghdad and destroy it next time, we may elect to leave it standing so we can better exploit it through our advances in information warfare.

So, there will be trade-offs between lethal and non-lethal dimensions in the IW arena. In the same manner, we have been doing some things along the way that we could properly classify as offensive information operations. There are ways that we corrupt information available to the enemy to deceive him. They include using psychological operations and our electronic warfare assets, like the Compass Call aircraft. We think that these kinds of measures that are designed to corrupt information the enemy has are really critical tools that we provide to the CINCs today. They open the envelope for the potential of further operations tomorrow. Again, if you think back to what we did on D-Day with disinformation, and you consider the tremendous advances in technology since 1944, you begin to appreciate the tremendous potential that exists in this area.

If we recognize an adversary's information network as a lucrative target, an adversary will view our data banks and weapon systems the same way. Information security -- the classic OPSEC, COMSEC, and the more recently stressed computer security -- takes on a whole new level of urgency. As a result, the Air Force is taking some rather significant measures to safeguard our assets. This year, we are spending more than $80 million on defensive measures alone, including establishing a base network control center to protect access to computers and communications. This same center will permit us to see if someone has tried to gain access to our system and, hopefully, will allow us to track down who tried to intrude on the system. These initiatives are important because we run a tremendous risk if we look at information warfare as something that is unique to America. It is not, and by the same token, the U.S. military is not alone in this vulnerability.

Our commercial sector, other elements of the government, and our industrial sectors rely on information systems just as much, if not more, than the military. If you've read Tom Clancy's recent thriller, Debt of Honor, you're familiar with what may be plausible. In this fictional tale, Clancy describes the problems caused when someone infects the stock exchange's computers with a virus, literally bringing the stock market to a standstill. To me, Clancy's work reinforces how the information threat is more than just a unique military concern.

As we look at information warfare and how it relates to the services, I'm reminded of a story about a football team. It seems that during one of the games, the local team had to put in a back-up quarterback late in the fourth quarter. They were ahead, and they were just trying to hang on. So, they put this relatively untested young man into the game, and all he had to do was avoid making a mistake and the team would win. So, the coach grabbed the guy as he was about to go on the field and said, "OK, here's what I want you to do. Run the ball three times, and then punt." So, the kid understood that and goes out onto the field. His first run gains 20 yards -- great. On the second play, he gains 30 yards. Now, this is going a lot better than he ever expected. On the third play, he gains 30 more yards. Now they are down on the 10-yard line, the fans are going crazy, and it appears they're going to wrap this thing up. All he has to do is score, and he'll seal the victory for sure. So, the center snaps the ball to him and he punts. Everyone is stunned by this. His coach pulls him over to the sidelines and asks him what he was thinking. And the quarterback replied, "I was thinking that since you didn't change that play, I must have the dumbest coach around."

It is not enough to make a game plan and go with it. You must act and react to what is happening around you. What we're doing today with information warfare is a little bit like that football game -- IW gives us the ability to plan faster with better information so that we can call the optimum play. It may allow us to know what defensive stunt the other team is going to use. It may allow us to give our opponent false information on what play we're about to use. And, most importantly, it may allow us to call an audible and adjust to a fluid situation.

But unlike the game that I just described, when America sends her military forces into action, we don't want a close, exciting game, and we don't want an inexperienced quarterback. This nation has come to expect in our military operations nothing but blow-outs -- 100 to nothing is a good score. And, I believe that exploiting this new and emerging information technology is going to be the key to making this happen. As we approach tomorrow, we need to do more as a service and with the other services. Let me touch just briefly on what we are doing in terms of changing the way we organize, train, and equip our forces.

First, in terms of organizing, in September 1993, the United States Air Force stood up the Air Force Information Warfare Center in San Antonio. This center has more than 1,000 men and women chartered to support IW planning, intelligence gathering, weapon system analysis, and related activities. This group will be a source of IW support teams to go out and assist the CINCs and JFACCs during crises or exercises. They will help build information warfare into the air campaign planning and execution. The Air Force is not alone in this. The Army has an Information Warfare Center at Fort Belvoir, Virginia, and the Navy has created a center at Fort Meade, Maryland.

Additionally, the Air Force is adjusting our training and education programs to include IW concepts. We have had a course for our major air command and numbered air force staffs to give them basic understanding of the issues. We are incorporating IW into our doctrine, so that airmen everywhere will share a common foundation and a common terminology. We're adjusting our mid- and senior-level professional military education schools at Maxwell Air Force Base, Alabama. You see part of this effort here today. We have four Air Force officers attending the inaugural class of the National Defense University's School for Information Warfare.

Finally, and most significantly, we are beginning to procure weapon systems with a mindset that places high priority on maximizing their performance as an information warfare platform. One example of that is the United States' new air superiority fighter, the F-22. This aircraft is the first platform to be built around information technologies. This was an established objective when we started the program, not something added after the fact. A lot of people have heard about the F-22's stealth. You've heard about its supercruise capability -- that is the ability to cruise faster than the speed of sound in military power. And possibly you've heard about the fact that it has tremendous agility in the air-to-air arena. But, you cannot begin to appreciate its potential until you sit in the concept demonstrator and see how the F-22's integrated avionics work. The quality of the composite picture that's compiled from a variety of sources will literally water your eyes, particularly if you're an old-time fighter pilot. For the first time, you'll be able to sit with those flat glass displays and have tremendous situational awareness readily available to you. That is something we've needed for years, and we're finally in the process of getting it.

It will allow our pilots to act and assess faster even when outnumbered. And I tell you it isn't just a concept -- it's being put into production today! The F-22 is just one of many Air Force programs that we're continuing to push forward. You see the same thought processes in the space-based infrared system, in our Joint STARS, and in our precision munitions program. As we move forward, we are establishing an additional requirement for our weapon systems -- that is security against the information threat -- that's being written into the requirements documents.

This new mindset is found throughout our acquisition strategy. We are changing how we view our modernization needs. We're taking another look at IW capabilities, like those associated with command and control, and we're treating them more like force structure than support structure. It's part of how we must change the way we do business to incorporate the fundamentals of information warfare.

This broad approach means that we must get the lawyers involved. When I first heard about bringing in the lawyers, I thought we had really slipped off the deep end one more time. I apologize if I offend any lawyers out there -- I always have held lawyers in fairly high esteem. The more I thought about bringing the lawyers into the equation, the more I realized we need their expertise. Because exploiting the information spectrum will readily cross international borders, we must be cognizant of what the law allows and will not allow.

When do you begin information warfare in the spin up to a conflict? When do you begin to go out there and intrude in somebody's banking system? When do you begin to get into somebody's telecommunications system? These are all very difficult questions. Clearly, information warfare is not something that is focused solely on the confines of a constrained battle area. While we will fight in a theater, information warfare will force us to be engaged worldwide. Thus, we must have some good advice as we pursue this capability.

I appreciate this opportunity to share with you what the Air Force is doing to try and keep up with the information technology explosion. The American way of war has very strong roots in understanding the value of exploiting information to deny information to our adversary, to corrupt what data he has, and to exploit what we know. World War II was filled with many examples of information warfare. Perhaps Winston Churchill offered the best summary of its importance. At the Tehran conference, when discussing the Allied plans to manipulate information before D-Day, many of these same ethical questions came up. When do we do it? How do we do it? Who are the innocent victims of this thing? And Churchill, addressing the other Allied leaders said, "In wartime, truth is so precious that she should always be attended by a bodyguard of lies" (Anthony Cave Brown, Bodyguard of Lies (New York: Harper and Row, 1975), p. 10). Something to think about. Later, there was a book written with that title by Anthony Brown. If you read his thick volume, it is rather chilling to see what was possible in that era, and then think about how much more is possible today with the technology that's available.

Today and in the future, information warfare is, in fact, going to be this nation's bodyguard. It is essential for the success of our joint forces. To succeed, we are going to need help from a lot of people, including all the very interested people in this room. You understand the far-reaching implications of systems like LANDSAT or SATCOM which are readily available and widely employed at relatively low cost. You appreciate the potential for information technology to allow an adversary to build small, capable, autonomous, operating systems that can threaten U.S. forces on land, sea, or in the air. Such devices might operate relatively unseen and unobserved until they unleash their destructive power.

THE DOMAIN OF INFORMATION AND INFORMATION WARFARE

The read-ahead package for the workshop included a paper that stressed the size and complexity of the information warfare domain. As illustrated in the paper, three relatively independent dimensions are required to capture and describe the information warfare arena: the degree of conflict/cooperation, substantive focus (political, military, social, economic, etc.), and the nature of the actors involved (individuals, private organizations, nation states, international organizations, the general public, media, etc.).

The workshop participants generally accepted the broad nature of the information warfare domain and the central role of information systems and processes in the world today. However, they inferred several very important implications from this broad characterization of the relevant domain.

- First, the term "information warfare" is used to mean many things, but is often focused on the military domain or the cyber-war domain dominated by computers. This narrow definition is inconsistent with the broad policy questions relevant to competition and conflict using information media.
- Because information warfare is really a broad and diverse arena, analysis of it must be focused on selected elements, which must be clearly defined in each application. Overall, the field is so broad that virtually no meaningful generalizations can be drawn about it.
- Isolation, except in rare instances, of military, national, public, and private information systems is all but impossible today. Even very important military traffic is likely to be carried on national infrastructure systems. Public and private sectors are heavily interdependent, and this linkage will continue to grow.
- A whole raft of information systems make potential targets -- banking systems, control systems for railway operations, air control systems, control systems for pipelines, media systems, and others. Only a fraction of these are primarily military or under the direct protection of the Department of Defense (DoD).
- As has been stressed by ADM Owens as Vice Chairman of the Joint Chiefs of Staff, the civilian sector is no longer a sanctuary that can be protected by interposing military forces between adversaries and their targets. Traditional military forces can be flanked at the speed of light by information age attacks on the general population or key economic systems.
- More profoundly, there is no consensus on the appropriate boundary between the military and Department of Defense roles and missions, those of the law enforcement and intelligence systems, and those of the commercial sector.

Workshop participants were aware of a variety of policy initiatives to create interagency working groups and coordinating mechanisms as well as public-private dialogues and mechanisms for both exchanging information and developing plans for dealing with information age threats that cut across communities. Considerable progress has been made in generating better awareness of the threat and some effort has been made toward cooperation.

However, the general consensus was that these helpful activities were only now developing momentum and were far from successful completion.

INFORMATION WARFARE AND INFORMATION STRATEGY

Information warfare is often thought of as being defined by a particular target setudecision makers, information, information processes, and information systems. The "battlespace" associated with IW has been a constantly expanding one, moving far beyond traditional military situations. In some quarters, IW has even been associated with the leveraging of information technologies to achieve greater effectiveness and efficiency. This has stretched the meaning of IW to the breaking point and has sowed more confusion than enlightenment. For this reason, this treatment of the subject uses the term "information strategies" to refer to the recognition and utilization of information and information technologies as an instrument of national power that can be independent of, or complementary to, military presence and operations.

The scope, or battlespace, of information warfare and strategy (IWS) can be defined by the players and three dimensionsùthe nature of their interactions, the level of their interactions, and the arena of their interactions. Nation states or combinations of nation states are not the only players. Non-state actors (including political, ethnic, and religious groups; organized crime; international and transnational organizations; and even individuals empowered by information technology) are able to engage in information attacks and to develop information strategies to achieve their desired ends. The term "war" has been used so loosely in recent times (e.g., War on Poverty, War on Drugs, War on Crime) that is should be no surprise that IW has evolved over the past several years to become a "catch-all" term that encompasses many disparate activities, some of which have long been associated with competition, conflict, and warfare, and others that are of more recent origin.

These include activities that range from propaganda campaigns (including Media War), to attacks (both physical and non-physical) against commanders, their information sources, and the means of communicating with their forces. Under this rather large umbrella that has become known as IW, one can find activities long associated with military concepts and operations, including deception, command and control warfare (C2W), and psychological operations (Psyops). Technological advances have added new forms such as electronic warfare (EW) and "hacker warfare."

The term "defensive information warfare" (IW-D) is used here to refer to all actions taken to defend against information attacks, that is, attacks on decision makers, the information and information-based processes they rely on, and their means of communicating their decisions. Strictly speaking, since these attacks can be launched during peace time at nonmilitary targets by nonmilitary groups, both foreign and domestic, the term IW-D should be IWS-D. However, IW-D is currently in wide use. This overview of IW-D does not attempt to deal with the problems of defending against all of the different kinds of information attacks, but rather focuses its attention on the subset of IW that involves attacks against our information infrastructure, including what has become known as "hacker warfare" and in its more serious form, "digital warfare."

Analogies and Realities

Defending against information attacks has a number of characteristics in common with societal efforts to combat disease, drugs, and crime. Noting these similarities helps to put this problem into perspective, provides some potential useful lessons learned, and serves as a benchmark.

Before reviewing the specific similarities between combating IWS and these long-standing problems, it should be noted that, while eradicating information attacks may not be a realistic expectation, significant progress can be made in defending against all forms of information attacks, enough so that the risks can be kept at acceptable levels. Defending, as it is used here, includes preventing attacks, blunting attacks, and controlling the damage caused by attacks.

The problem of IW-D is similar to the problems encountered in the "wars" on disease, drugs, and crime in a number of dimensions. First, the solution to any of these problems requires the efforts of a number of organizations, both public and private. Second, it is unlikely, given the competition for resources, that any of these efforts will be fully funded.

Therefore, we can expect that there will never be what those who have IW-D responsibilities think are a sufficient level of funding for IW-D programs. Third, these are not static problems. Drug cartels and criminals certainly learn from their mistakes. Even viruses "learn." Thus, defense forces will be continuously locked in a battle to keep up with attackers. Fourth, public awareness and concern will reach peaks, often accompanied by frenzied efforts to solve the problem.

These relatively short periods of interest will be followed by longer periods when the urgency to solve the problem will give way to apathy. Maintaining funding and progress during these periods of waning public interest will be one of the key challenges of leadership in this area. Fifth, organizations and individuals will learn to make adjustments in their behavior to deal with IW attacks and their often unintended consequences. These adjustments will be made so that those organizations and individuals can accommodate some level of painùa dynamic equilibrium of sortsùas the cost of doing business in the Information Age. Finally, solutions will, of necessity, involve compromises. This is due to the natural tensions that exist among the various stakeholders. Tensions between the law enforcement and the protection of civil liberties are classic examples that have already arisen in the information domain.

Current Situation

Attacks on information systems are already a fact of life in the Information Age. Although a small portion of these attacks result in significant loss or damage, the vast majority of them result in little or no damage the crime equivalents of trespassing, public nuisance, minor vandalism, and petty theft.

It has been estimated that more than 90 percent of these attacks are perpetrated using available tools and techniques (based upon incidents reported to CERT), that only 1 attack in 20 is noticed by the victim, and that only 1 in 20 gets reported (these last two statistics were a result of a Defense Information Systems Agency (DISA) study and similar rates have been reported by others). However, it appears that reporting rates may be on the increase.

Of more concern is the presence of a technically feasible "strategic" threat. That is, the means exist to cause significant damage and disruption to U.S. public and private information assets, processes, and systems, and to compromise the integrity of vital information.

Analysts also have no difficulty identifying groups with the motivations and opportunities to launch such attacks. Given our present vulnerabilities as a nation, a well-planned, coordinated IW attack could have strategic consequences. Such an attack, or the threat of such an attack, could thwart our foreign policy objectives, degrade military performance, result in significant economic loss, and perhaps even undermine the confidence of our citizens in the Government's ability to protect its citizens and interests.

While no "smoking keyboard" has been found to validate such a threat, the very existence of the means to carry out such an attack, when coupled with the myriad of motives and opportunities that exist, results in our present state of vulnerability. These circumstances have created a situation that calls for prudent defensive actions to be taken in the public interest. We need to be proactive rather than be forced to react after an Information Age "Pearl Harbor." Moreover, a successful strategic attack would point the way and encourage others to plan similar attacks. Hence, we need to go on the offensive with a vigorous defense.

INFORMATION BASED WARFARE -THE NEW BATTLEFIELDS

Exiled to France, the Ayatollah Khomeni sought to maintain contact with the faithful. A cleric who espoused the return of his country to an Islamic theocracy-something: that many argued would move Iran back into the 16th century-the Ayatollah turned to 20th century tools to begin his crusade. Through the medium of cassettes, he began to record his message. After being mass-produced m 20th century studios, his 16th century message was smuggled back to Iran. Those tapes both planted the seed and inspired the flowering of a movement that brought Khomeni back to power m 1979.

For at least a decade, the American military had tinkered with devices for sabotaging enemy electrical systems. Some of the results were serendipitous. In the early 1980's, during a Navy exercise code-named Hey [Rube, long strands of rope chaff-glass filaments in which metal shards were embedded-had been dropped over the Pacific Ocean as part of a standard tactic to befuddle an opponent's radar. An unexpectedly skiff wind carried some of the chaff ninety miles to the coastline, where it got draped across power lines, shorting out transformers and causing power failures in parts of San Diego. The Navy quietly settled the damages- while carefully noting the effects of its unintended attack.

Information warfare has as many meanings as it has proponents, detractors and observers. Airpower theorists see it on the wings of Desert Storm; tank commanders see it in the American army's Force XXI; simulator designers see it in their virtual realities...and strategic-war planners see it as a way to lay waste to whole societies. Information warfare studies are proliferating within the American armed forces almost as quickly as the networks that carry them from desktop to desktop. The confusing planoply stems from the fact that the information revolution, whether it is in uniform or mufti, relies upon the fastest technology to do the oldest things. Thus it is always a peculiar mixture of the familiar and the shockingly new. In that war is all about strategies, command and morale, it has always been about information. All war is information war, and so every aspect of fighting wars in the information age can be called "information warfare" by someone. If information driven warfare means something new, it is the use of information as a substitute for traditional ways of fighting, rather than an adjunct to them. There are three ways that this might be achieved by:

- the high technology equivalent of brute force;
- subversion; and,

- a new form of deterrence.

For the purpose of this paper, we focus on the second element-subversion. It is our belief that because of the unique relationship between Americans and computers, IBW launched subversive acts-a prelude to, or the actual execution of "quiet wars"-may be accomplished.

The evolution and ultimate "blurring" of military and civilian sectors came about in large part because of the growth in hardware and software. It was not so long ago, in the early 1960's, that the Pentagon provided the market for sophisticated electronics. Today, it makes up less than 1% of that market. In many ways, the military is following the revolution, not leading it. In 1962 Paul Baran of RAND developed a concept that permitted the linking of computers from distant locations. It was designed to preserve the integrity of the military command and control network in case of a nuclear attack. In 1969, the Defense Advanced Research Projects Agency (DARPA) funded the first test of the concept, and the first node was installed at RAND. The test consisted of scientists from remote locations passing findings and research notes back and forth. However, a year later it was being used like a mail box for the users and it proceeded to grow rapidly in use. In 1983, the military part and the nonmilitary part grew apart and finally split, the nonmilitary section grew up into what is now called the Internet.

For the first time in our nation's history, technology is no longer the sole domain of the military. The speed of the growth and application of technology is clearly a concern for defense planners. While the US used some of the world's most advanced weaponry and technology in the Gulf War (much of which proved inaccurate) it also used a great deal of older technology, some of which dated back to the 1960's. As B.R. Inman and Daniel F. Burton Jr. note in their article "Technology and US. National Security, "the 8088 microprocessor used in the Patriot missile was developed by the Intel Corporation fifteen years ago." This technology is not competitive today.

Opening and Closing Pandora's Box

In the center of Strike the battleship's commander, Captain David S. Bill, Ferched in his high backed padded chair. Although he occasionally glanced at the screens above, the captain's attention was largely fixed on the men clustered around four computers lining the far bulkhead. Something had gone awry with the ship's Tomahawk missile system.. For reasons no one could fathom, the Tomahawk computers seemed confused, refusing to transfer the necessary commands from the engagement-planning console to the launch console. The resulting impasse_"casualty" in Navy jargon_meant the missiles could not be fired...On Wisconsin, where the scheduled launch was now just moments away, the men in Strike were running out of solutions...As the request for additional time flashed up the chain of command, an excited voice from one of the nearby ships crackled through Strike: "Alpha, alpha." This is the Paul F Foster. Happy trails." Happy trails: the code phrase for missiles away. Operation Desert Storm had begun without Wisconsin.

As the most technologically vulnerable nation, the US defense planners must recognize several concepts about the technical end of the IBW battlefield:

It must be assumed that everyone has access to technology, therefore the US is the most vulnerable to attack;

As the US's ability to wage IBW increases, so to do the IBW capabilities, and response capabilities, of other nation-states and non-state actors;

While at first glance it would appear that IBW is most effective against adversaries with like technological capabilities and infrastructure-the top end of the IBW target spectrum-it must be remembered that technology comes in two forms-high and appropriate-and it is the latter that will always defeat the former. Thus, the benefits of IBW in arena's of conflict as found in the Gray Areas are a target rich environment must be pursued alongside the force on force approach.

The technical realm of information based warfare can be split into two major areas: Netwar and Cyberwar. Netwar is the information related conflict between nations, societies, governments, or non-state actors with the targets being information systems and communications, and it consists of destruction of communications, acquisition of information, release of misinformation, and destruction or deletion of data. Cyberwar consists of militaries conducting their operations according to information based theories and principles. These terms can be broken down even further. Netwar can be broken into three main categories: Personal, Corporate, and Global.

We are constantly warned about the personal level of Netwar, we have passwords to computer accounts, never give our social security number over the telephone, and generally try to be careful about our own information. But protecting yourself from someone who genuinely wants to conduct information war against you is nearly impossible. Corporations are subject to a barrage of information security problems to an even greater extent. The stealing of company secrets is a new form of economic war that is plaguing many companies. It is also possible for one company to release false findings that indicate that a competitor has a poor or dangerous product. IBW spawned misinformation-a fertile area for denial and deception techniques-are very difficult to combat and correct. Finally, on the global level, Netwar can be waged against industries, economies, nations, or non-state groups. It ranges from intelligence and information leads, to the terrifying possibilities of terrorist groups breaking into such communications as an air traffic control system at a major US airport. The impact at the global level can be much more wide spread and all threatening than that of the personal or corporate levels of netwar.

On both sides of the war, Netwar and Cyberwar, the key to good protection and offence is good software to run the systems, encode the data, and peck holes in other's data. The vital link for the information and the technology is software, which relies heavily upon implanted logic. The newest and brightest theories and concepts of logic center around what is called 'fuzzy logic'. The name fuzzy logic makes one think of a system that is inexact, but that is not the case, instead it has an infinite exactness. Fuzzy logic expands our normal computer principle of 0 or 1, true or false, and in the place of this is infinite degrees between 0 and 1. Fuzzy logic is used every day in the development of everything from smart washers to train systems in Japan. With a smart washer, you merely press a start button and the machine figures the cycle, how much detergent, and the water use; the logic train systems are smooth as silk, quick, and always on time. The theory started with a few paradoxes one of which is The Paradox of Theseus' ship:

When Theseus returned from slaying the Minotaur, says Plutarch, the Athenians preserved his ship, and as planks rotted, replaced them with new ones. When the first plank was replaced, everyone agreed it was still the same ship. Adding a second plank made no difference either. At some point, the Athenians may have replaced every plank in the ship. Was it a different ship? At what point did it become one?

At different points in time the ship was certain degrees the original ship, for instance when half the planks were replaced, it was the original ship. This same principle of degrees can be applied to many concepts around us, and what you end up with is a very exact and reliable process for computers. When you tie this concept into ideas such as artificial intelligence, you may obtain a computer that has the capacity to learn because it can start to work with more than 0 and 1.

Because of the importance of the technical tools of IBW-and their fragility-we list below the possible contents of an IBW techno "kit-bag":

Computer Viruses - A piece of code, or code fragment, designed to begin replicating itself when a host program begins to run. It's objective is to erase data, software programs, or memory in order to interrupt the action of the computer it infests. These can be loaded unwittingly by a user off the Internet or some other disk.

Worms - Instead of being just a code fragment, a worm is an entire program in and of itself. The code begins to replicate as soon as it touches a computer system, not dependent on the start of execution of any other program. Its aim is to eat up computer resources and/or delete data to result in a crippling effect on the host computer.

Trojan Horses - As the name would suggest, a Trojan horse is a program, or code fragment inside a program, that performs a function unbeknownst to the user. It usually performs a simple task on the outside, while unleashing a virus or a worm on the inside. It can also perform information retrieval while performing a task, leaving no trace.

Logic Bombs - Similar to a Trojan horse, a logic bomb is used to release a virus, worm, or complete some other secret task. These are usually planted by a programmer or system developer. This could be useful in US military strategy, instead of open bombs, the US could plant logic bombs to retrieve specific data from foreign users. This is plausible because many of the main software development in the world occurs in the US.

Trap Doors - The use of this is similar to a logic bomb. It is a secret way back into a system left by a programmer or designer. Unlike a logic bomb that executes, a trap door is merely an unknown security flaw. Chipping - This is the term for doing any of the above to the hardware of a system instead of to the software. One can build in circuitry to a chip that performs specific functions.

Machines and Microbes - Although one thinks of Star Trek and other science fiction when the subject of nanny machines comes up, it is actually a feasible plan. machines and microbes are tiny machines, like a small insect, that "eat" electronic circuits, oil, plastics, etc. If unleashed on a computer center, the result would be total shut down.

Electronic Jamming, HERF guns, and EM bombs- These are all forms of electronic signal jamming. One can jam communications, stopping computer information flow; shoot radio signals at an electronic target to shut it down with a High Energy Radio Frequency (HERF) gun; or send out a high powered electromagnetic pulse, an EMP bomb.

Hitch-hiking- This is a group of people, a subsection of hackers, that merely sit on the net and wait. They wait for any information and interesting code to go by and then hitch a ride with it, they follow and delete it, or they simply copy and steal it. Thinking in terms of closing Pandora's Box, the following techniques will have to be considered as an IBW operational security plan is built:

Firewalls - A limited gateway to the Interment from a company or group. Only passwords and certain configurations can get in, and everything is checked for viruses, etc. Only privileged personnel, or personnel with certain system configurations can get out. If implemented correctly they can be useful.

Encryption - This growing area of interest consists on coding data so that others can not place bombs in or around it or read the data. This is growing more difficult as hackers and other groups become more efficient at breaking the codes. This is one of the areas that fuzzy logic could come into serious play. If, at first glance, the foregoing appears to be merely a "laundry list," a reading of the following paragraph will surely prove sobering to the IBW planner:

The Defense Information Security Agency (DISA) conducts vulnerability studies of military and government computer systems. Their figures are truly alarming: 88% of defense computer systems are easily penetrated. Of the successful penetrations, 96% are not detected. Even worse, 95% of the detected penetrations are not reported or responded to. Even when an intrusion is detected, it is usually impossible to determine who did it. DISA studies indicate that there were possibly 300,000 intrusions into government computer systems in 1994 alone.

INNATE FEATURES OF INFORMATION WARFARE

While information warfare in the true sense has not yet arrived in the battlefield arena, the repeated live-troop maneuvers and simulated drills of the armies of Western nations such as the United States, as well as the Gulf War, have enabled us to determine certain innate features of information warfare:

- Battlefield transparency. While "battlefield fog" used to be a major problem troubling battlefield commanders, with digitized units, the battlefield is transparent. All belligerent troops will have the battlefield situation at their fingertips both day and night, and be able to see clearly on computer terminal display screens both their own and the enemy's positions, postures, concentrations, and movements. Sullivan says that the transparency of coming wars will be "a quantitative step higher than in the Gulf War."
- Battlefield transparency will be the result of digitized technology. Digitized technology can transmit battlefield intelligence to commanders quickly and accurately in a noiseless and graphics-plus-words form. Digitized cameras on reconnaissance planes can send, in 30 seconds, a 24-power photo that was shot in the morning to an operational command center as far as 315 km away. Frontline troops using digitized infrared sights can detect maneuvers by over 100 enemy

tanks, immediately reporting them to their superiors with digitized information equipment. Digital compression technology can determine enemy detection distance, raising information processing capability, and transmitting intelligence in real time to all units (subunits), even to individual soldiers, for joint information sharing.

- Overall coordination. Overall coordination is another feature of information warfare. The building of the battlefield information superhighway will mean that all operational systems such as combat forces, combat support units, and combat logistics support units, as well as all operational functions such as battlefield intelligence, command, control, communications, and assaults, will be linked into an organic whole. Coordinated actions by all units of this whole can raise combat effectiveness. For instance, coordinated firepower can raise fire assault effectiveness. Air and land sensors detect enemy target activity, which is immediately displayed on screens at the support arm operational center, with the target positioning system accurately converting enemy target coordinates; the target assignment system then assigns suitable targets to the weapons-launching platforms (such as cannons, helicopters, and tanks) that are most suited to attack.
- Operations in real time. Real time is defined as the time of dealing with a certain event being almost the same as the real time of the occurrence of the event. Real-time operations mean immediate responses to all events that occur on the battlefield between ourselves and the enemy and involves the taking of countermeasures such as timely target detection, timely command, timely mobility, real-time strikes, and real-time support. The advantage of this is that missions that used to be hours or even longer can now be completed in minutes or even seconds, making decisionmaking and the course of battle nearly simultaneous.
- Precision strike. Long-range precision strikes without collateral damage will become the essential fire-assault form of future information warfare, making carpet bombing and area fire part of history. Future warfare will be as accurate, clean, and neat as a scalpel cutting out a brain tumor, because future wars will use smart weapons on a large scale. Such weapons include guided bombs, guided shells, guided shrapnel, cruise missiles, no-tip guided missiles, and antiradiation missiles. Their sensors will be capable of capturing all useable direct or indirect target information, such as sound waves, electric waves, visible light, infrared waves, lasers, and even odors and gasses, which information computers will be able to differentiate and analyze. Such smart ammunition not

only can hit targets 100 percent of the time, but can also hit predetermined target positions. To conduct and win information warfare, two major supports will be needed.

A Digitized Battlefield

A digitized battlefield is a composite network system covering the whole operational space. It is made up of a communications system, a command and control system, an intelligence transmission system, a computerized battlefield database, and user terminals, all of which can provide users with large amounts of operation-related information in real time or nearly real time. This network system's function is to use information technology to acquire, exchange, and use digitized information in real time, promptly meeting the information demand of commanders, combat personnel, and combat support personnel, so that they can clearly and accurately grasp all battlefield conditions needed to draw up and apply operational plans. This system can transmit information such as voice, graphics, text, and data, and can also provide users with a battlefield image portrayed by a common database and the supreme battlefield command knowledge-base (including substance such as one's own posture, the enemy's posture, combat readiness, logistics conditions, and operating environment).

This picture is dynamic, changing with the movements of both combatants and changes in terrain and weather. A digitized battlefield is a prerequisite for information warfare. The establishment of a digitized battlefield has many advantages. For instance, information sharing clarifies the position of the enemy and one's own units, sharply lowering accidental injuries; it enables battlefield commanders to amass key units at crucial sites at critical times; it can effectively coordinate short-distance, in-depth, and rear operations, providing intelligence support for all-out, in-depth, simultaneous offensive operations. As all come to know the battlefield conditions, subordinate commanders can bring their initiative into play, acting promptly at their own discretion in line with their superiors' intentions; it makes logistics support "very accurate," for such activities as material provision variety and quantity "accuracy," logistics support provision-time "accuracy," and wounded treatment "timely accuracy."

The establishment of a digitized battlefield is a sort of systems engineering. Many U.S. military specialists claim that this project is more challenging than the Manhattan Project. To carry out this project, the United States is taking many steps.

In line with Clinton's Presidential Order #29 issued in September 1994, the U.S. Defense Department has set up the National Security Policy

Commission and the National Information System Security Commission. The former is charged with formulating military security policy and digitized battlefield establishment principles, while the latter is responsible for controlling the security and secrecy of classified and sensitive information on the military information superhighway and the digitized battlefield.

The U.S. Army set up in January 1994 the Army Digitized Special Taskforce under the direct leadership of the Army's first deputy chief of staff. In June 1994, that taskforce was expanded into the Army Digitized Office, and charged with the design and establishment of the digitized army battlefield. In July 1994, the U.S. Navy set up the Theatre of Operations Information Warfare Center; in January 1995, it established the Fleet Information Warfare Center. Their joint responsibilities are to study and design the technology and software needed for the digitized naval battlefield. The U.S. Air Force Information Warfare Center was set up in October 1993, and charged with establishing a digitized air battlefield.

To build a digitized land, sea, and air battlefield, the computer system structures, operating programs, program design languages, software applications, database languages, and communications rules of all information systems must be standardized and interchangeable throughout all branches of the military. Thus the U.S. military is now pursuing two information resource standardization plans: 1) the all-service command, control, communications, computer, and intelligence system standardization plan, which will set up a global military information database and a global joint network system, thus deploying throughout the world global information sharing for the U.S. military; and 2) the defense information control standardization plan, which is aimed at upgrading the interchangeable software technology of all Defense Department information systems, to eventually make information control and usage standardized and interchangeable.

To achieve battlefield digitization for all arms of the service, the U.S. military is now pursuing a diversified C&C digitized joint-network plan. For instance, the U.S. Army has seven plans:

- The "composite unit C&C, a high-tech demonstration" plan aimed at improving and developing the computer assisted C&C system
- The "joint ground station" plan to provide rapid operational intelligence information to brigade commanders
- The "global network grid" plan to bring many combat units into a single working network
- The "survival adaptation system demonstration" plan that uses multi-media technology to transmit information such as voice, graphics, and data to combat troops

- The "21st century ground warrior" plan to achieve a free battlefield dialogue between man and machine
- The "brigade and below unit (subunit) C&C plan" to provide battlefield information to units (subunits) at the brigade level and below
- The "battlefield combat friend and foe recognition demonstration" plan.

An Informationized Military

The second major support for information warfare [IW] is an informationized military. While many developed Western nations are now considering the establishment of technology-intensive informationized armies, the United States is the only one that has drawn up and started to implement plans for an informationized military establishment.

An informationized army is a brand-new "information-based" military category, with its combat theory, system establishment, personnel quality, and weaponry being completely suited to IW needs. The U.S. informationized military establishment plans are in two stages, which are estimated to be completed by the mid-21st century.

In the first stage, the U.S. Army will first be digitized. While digitized units will be essentially the same in authorized strength and structure as units with ordinary equipment, they will be units with digitized communications technology; integrated command, control, communications, and intelligence; smart weaponry; and networking of all operating systems. The major signs that a unit is digitized will be that its main outfits will be equipped with digitized communications equipment, second-generation forward-looking radar, identification friend-and-foe [IFF] equipment, and the global positioning system [GPS]. Such equipment will include M1A2 tanks, M2A2 fire support vehicles, M2A3 fighting vehicles, Black Eagle command helicopters, Apache attack choppers, Kiowa Brave reconnaissance choppers, M109A6 Warrior self-propelled guns, and M106A2 mortars. The U.S. Army now has a digitized battalion and will have established a digitized army by 1999, with all Army units digitized by 2010.

To test the combat capability of digitized units, the U.S. Army has conducted repeated simulated tests and live-troop confrontation exercises between digitized task forces and nondigitized units. The simulated tests show that digitized technology can shorten the time of choppers going into action from 26 minutes to 18 minutes, while raising the hit rate of antitank missiles from 55 percent to 90 percent. The live-troop exercises show that using conventional communications means to send on-site reports to battalion headquarters takes 9 minutes, while digitized communications means takes only 5 minutes; that the repetition rate is 30 percent for (telegram) text sent by conventional means, but only 4 percent for that sent by digitized means; and that the completion rate of on-site reports is only 22 percent by phone, but as high as 98 percent by digitized means. Through repeated demonstrations the U.S. Army has reached the initial conclusion that "digitized units have enormous combat potential," with their combat effectiveness being "about three times that of ordinary units."

In the second stage, the U.S. Army will grow more informationized on that digitized foundation, as well as build the entire U.S. military, including the Navy and Air Force, into a fully informationized force. After 2010, the U.S. Army will probably be the first to draw up "IW theory," as well as act in line with that theory to reform its system establishment, carry out military training, and develop weaponry, to informationize its units. For two reasons this will probably take about three decades, with completion by 2040:

- The shortage of money for military expenditures dictates that, only once its key combat equipment is digitized, can its related combat support and combat logistics support equipment be gradually digitized. Also, it will have to develop a batch of new smart weapons. So projected from an arms development cycle of about 15 years, it is estimated that its equipment will be completely informationized by 2030.
- The conversion of a military establishment from one structure to another that can operate effectively will take roughly two decades. The U.S. military that can begin to adjust its troop structure after 2010 will still need around two decades to establish the mechanisms suited to fight an information war. Also, as weaponry informationization and military establishment reform cannot be completely synchronous, with an approximate time lag of at least a decade, it is projected that the U.S. Army will be fully informationized only by 2040. The U.S. Navy and Air Force are now also informationizing. By about 2040, once all services are informationized, it will still take more than a decade to get the entire military into a digitized joint network. So it is obvious that by mid-century, the United States probably will have built the world's first completely smart military.

While IW has not yet occurred or at most has only started to show up, as it is an exceptional and new form of warfare with milestone significance, it will have an enormous impact on all aspects of the military arena.

The IW Impact on Combat Concepts

The IW proposition will have an impact on many aspects of combat concepts:

- It will make the rivalry over "information dominance" particularly intense. Certain experts note, "information dominance can be defined most easily and accurately as knowing all enemy information, while keeping the enemy from learning one's own." In future wars, most participating troops in most situations will be dealing not with material, but rather with information. The formation and development of troop combat effectiveness will rely mainly on information collection, processing, transmission, control, and usage. A superior force that loses "information dominance" will be passive, beaten, and in trouble, while an inferior one that seizes the information advantage will be able to win the battlefield initiative. As future combat actions will all be dependent and focused on information, the struggle to wrest information dominance will permeate everything and will be exceptionally fierce and intense.
- It will expand the implications of warfare. This will be manifested mainly in two areas. 1) It will make it harder to win wars. In the agricultural age, it was necessary only to exterminate the enemy's armed forces to win the war. In the industrial age, in addition to wiping out the enemy country's military, it has also been necessary to destroy its military-industrial base. However, in the information age, it will be necessary not only to eliminate the enemy country's war making "material base," but also to control and destroy the enemy's information systems, which will be the primary assault targets. 2) It will expand the limits of war into outer space. That is because the key IW systems space monitoring, positioning, guidance, and communications systems will all be deployed there.
- It will shorten the time of battle. The institution of IW will shorten future wars for two reasons: 1) On one hand, attack means will be highly precise, with the strike targets also being key enemy military positions such as "brain centers," which can be forced to submit very quickly. 2) On the other, in the information age as compared to the industrial age, the combat objectives pursued by both belligerents will be more limited, not total surrender or extermination of the other side, but rather limited political objectives.
- It will make combat more integrated. As information will flow more quickly and not be subject to service branch or time-space limitations, future wars are going to be unprecedentedly integrated.

-Land, sea, air, and space warfare will be highly integrated, which will be the case not only in large-scale wars, but also in small-scale armed conflicts.

- The combat lines among service arms will be hard to distinguish. For instance, the weapons that destroy enemy tanks may not be one's own [friendly] tanks, but rather smart missiles fired from friendly naval submarines. -War zone combat operations will be integrated. As information-age units will have real-time information for rapid mobility both day and night, "the decentralized campaigns developed in the industrial age will no longer exist, being replaced by integrated combat operations in the entire theatre of operations." -The lines among the strategic, campaign, and tactical levels will be blurred. As smart weapons will provide effective means of meeting combat objectives, it will be possible at times to meet strategic and campaign objectives without losing large units.

- It will change the substance of force concentrations. As the use of precision-strike and stealth weapons will make it possible for force concentrations to meet campaign and even strategic objectives, the force-concentration priority will change from the tactical to the campaign and strategic level. A concentration of mostly personnel will change to a concentration of mainly firepower and information, and a concentration of mostly troop and weapons quantity will change to mainly quality. Force concentrations will occur faster, more precisely, and more often during operations.

IMPORTANCE OF INFORMATION WARFARE

Given the above context, one can get an insight into evolution of Chinese theories and concepts on Information Warfare (IW). As with all its military theories and strategic perspectives, Chinese traditional wisdom and strategic thought is applied to all new concepts and precepts originating from the US, Russia or elsewhere. The first wave of Chinese writings on IW appeared in the mid-1990s following the success of US information technologies in the first Gulf War of 1991. Though this war was a defining event for all militaries of the world, its impact on the PLA was greater because of the aspirations of the Chinese political and military leadership towards acquiring comprehensive national strength. The PLA was first off the block in developing theories of IW and adapting Western concepts to suit local conditions. A PLA General, writing on challenges and importance of IW, observed: In near future, Information warfare will control the form and future of war. We recognise this developmental trend of information warfare and see it as a driving force in China's military and combat readiness. This trend will be highly critical to achieve victory in future wars.

The General further emphasised that China must use a practical combination of IW and Maoist and Marxist military thought to guide IW issues under military construction. The military must study ways of using inferior equipment to achieve victory over the enemy's superior equipment. He advocated study on how to conduct 'People's war in IW domain'. The underlying theme of Chinese concepts on IW has been emphasis on devising ways and means to attack an enemy's weaknesses and vulnerabilities, and on exploiting own strengths. The other fundamental assumption is that superior tactics can compensate for inferior technology.

People's Warfare in Information Warfare Context

According to some Chinese military analysts, because of the increasing relevance of information technology (IT) to people's lives, individuals who take part in IW are not all soldiers and that anybody who understands computers may become a fighter. IW is inexpensive as the targeted party can be delivered a paralysing blow through the net and it may be difficult for the latter to discern where the attack originated. Large amount of useless information can be created to block or stop the functioning of an adversary's information system.

Thus, a People's War in context of IW can be carried out by hundreds of millions of people, using open-type modern information systems. Even political mobilisation for war can be achieved via the internet, by sending patriotic e-mail messages and by setting up databases for education.

This finds further support from another Chinese author, who observes that "even as ... government mobilised troops, the numbers and roles of traditional warriors will be sharply less than those of technical experts...since thousand of personal computers can be linked up to perform a common operation, to perform many tasks in place of a large-scale military computer, an IW victory will very likely be determined by which country can mobilise the most computer experts and part-time fans... That will be a real People's War."

Preparing for people's war is a recurring theme in Chinese writing, as IW will be carried out by the PLA and society as a whole. This concept has found practical expression in turning some of the 1.5 million reserve forces into mini-IW regiments. The People's Armed Forces Department (PAFD) has reportedly organised militia/ reserve IW regiments at district levels in many provinces.For instance, in Echeng district of Hubei province, the PAFD has a network warfare battalion as well as electronic warfare, intelligence and psychological warfare battalions, and also a training base for IW activities. The PAFD has also carried out 'Informaticised People's Warfare Network Simulation Exercise'. A version of this concept was also put into practice following the bombing of the Chinese embassy in Belgrade on May 8, 1999, during 'Operation Allied Force'. The Chinese hacked a number of US political, military and diplomatic web sites, and also carried out a network battle by mobilising thousands of net users for sending emails and viruses. This caused servers to crash, paralysing a large number of web sites.

Cyber Warfare

Concerns about China's net force were heightened after the aforementioned attacks on US computer systems and after the Chinese militia carried out IW exercises, which included India, the US, Taiwan and Japan as target countries.

The aim of such training was to disrupt critical infrastructure like banking, power supply and telecommunication networks in the target country as part of China's strategy of asymmetric approach to warfare. In the cyber domain, the Chinese have adopted three methods for targetting such networks; the first is the use of e-mails for planting viruses; then phishing and lastly, the introduction of 'intelligent trojans' and 'vacuum trojans'. Diverse routes of planting trojans and viruses have been used to attack critical PCs, which in turn send out files or cause Chinese Concepts and Capabilities of Information Warfare 785 malfunction. Hackers' tools are becoming more robotic and simple; for instance, a vacuum trojan will extract information from a pen drive automatically when connected to a USB port. It is also believed that the next step could be planting the targeted sites with the more difficult to detect fake data or partially fake data.

In Nanjing, the PLA has developed more than 250 trojans and similar tools. Here, it needs to be remembered that foreign companies like Network Solutions, were made to hand over 300 computer viruses by the Ministry of Public Security's lab in an effort to speed up the certification of antivirus products. Further, the Chinese Academy of Sciences, which provides suggestions about national information security policy and law, has established the State Lab for Information Security. The lab has 'National Attack Project' as one of its research programmes. Also, select professionals have been inducted into militia organisations to boost combat capabilities in future wars. Thus, China has been paying much attention to offensive strategies in cyberspace even as it concentrates on defensive IW.

Definition and Goals of Information Warfare

The Chinese understanding of IW, which was initially based on western concepts, has increasingly moved towards evolving its own orientation. Chinese experts believe that IW's essence is the sum of information capabilities capable of breaking the will to resist by attacking an enemy's cognitive understanding and convictions, forcing it to give up all resistance and terminate the war. The goal is to "force enemy to regard their goal as our goal, to force the opponent to give up the will to resist and end confrontation and stop fight by attacking enemy's perceptions and belief via information energy." Xie Guang, the then Vice Minister of Science and Technology and Industry for National Defence, defined IW in December 1999 thus: "IW in military sense means overall use of various types (of) information technologies, equipment and systems, particularly his command systems, to shake determination of enemy's policy makers and at the same time, the use of all the means possible to ensure that one's own systems are not damaged or disturbed." This definition apparently includes the aspects of IW's goals at the larger national level. A further elaboration was done by two senior PLA colonels, who described IW as consisting of five major elements and two general areas. The five elements are:

- Substantive destruction, the use of hard weapons to destroy enemy headquarters, command posts, and command and control (C2) information centres
- Electronic warfare, the use of electronic means of jamming or the use of anti-radiation [electromagnetic] weapons to attack enemy information and intelligence collection systems such as communications and radar
- Military deception, the use of operations such as tactical feints [simulated attacks] to shield or deceive enemy intelligence collection systems
- Operational secrecy, the use of all means to maintain secrecy and keep the enemy from collecting intelligence on our operations.
- Psychological warfare, the use of TV, radio, and leaflets to undermine the enemy's military morale.

The two general areas are information protection (defence) and information attack (offence). Information defence means preventing the destruction of one's own information systems, ensuring that these systems can perform their normal functions. In future wars, key information and information systems will become "combat priorities", the key targets of enemy attack. It also includes many other manifestations of IW like computer virus warfare, precision warfare and stealth warfare, all dependent in some manner on information and software programmes.

Information Operations

Information Operations (IO) are specific operations and are considered to be at the core of IW, in the same manner as IW is considered to be at the core of informationalisation. In fact, IO is a manifestation of IW on the battlefield. It can be both of the defensive and offensive types, and can be conducted at the strategic, operational, campaign and tactical levels at times of peace, wars and crises. Principles of IO have been defined by Chinese military authors to include centralised command, decentralised control (multi-level power delegation), multi-dimension inspection and testing, timely decision-making and integration of military and civil actions with focus on key links. Major General Dai Qingmin, Director of PLA's General Staff responsible for IW and IO (and also ex-Commander of PLA's IW Centre in Wuhan) observes that integrated and joint information operations give more scope and purpose to people's war. (In fact, jointness and integration is a major theme of the 2004 White Paper). He defines IO as a series of operations with an informationalised environment as the basic battlefield condition, with military information and information systems as the direct operational targets and electronic warfare (EW) and computer networks as the principal form. He has outlined various IO strategies because, as mentioned earlier, according to the traditional Chinese approach strategies can compensate for inferior equipment and technologies and, in the case of IO, it may also compensate for gaps in information or poor information about the enemy. Some of the IO strategies are:

- Jamming or sabotaging an enemy's information or information system.
- Sabotaging an enemy's overall information operational structure.
- Weakening an enemy's information fighting capacity.
- Dispersing enemy forces, arms and fires while concentrating own forces, arms and fire.
- Confusing or diverting an enemy and creating an excellent combat opportunity for on self.
- Diverting an enemy's reconnaissance attempt and making sufficient preparations for it.
- Giving the enemy a false impression and launching surprise information attack on him at the same time.
- Blinding or deafening an enemy with false impressions.
- Confusing an enemy or disrupting his thinking.
- Making an enemy believe that what is true is false and what is false is true.
- Causing an enemy to make a wrong judgement or take wrong action.

In the IW exercises conducted by PAFD, 10 methods of IO were practised and these can be viewed as tactics in the electronic battlefield. These are:

- Planting information mines
- Conducting information reconnaissance
- Changing network data

- Releasing information bombs
- Dumping information garbage
- Disseminating propaganda
- Applying information deception
- Releasing clone information
- Organising information defence
- Establishing network spy stations.

Computer Network Operations

In Chinese writings on Information Warfare, networking has also been the focus of discussions. The recent emphasis on jointness and integration apply equally to integrating various military networks. A critique by Timothy Thomas notes that the Chinese feel it necessary to prepare for a "network people's war". Computer network warfare has been included by Dai Qing as one of the six forms of IW (i.e. operational security, military deception, psychological warfare, electronic warfare, computer network warfare and physical destruction). Though there is no evidence of a formal Chinese doctrine, Chinese theorists have coined the term "Integrated Network Electronic Warfare" (INEW) and this has also been referred to by Timothy Thomas as a half cousin, given its similarities and points of divergences to the US approach.

INEW has been described as a series of combat operations that integrate electronic warfare and computer network warfare measures to disrupt the normal operation of an enemy's battlefield systems while protecting one's own with the objective of attaining information superiority. The essence of computer network warfare (CNW) is "to disrupt layers in which information is processed, by seizing and maintaining control of network space". EW is targeted at networked information systems and informationalised weapon systems in order to increase combat effectiveness. According to Dai, INEW is necessary for system to system confrontation on the informationalised battlefield, as systems are centres of gravity. Any disruption in system will lead to a disconnect between the people and weapons.

Thus, INEW lays stress on coordinating and integrating all aspects of C4ISR and weapon platforms and weapon systems to produce the desired effects at the target end. The effectiveness of weapon platforms and network systems is directly proportional to its levels of integration. As in other spheres, integration produces a combat capability greater than the sum of its parts and, this is true for information operations as well.

China's computer network operations (CNO) comprise network attacks, defence, and exploitation. According to the Pentagon's Annual Report for 2005 to the Congress on China's military power, the PLA views CNO as critical to seize the initiative and "electromagnetic dominance" early in a conflict, and as a force multiplier. This concept outlines the integrated use of electronic warfare, CNO and limited physical strikes against key C4ISR nodes to disrupt an enemy's battlefield network information systems. It is believed that the PLA has established information warfare units to develop viruses to attack enemy computer systems and networks, and tactics to protect friendly computer systems and networks. The PLA has increased the role of CNO in its military exercises. Although initial training efforts focused on increasing the PLA's proficiency in defensive measures, recent exercises have incorporated offensive operations, primarily as first strikes against enemy networks.

The main area of weakness that the Chinese espy, especially with regard to US forces, is the deployment phase. US forces are largely dependent upon computer and communication systems, both military and nonmilitary, and the particularly weak links in the logistics network systems make them susceptible to computer network attacks. Logistics network systems may be relatively easy to penetrate compared to other C4 systems though it will be more useful to penetrate command and information links. However, the priority of Chinese CNW seems to be to prevent the force from deploying at the first place and thereafter breaking the linkages between decision-makers and weapon platforms. This approach rhymes with the oft-stated Chinese strategy of attacking weaknesses and avoiding strengths of the enemy. As observed by James Mulvenon, Chinese strategists theorise that:

- Computer network attack is the most effective means for a weak adversary to fight a strong one.
- It can be used as a means to deter the enemy.
- It has longer range than the conventional power projection assets, as long distance surveillance and precise powerful and long distance attacks are available to the military.

Psychological Operations and Information Warfare

Another important component of information Warfare with Chinese characteristics is psychological warfare. Chinese doctrine has traditionally focused more attention on the psychological dimensions of IW, including deception, though of late they have also been paying equal, if not more, attention to the technological dimensions. The target in psychological operations is always the people and decision-makers, so that their will and perceptions are attacked to alter their beliefs, goals and behaviour. This is aimed at both military and civil components of an adversary's populace. Psychological operations comprise of manipulation of media to support military efforts and include conventional methods of propaganda like distribution of leaflets, radio and TV broadcasts, and other means of communication. Like most of the components of IW, psychological operations are a continuum of actions in peacetime, crisis time and war time.

In August 2005, the PLA conducted a joint exercise, involving not only all its services but also troops from Russia. The exercise involved distribution of leaflets over the opponent, electronic warfare to confuse incoming missiles and adoption of electronic counter measures. These exercises involved the use of live missiles and ammunition, and showcased precision warfare capabilities as well as the latest military equipment. These exercises could also be said to have had a psychological dimension for deterring Taiwan or those aiding it in its political objectives.

Here, it can be argued that the Chinese appear to have taken a leaf out of the US forces' tom-tomming of the awesome power of their arsenal and military capabilities before the start of 'Operation Iraqi Freedom', which had the effect of lowering the morale of the Iraqi military. The US forces also air dropped over 31 million leaflets for propaganda purposes besides physically attacking Iraqi forces' command and control networks based on fibre optic lines and radio and computer servers. US forces had been issued cyber-guidance as early as February 2003 for operations in Iraq. The PLA has thus been quick to absorb lessons on IW from 'Operation Iraqi Freedom'.

The Chinese also observed the power of media when CNN's broadcast of a US soldier's body being dragged through the streets of Mogadishu transformed perceptions of victory into defeat. Authors of the Chinese book titled Unrestricted Warfare reflected on the incident thus: Did CNN's broadcast of an exposed corpse of a US soldier in the streets of Mogadishu shake the determination of the Americans to act as the world's policeman, thereby altering the world's strategic situation? And should an assessment of wartime actions look at the means or the results?

PLA's IW/EW Capabilities

The 2004 White Paper shows that the Chinese military has understood that there is a large and expanding technology gap between it and modern militaries, especially that of the US. China's leaders, including President Hu Jintao, have ordered the PLA to pursue "leap ahead" technologies and "informationalised" capabilities to increase weapons' mobility, firepower and precision. This perspective applies to IW also.

The Central Military Commission's (CMC) Third or Technical Department of General Service Headquarters is responsible for strategic SIGINT and has established a number of monitoring stations to intercept signals from countries like India, Taiwan, Japan, South Korea and others. The PRC also established a Fourth Armed Forces Department in 1990 to look after offensive and defensive IW activities. It has also built "an information warfare simulation centre" for training its corps of network warriors. The centre uses high technology simulation skills and equipment to simulate information warfare and its environment. The Fourth Department has special detachments and units that manage and direct SIGINT and EW operations for the PLA at all levels and includes operations of the Air Force and the Navy.

The PRC has completed one million km of fibre optics line and communication infrastructure called "Eight Horizontal Grids and Eight Vertical Grids" supported by satellite, ground mobile receiving stations and ground to air data links. With technologies obtained from Western countries and by exploiting its booming commercial IT and telecommunications sector, it has improved the quality of its military programmes. The PLA has acquired and deployed a wide variety of air, sea and land-based intelligence, surveillance and reconnaissance (ISR) systems to enhance its ability to detect monitor and target military activities in Asia and West Pacific Ocean. Some of the latest programmes include electro-optics, synthetic aperture radar, over the horizon radars, and surveillance systems that can detect stealth aircraft.

EW is a key element in the PLA's 'Three Attacks and Three Defences' strategy (attack stealth aircraft, cruise missiles and helicopters; defend against precision strikes, electronic warfare, and enemy reconnaissance) to meet the requirements of 'local war under high tech conditions' which has now progressed to 'local war under informationalised conditions'. Both military and civil sectors are actively exploring IW concepts which could lead to developing a corps of network warriors to defend China's telecommunication, command and information networks while uncovering vulnerabilities of adversaries' networks.

At the national level, China has a C3I system based on fibre optic cables, satellite communications, micro-wave links, tropo-scatter communications and automated command and control systems. The PLA has both secured and non-secured telecommunications and has an army wide data communication network and integrated field operations communication system. Its WAN is capable of supporting peacetime operations within Chinese borders and limited pre-planned operations along China's periphery but is inadequate for large-scale joint operations.

The Chinese Army has a family of battlefield ELINT systems like DZ 9002 that detect, intercept, analyse and record an adversary's signal emissions. DZ 9001 has been developed both for defensive and offensive electronic counter measures (ECM). DZ 9300 is a man-packed radar reconnaissance system meant for special operations forces and rapid reaction forces. A bodyguard laser countermeasures system has also been developed to counter precision-guided munitions guided by laser emissions. There are also a variety of jamming systems with the ground forces.

The PLA Air Force is developing capabilities in airborne warning and control systems (AWACS), airborne early warning, and ECM aircraft and UAVs. Shaanxi Y-8 has been designed for special EW, ELINT and ECM missions. This aircraft was first observed in operation in the summer of 2004 and it is believed that some of its equipment may be from the US Navy's EP-3 ELINT aircraft that made an emergency landing in Hainan in April 2001. Another version of the Y-8 aircraft is 'Balance Beam' airborne early warning aircraft meant for tactical ISR, EW and ELINT missions. It made its maiden flight in 2001 and its finalised version Y-8 F600 flew in January 2005. The PLA Air Force is planning for 4-6 AWACS and has about 20 other dedicated ELINT aircraft like HD-5, TU-154M and HZ-6. HD-5, an older version, is being replaced by HZ-6 which has improved capabilities. UAV's configured for ELINT and EW missions are also in use. In July 2002, the PLA inducted the Israeli anti-radar hunter killer HARPY UAV. The Chinese Navy also has over a dozen ships and several trawlers for various electronic warfare missions. Four Yuan Wang and Shiyan class ships monitor space events and are capable of collecting and monitoring missile and satellite telemetry data and communications. Chinese industry has developed three types of systems, based on Soviet-era systems, which have been further upgraded and modernised.

Space is another area where the Chinese have been making rapid advances, especially in the field of ISR and anti-satellite technologies. China considers space as a 'commanding height' and it plans to control space and win the information war after having built up an informationalised PLA. In 2003, the PLA had six dual-use dedicated satellites for military purposes. In 2004, China placed 10 satellites into orbit and has a similar schedule through 2006. It hopes to have more than 100 satellites in orbit by 2010, and launch an additional 100 satellites by 2020. In the next decade, Beijing will most likely field radar, ocean surveillance, and improved filmbased photo-reconnaissance satellites. China will eventually deploy advanced imagery, reconnaissance, and Earth resource systems with military applications. China's ZY-2 payloads have digital imagery reconnaissance capabilities and have worldwide coverage. Beijing also tested new film-based imagery satellites and small digital imagery satellites in 2003 and 2004. It is also developing its own GPS navigation system based on the Beidou series of navigational satellites. The PLA possesses anti-GPS jammers obtained from Russia, which however may not be very effective against the NAVSAT satellite system of the US.

China is also developing electronic intelligence (ELINT) and signals intelligence (SIGINT) reconnaissance satellites. These digital data systems will be able to transmit directly to ground sites, and China may be developing a system of data relay satellites to support global coverage. Furthermore, Beijing has acquired mobile data reception equipment that can support more rapid data transmission to deployed military forces and units. China is developing micro satellites for remote sensing as well as for putting into place networks of electro-optical and radar satellites. In April 2004, Beijing launched a micro satellite with a probable imagery mission. China is also conducting research to develop ground-based laser ASAT Weapons. All these capabilities will contribute to China's prowess in the field of information warfare.

Implications for India

Attaining information superiority has become one of the most important objectives to be achieved in the era of knowledge age warfare. The concept of information superiority is somewhat analogous to similar concepts of air, sea or space superiority.

This is because proper use of information is as lethal as other kinds of power. Further, the concept of information superiority leads us to attainment of decision superiority. Information operations are increasingly being considered as important as sea, land and air operations. Information operations can vary from physical destruction to psychological operations to computer network defence. Wellconducted joint information operations with new RMA technologies, improved organisations and doctrine will greatly contribute to a successful and decisive outcome.

It is in this context that a Defence Information Warfare Agency (DIWA) under the Integrated Defence Staff Headquarters has been formed to coordinate efforts of the three services and certain other agencies to handle all aspects of information warfare. The Indian concepts of IW are generally based on Western concepts and according to the 2004 Army Doctrine, IW encompasses the elements of command and control warfare, intelligencebased warfare, electronic warfare, cyber warfare, psychological warfare and network centric warfare, military deception and secrecy as well as media support. Though the three Services have different set ups for IW activity, DIWA is the nodal and apex policy-making body to formulate joint and integrated responses to IW challenges. Therefore, an IW doctrine needs to be formulated, which it is believed, is under the process of being evolved by DIWA. However, it is at operational levels that weaknesses in our IW efforts exist. There is a need for joint linkages and joint planning to synchronise our response to all elements of information warfare.

INFORMATION WARFARE AND DETERRENCE

It is clear that the information age has spawned new relationships and greatly expanded the range of possible interactions. It is no longer possible to separate and isolate military, national, public, and private systems. Thus, concepts of national security, to include protecting information systems and deterring attacks, need to be expanded to consider the full range of likely interactions. This would help to determine where the boundary between DoD and the rest of the national information infrastructure should lie. It was in this context that the workshop primarily addressed the relationship between information warfare and deterrence.

At the abstract level, the interface between these two concepts is dependent on setting the context clearly. First, deterrence is always from an actor toward a target. The very nature of the actor and target, as well as the degree of asymmetry between them is important. A nation state has much greater power than an individual hacker and has broad powers of law enforcement that can be brought to bear if the individual is within its borders or the reach of accepted international laws. However, two nation states are, at least in legal terms, equal and must exercise the international system (diplomacy, warfare, etc.) to influence one another's behavior. Moreover, the nature of the relationship between the parties is important to the analysis. The use of deterrence is unlikely in cooperative arrangements, more likely in competitive ones, and most likely in conflictual patterns. Finally, substantive context may also make a difference. For example, deterrence is most likely in military arenas where the credibility of threats is greatest and easiest to assess. Hence, specification of the context (type of relationship, nature of the actors, substantive domain) is essential before any conclusion is possible about the effectiveness of deterrence.

The Steamroller and the Wrench

The most important insight arising from looking at the two concepts however, is the fact that they are only relevant to one another in highly selective contexts. The analogy that emerged was that of a steamroller and a wrench. Both are tools and depending on the situation, appropriate wrenches may be useful for, or even crucial to, the operation of the steamroller. However, most of the things the steamroller does are irrelevant to the wrench and most of the things the wrench can be used for do not involve a steamroller. In many cases, therefore, the workshop found itself venturing away from a pure consideration of the two concepts and into meaningful discussions in areas related to one or the other of the two central topics. These discussions revolved around the concepts, but kept slipping tangentially to more familiar issues such as command and control warfare (C2W), or IW in some other context such as retaliation in kind for an IW attack. It eventually became apparent that the main reason for frustration was that the related concepts and issues are grossly mismatched. IW is just too big and encompasses so much (particularly in the context of information dominance), while deterrence is limited and almost always case specific.

In retrospect, the revelation should not have been surprising. While workshop participants noted that certain IW actions are as old as warfare (a bluff for example), the exploding vistas of information technology and cyberspace are only beginning to be understood. Several of the participants were comfortable discussing deterrence as it might be related to command and control warfare (C2W). In this application there are five clearly defined "Pillars" which include Operational Security (OPSEC), Electronic Warfare (EW), Psychological Operations (PSYOPS), Military Deception, and Physical Destruction.

The pillars are arrayed both offensively as "Counter-Command and Control" and defensively as "Command and Control Protection." Both arrays are dependent on and supported by intelligence. Any one of the pillars can have a deterrent effect. For example, in EW the presence of anti-radiation missiles may deter the use of air defense radar. Likewise, the adroit use of psychological operations might disrupt the enemy decision making process to the point where they are deterred from action, or at least their C2 process is greatly slowed.

While we believe that we understand C2W, the workshop brought into clear focus the fact that C2W is only a very small subset of IW, and it is that larger context that needs further exploration and analysis. Likewise, one size IW deterrence does not fit all. Equally important to the action itself is the intended recipient. Without getting into the adversary's mind and understanding his social, cultural, and religious values, as well as his education and past history, IW deterrence actions may be like the tree that falls in the forest and goes unheard. They may even be misunderstood and, therefore, have unintended consequences. The earlier discussion of deterrence stressed that creditable deterrence requires that the message be communicated clearly. Knowing how the adversary receives and understands messages is essential. It also became increasingly clear that IW deterrent actions must be part of an orchestrated and integrated effort. Seldom will an IW action in and of itself be a creditable deterrent. However, skillfully combined as part of an overall information dominance concept, some combination of IW and other actions may produce the desired deterrence.

ESTABLISHING CONCEPTS OF VICTORY IN FUTURE INFORMATION WARFARE

Looking at the current situation, it can be seen that the authorized strength and equipment, strategy, tactics, and military theory of China's military are still basically the products of the industrial era and are far from satisfying the demands of information warfare. We have much work to do to shrink this gap, and our first task is to clarify our war preparation concepts. We have already made it clear that the basis of war preparation is to achieve victory in modern warfare, especially high-tech warfare, and this is quite correct. High-tech warfare, however, has already developed from an emphasis on guided missiles to an emphasis on information. Firepower superiority depends on information superiority. This has been a phased transition. In keeping with the demands of information warfare, we must base our war preparations on achieving victory in this area and use it to plan China's military and national defense modernization. When we engage in war with strong enemies in the future, we will face comprehensive and powerful information suppression.

There is a question of how to use weakness to defeat strength and how to conduct war against weak enemies in order to use information superiority to achieve greater victories at a smaller cost. It must be confirmed that information and weapons are all controlled by people. People are the main factor in combat power. However, it must also be confirmed that the functions of people and weapons will primarily be determined by the control of information, because information can play an important role in warfare. Hence, the flow of information, under the control of people, is injected into the flow of manpower, capacity, and materials, and will influence the form of warfare and determine victory or defeat.

During the industrial age, the combat power of a military was measured primarily by how much capacity that military held and could utilize. During the information age, the efficiency of capacity utilization is even more important. Generally speaking, a military with capacity but no means to use it cannot become a true combat power. If capacity is used to no effect, it will only cause unnecessary damage and waste and will not have practical significance to victory or defeat in the war. A military can become a truly effective combat power only if it can use its capacity effectively. Capacity utilization controlled by information technology can successfully solve this problem. In this way, the thrust of China's military construction and development of weapons and equipment will no longer be toward strengthening the "firepower antipersonnel system" of the industrial age, but toward the strengthening of information technology, information weapons systems, and information networking. Our sights must not be fixed on the firepower warfare of the industrial age, rather they must be trained on the information warfare of the information age. This must be the starting point from which to propel China's military construction forward and raise that construction to a higher grade and standard.

Theory is the new guide to action, and information warfare theory is a new warfare theory. We must understand it, study it, and use it to guide military construction and combat. China's military, which has always had advanced Marxist and Maoist warfare theory, absolutely must not fall behind the times. We must use a practical combination of information warfare and Marxist and Maoist military thought to guide information warfare and issues in military construction. In light of the fact that the military lags behind its strong enemies in information technology and information weapons, the military must emphasize the study of ways to use inferior equipment to achieve victory over enemies with superior equipment. "Using the inferior to overcome the superior" is a tradition of China's military. However, "using the inferior to overcome the superior" in information warfare is definitely much different in content and form from the techniques of war used in the past. The question of how to conduct a people's war in information warfare also requires study. The people's war of the past was conducted in tangible space, but information warfare, in addition to occurring in tangible space on the ground, on the sea, and in the air, is conducted even more in intangible space, such as in electromagnetic fields. It is not only a battlefield in which guns and bombs proliferate, but also a "computer battlefield" in sheltered laboratories and control rooms. There are many new issues here we need to explore.

IMPROVING WEAPONS AND EQUIPMENT THROUGH INFORMATION TECHNOLOGY

We must put effort into information technology, information weapons systems, and information networking. These are the important aspects of hardware construction for the military when adapting to information warfare. Information is a material good, and information sources, information channels, and information storage are all material goods. The gathering, transmission, processing, and use of information and the development of information into combat power all depend on certain material goods, energy, and technology carriers. Information technology itself is a pinnacle of high technology. The key technologies are remote-sensing technology, communications technology, and computer technology. Key information weapons include precision-guided weapons systems and electronic warfare weapons systems as well as C4I systems (communications, guidance, control, computers, and intelligence) which form the central nervous system. These hardware items are necessary and essential to adapt to and achieve victory in information warfare, and we must make efforts here. Developing this hardware, however, is not easy. It will be restricted by the level of our information technology base and funds. Hence, comprehensive consideration must be given to the direction, goals, and emphases of this development. The overarching demand, for long-term planning as well as short-term arrangements, is to consider fully the threat faced by China, the possible warfare tasks of the near future, the battle regions and battlefield conditions, the state of China's defense technology development, as well as the possible support for military funding. Thus, it appears that we should emphasize in our development the following aspects of information technology.

A Reliable Reconnaissance and Remote-Sensing System

The goal is to obtain timely information, to understand the enemy and ourselves, and to achieve clarity about our situation with great determination. It is especially necessary to establish a strategic reconnaissance warning and air defense system to achieve a capacity for early detection of enemy movements, in order to be forewarned and ready.

Information Weapons Systems

The most important of these are air defense weapons systems, offensive tactical guided missile attack systems, landing and touchdown operations equipment systems, electronic warfare equipment systems, and underwater minelaying systems. These will give China over-the-horizon, high-precision, concealed, sudden defensive attack capability and a stronger survival capacity and make the enemy terrified and worried, providing an effective threat.

4

The Computer Technology and Cybernetic Warfare

As the intensity and breadth of the battlefield grew along with its logistical requirements, new communication technologies became necessary to achieve the required integration and coordination of increasingly large and intricate military systems.

The harnessing of electromagnetic forces for telecommunication purposes proceeded with telegraphy and telephony, simultaneously stimulating growing scientific interest in the concept of information. Cybernetics emerged from the unprecedented technological and industrial effort of the Second World War, in particular the work on the automation of anti-aircraft defences. The selfproclaimed 'science of communications and control' promised to manage chaos and disruption through self-regulating mechanisms of negative information feedback. By being defined in terms of negative entropy (negentropy), information became conceptualized as the source of all order. The computer, also developed during the war for the purposes of code-breaking and the computation of nuclear physics, emerged as the new dominant technology and abstract model through which the world came to be understood chiefly in terms of information processing.

The drive for complete predictability and centralized control over armed conflict was renewed under cybernetic warfare with the deployment of computers and automated control technologies, and the widespread application of the analytical tools of operations research and systems analysis.

The Cold War and the constant threat of nuclear annihilation required ever greater levels of automation and centralization of the war machine; and cybernetics, with its promise of stability in the face of perturbation, appeared best suited to the containment and management of a conflict of potentially apocalyptic proportions. Vast command and control architectures were established to organize the global projection of armed force and the rapid mobilization of military systems within the shrinking windows of opportunity afforded by nuclear weaponry. Scientific methodology was applied to warfare more systematically than ever, with operations research and systems analysis applied comprehensively to both tactical and strategic questions. The first two decades of the postwar era saw the rise of the defence intellectuals and their analytical tools in the United States, culminating in the nomination of Robert McNamara as Secretary of Defence.

In its most pristine form, cybernetic warfare fuelled wild yet enduring fantasies of omniscience and omnipotence on the battlefield. In 1969 General William Westmoreland, commander-in-chief of US forces in Vietnam, formulated his vision of the military's future, encapsulating this cybernetic ideal:

On the battlefield of the future, enemy forces will be located, tracked, and targeted almost instantaneously through the use of data links, computer assisted intelligence evaluation, and automated fire control. With first round kill probabilities approaching certainty, and with surveillance devices that can continually track the enemy, the need for large forces to fix the opponent becomes less important.

Towards Chaoplexic Warfare

Since the mid-1970s, the cybernetic mode of warfare has come under increasing challenge from the military reversal for US forces in Vietnam, geopolitical transformation following the end of the Cold War, and novel scientific developments growing out of the original corpus of cybernetics.

The increasing application of computers to the study of scientific problems, the exploration of non-linear mathematics, and an extension of the cybernetic analysis of systems to questions of self-organization opened the way for novel scientific approaches which eventually crystallized into the theories of chaos and complexity (here referred to together as *chaoplexity*). Information remains the central concept, and in this sense chaoplexity is an outgrowth of cybernetics; but the focus on change, evolution and positive feedback breaks with the cybernetic pioneers' concern for stability.

Chaos is seen no longer as simply a threat to order which must be averted at all costs, but as the very condition of possibility of order. The key notions here are those of non-linearity, self-organization and emergence, and the pivotal technological figure is that of the network, the distributed model of information exchange perhaps best embodied by the internet.

The Science of Chaoplexity

Although still firmly set in the informational paradigm, chaos theory and complexity science departed from cybernetics in shifting the focus away from the stabilizing self-regulation (or homeostasis) underlying the persistence of existing systems towards runaway processes of change leading to the emergence of new systems or patterns of behaviour.

Non-linear dynamics and positive feedback processes, whereby small causes can amplify into large effects, are crucial here. Chaos theorists have used computer simulations of non-linear systems to reveal how initially minute variations can ramp up into dramatic changes in the long-term behaviour of the system. The popular image invoked to illustrate this phenomenon is the 'butterfly effect': the notion that a butterfly flapping its wings in (say) Tokyo can cause a tornado in (say) California. While chaos theory has imposed serious limits on the ability to predict the long-term behaviour of systems, it has also provided new insights, uncovering a subtle order and structure to phenomena previously believed to be completely devoid of recognizable patterns, such as the turbulence of fluids or plate tectonics.

Building on the original insights of chaos theory, complexity scientists turned to the interactions of the different component parts of living systems, and particularly to the new properties and behaviours constituted through the networked selforganization of autonomous agents.

Self-organization is the process by which the autonomous interaction of individual entities results in the bottom-up emergence of complex systems, systems composed of many parts which are connected in a non-linear fashion.

The notion of the network is central to describing the patterns of interaction which are constituted by the interplay of entities in a complex system: 'The first and most obvious property of any network is its non-linearity— it goes in all directions. Thus the relationships in a network pattern are non-linear relationships. In particular, an influence, or message, may travel along a cyclical path, which may become a feedback loop. The concept of feedback is intimately connected with the network pattern.'

Of special interest are the 'complex adaptive systems' which display the ability to change and learn from experience. Complexity theorist John Holland defines a complex adaptive system as a dynamic network of many agents acting simultaneously, constantly both acting and reacting to what the other agents are doing. Since the control of a complex adaptive system tends to be highly dispersed and decentralized, any coherent behaviour in the system arises from competition and cooperation among the agents themselves. It is the accumulation of all the individual decisions taken by the multitude of agents which produces the overall behaviour of the system, which can thus be said to be emergent. Complex adaptive systems include living organisms, insect colonies, bird flocks, ecosystems, businesses, stock markets and other forms of social organization; the constituent agents may be cells, species, individuals, firms or nations. From the perspective of chaoplexity, the most successful systems are those that retain flexibility and openness in the interaction and organization of their parts within environments which elude complete predictability.

No longer is order to be sought in a natural tendency towards equilibrium. On the contrary, it is with non-equilibrium that order emerges from chaos, at the point where instability and creative mutation allow for the genesis of new forms and actions. As Ian King puts it, 'networking [is] a way of maintaining a low-level chaotic substrate so that—as in the brain—the chaos will from time to time give birth to an intellectual self-organizing structure'.

Decentralized self-organizing systems are inherently better equipped than centralized systems to deal with limited predictability and contingency. According to the biologist Christopher Langton, 'since it's effectively impossible to cover every conceivable situation, top-down systems are forever running into combinations of events they don't know how to handle. They tend to be touchy and fragile, and they all too often grind to a halt in a dither of indecision.' In contrast, decentralized systems of quasi-autonomous units can operate more effectively and with a greater degree of adaptability on the basis of the local calculations of the networked agents constituting them. For Stuart Kauffman, 'networks in the regime near the edge of chaos—this compromise between order and surprise—appear best able to coordinate complex activities and best able to evolve as well'.

Chaoplexity has challenged some of the most deeply held scientific convictions about the natural world and opened up whole new areas of research. It is now also increasingly weighing on the debates about military organization, heralding a new era in the scientific way of warfare.

COMPUTER TECHNOLOGY AND BATTLEFIELD INFORMATION NETWORKS

First, we should establish battlefield information networks and battlefield databases for the battlefields in priority strategic directions. By bringing all branches of the military into an information network, information may be shared on the network. Near-real-time communication can be gained in all directions and a better solution can be achieved for the problem of vertical and horizontal coordination in warfare.

Firm Control of Battlefield Information

To achieve victory in information warfare, the central issue is control of information.

Preparation and Defense with Attacking and Fighting

In comparison with the strength of potential enemies, the information technology and information weapons of China's military may all be inferior for quite some time. When China's enemies mainly use their air forces and navies to conduct strategic information warfare, China will be in the strategic position of engaging in defensive warfare along interior lines. The progress and outcome of the war will be determined by the state of China's advance preparations and defensive situation during the war. In defensive warfare, China should still thoroughly implement an active defensive strategy. In addition to hiding and concealing forces, in combat, especially during key phases in key areas, we must engage even more actively in air defense warfare and intercept and attack enemy weapons as they arrive in surprise attack. When conditions permit, we should also engage in counterattacks against the enemy and interfere with or misguide their guided weapons, thus damaging or destroying their equipment. Strategically, we should use preparation and defense, and in combat we should use attacking and fighting to achieve victory.

Organize Offensive and Defensive Information Warfare

Information warfare includes engaging in an active offense of information suppression and attack, as well as in the reactive defense of information counter-reconnaissance, resistance to interference, and defense against destruction. The issue of an information offensive can only be discussed if one has superior technology for information suppression. In a strategic defense situation, sometimes information offensives can be undertaken during warfare actions in limited areas. In that case, information technology suppression superiority must first be achieved in warfare actions in that limited area. Under the conditions of modern high technology, an information offensive is often a prelude to a strategic offensive. Take, for example, the surprise attack on Libya by the United States. Before the attack, 18 electronic-warfare aircraft were sent to Libya to engage in powerful interference.

Fighter aircraft were then sent to launch counterradiation guided missiles to destroy Libya's air defense radar stations, then fighter aircraft were sent to launch precision-guided bombs to attack five important targets. The information offensives in this raid included: 1) information reconnaissance to gain information on targets of the raid and to study the target in detail;

2) electronic interference to paralyze the opponents's communications and blind the opponent's air defense guided missiles; 3) information suppression by using counter radiation guided missiles to destroy air defense radar stations, and 4) information attack by using precision-guided warheads to attack pre-set targets.

During the Gulf War, the information offensives of the multilateral forces were even more representative. In addition to the four types listed above at least the following should be added: 1) Computer viruses were used to destroy the computer systems of Iraq's air defense system and thus paralyze it, and 2) stealth aircraft were used to launch precision-guided bombs against the communications building and the command center, thus achieving information suppression.

In situations of information defense, we must strive for an active approach in a reactive situation and use every means possible to destroy the opponent's information superiority and transform our inferior position in information. We must pay attention to:

- Counter reconnaissance to prevent the opponent from obtaining information about the true situation. For example, secret falsification can be used to plant false intelligence and false targets in the place of true intelligence and true targets to confuse the real and the false and muddle the opponent's perceptions and inspire false assessments. When conditions exist, active methods may be used to engage in interference to blind or even destroy the opponent's reconnaissance instruments.
- Resistance to interference to maintain one's own channels of information. By using defense advantages, multiple-communication methods can be used to weaken the impact of the enemy's interference.
- Resist viruses to protect the normal operations of information processing in computer systems.
- Information counterattack. This is an important action to be carried out according to the general strategic plan and in coordination with strategic and combat counterattacks. The specific content and form is the same as that of information offensives.

The information offenses and defenses outlined above, in addition to using information technology extensively, also use information weapons extensively. Thus, during the process of a war, these do not exist alone but accompany strategic offenses and defenses and are consistent with the overall situation of strategic offenses and defenses. Before and after war, information hassling never stops for a moment but usually does not involve the use of information weapons.

Using Strengths to Attack Weaknesses

This is the basic warfare style which Mao Zedong taught us, and it is an excellent tradition of China's military. Strengths and weaknesses are in comparison with those of the enemy. What then will China's strengths be in future wars? What will be China's weaknesses? Politically speaking, China's military has the advantage of justness, which is conducive to gaining international sympathy and support, and it has the support of the people domestically. In terms of warfare space, when China's military engages in war on China's soil, it will have the advantages of topography and position. In air, sea, space, and electronic warfare, however, the enemy will have the advantage. In terms of the choice of timing for warfare, because the enemy will have more advanced night-vision instruments, the advantage will not be China's, especially in air and sea warfare at night. The enemy will have advantages in instrumentation. China will have advantages in familiarity with the topography. Each will have half the advantages. In terms of warfare techniques, China's military has a tradition of flexible fighting methods and is more adapted to nonlinear warfare, but lacks practical battle experience in information warfare with high technology. In terms of weapons and equipment, generally speaking the enemy will have the advantage, but in some areas, such as guided missiles and submarines, China can still shock the enemy to a certain degree. China is strong in close warfare; the enemy is strong in distant warfare.

In wars of the future, China will face the enemy's more complete information technology with incomplete information technology. Because sometimes superior tactics can make up for inferior technology, China will still carry out its traditional warfare method of "you fight your way, I'll fight my way," and use its strengths to attack the enemy's weaknesses and adhere to an active role in warfare. To do this, it appears that we must pay even more attention to:

- Fully utilizing the advantages of national territory and front information facilities to carry out reconnaissance on the enemy's situation and protect ourselves and attack the enemy
- Developing, improving, and utilizing China's information weapons in a concentrated way to carry out raids on enemy operation platforms and bases and damage and foil the enemy's offensive
- Emphasizing mobile war in the context of information warfare
- Conscientiously organizing sabotage operations by the Army, Navy, and Air Force, grasp exploitable opportunities, and make continuous raids to exhaust and wear down the enemy

- Organizing specialized combined special warfare troops and equip these with information technology weapons to carry out powerful special warfare.

In summary, our warfare methods must adapt to the needs of information warfare. We must use all types, forms, and methods of force, and especially make more use of nonlinear warfare and many types of information warfare methods which combine native and Western elements to use our strengths in order to attack the enemy's weaknesses, avoid being reactive, and strive for being active. In this way, it will be entirely possible for China to achieve comprehensive victory over the enemy even under the conditions of inferiority in information technology.

Cultivating Talent

In the final analysis, information warfare is conducted by people. The basic great plan is to cultivate talented people suited to information warfare. One aspect is to cultivate talent in information science and technology. The development and resolution of information warfare can be predicted to a great degree in the laboratory. Information science and technology talent is the forerunners of science and technology talent is the forerunner of science and technology research. The achievements and practical use of their research will play a key role in the development and advancement of society and military construction and warfare. The second aspect is talented people in command and control. They especially need to have the ability to conduct comprehensive analysis and policy-information processing, to understand themselves and the enemy, as well as the battlefield, and also to have a capacity for scientific strategic thinking and a comprehensive point of view. Senior command personnel especially need to have information knowledge and the ability to control information warfare and must be adept at using information technology to organize and command warfare. They must be very knowledgeable, brave, and talented people.

Combat personnel must also be familiar with the technical and strategic aspects of the weapons and equipment in their hands and must be very well versed in the operation of those weapons and equipment. They must be able to understand accurately the combat plan and resolutely and flexibly utilize weapons and equipment to wipe out the enemy. The combat personnel of information warfare are not only the warriors who charge enemy lines for face to face struggles of life or death, but sometimes are the operating technical personnel who sit before computers and instruments. They stand at the first line in electronic warfare and in the resistance against C4I systems and on the front line in information technology conflicts.

Rear support and technical support are very important in information warfare. Information technology relates to a number of high-technology groups of people and touches on new energy, new materials, artificial intelligence, space travel, marine engineering, systems engineering, and other high-technology subjects. The demands for the technical level of support personnel are quite high. They are required to be able to guarantee that weapons and equipment are always kept in excellent condition. While carrying out rear and front-line support, the use of information technology is a support method just like other methods. In information warfare, the support of information technology penetrates the contents of information resistance and is also one method of warfare support.

The main methods of cultivating talent are study and training. In addition to conducting training in politics, ethics, and psychology, there must also be study of high-tech knowledge and the fundamental knowledge of and warfare techniques related to information warfare. If conditions permit, we want to create as much as possible the conditions necessary for implementing simulation training.

We can first consider creating stimulated battlefields with information in key areas of the army, navy, air force, and artillery, and, second, conducting rotational training of cadres and key troops. Colleges and universities should also establish curriculae in information warfare. Scientific research institutions should also engage in research on information warfare.

The large-scale importation of information technology deep into the field of warfare will inevitably bring about a military revolution. This revolution has actually already started. Those who perceive it first will swiftly rise to the top and have the advantage of the first opportunities. Those who perceive it late will unavoidably also be caught up in the vortex of this revolution. Every military will receive this baptism. This revolution is first a revolution in concepts, then it is a revolution in science and technology, equipment, troop strength, strategy, and tactics as well as a revolution in training. Thus, the issue of how to adapt to and achieve victory in the information warfare which we will face from now on is an important question which we need to study carefully.

ATTACKS ON COMPUTER SYSTEMS

While the public has perceived buildings and airplanes as the primary targets of terrorists, attacks on computers were involved in 60% of conventional terrorist acts by 1989. The pattern of criminal computer attacks, together with terrorist activity, suggest that there may be a shift toward cyberterrorism as a physically less risky means to achieve both criminal and terrorist ends.

Europe and the United States

In the 1970s the Italian Red Brigades launched 27 attacks against companies that did business in the electronics, computer and weapons sectors. In 1980, the French organization Comite Liquidant ou Detournant les Ordinateurs (Computer Liquidation and Deterrence Committee or CLODO) undertook a series of attacks on computer companies in the Toulouse region.

The organization released a statement to the press, "We are workers in the field of dp (data processing) and consequently well place to know the current and future dangers of dp and telecommunications.

The computer is the favorite tool of the dominant. It is used to exploit, to put on file, to control, and to repress."

A Belgian Group, the Cellueles Communistes Combattants (Fighting Communist Cells) conducted a series of bombings in September 1984 directed against Honeywell Controls and Litton Industries. In November 1984, the same group attacked the Brussels office of Motorola. Computers were prime targets in each of these attacks.

Similar attacks have occurred in the United States. IBM's offices in White Plains N.Y. were bombed in March1984. The group claiming responsibility for the attack, the United Freedom Front, distributed a newsletter that stated "IBM is a death merchant... The computer is an integral part of the fascist South African government's policies of racist repression and control."

The CLODO group struck again in 1983 by firebombing a Sperry-Univac computer room in Toulouse to protest the U.S. invasion of Grenada. Upon putting out the fire, the message, "Reagan attacks Grenada- Sperry Multinational is an American accomplice." was found spray painted on an interior wall.

While the attacks on computer systems failed to cause any major political victory for CLODO, they did heighten the awareness that European computers are vulnerable to attack.

A 1979 report by the Swedish Defense Ministry recommended that the government become involved in monitoring computer security of both public and private computers. While the proper role of the government in computer security remains open for debate, an article in the French daily *Le Figaro* states that computer attacks might be more harmful to national security than the assassination of random politicians.

Japan

In 1985 in Japan, the Middle Core Faction, a terrorist group consisting of approximately 300 individuals, attacked the commuter rail system to cause massive disruption during the height of rush hour. The group used C2W techniques to carry out its attack by first cutting strategic power and communications cables that fed the computer controls for the rail system. Secondly, the group jammed police and rescue radio frequencies in an attempt to hamper and delay response by the authorities. While no one was injured in this attack, it caused a major commuting delay affecting 6.5 million commuters and cost the Japan National Railways more than $6 million in lost ticket sales. Rather than blowing up or tampering with the physical destruction of one rail, the group focused on the critical node (control circuits) and disabled the entire system by using technoterror, attacking physical targets to cause a disruption in cyberspace. The disruption was extensive enough that the Centralized Traffic control Office of Japan National Railways (JNR) was forced to stop operation. While the attacks were successful in creating disruption, the effects were short lived, with most of the severed cables back in full service within 24 hours. This attack, while creating problems for millions of commuters, was also linked to specific objectives. The first was to show solidarity with the National Railways Locomotive Engineers' Union, which was on strike to protest the planned privatization of the JNR. The second goal may have been to influence the trial of Hiroko Nagata, the leader of the Extreme Leftist United Red Army. Her hearing was delayed because the rail shutdown prevented her defense lawyer from making it to court on time.

The combination of computer controls and energy systems raises new possibilities for terrorists. While targeting of energy systems in the past has relied primarily on the physical destruction of key assets to disrupt service, the potential vulnerability of the control systems poses an even greater risk.

Political Motivation

The rise of Information Warfare tactics may allow tomorrow's terrorists to focus their attacks on certain individuals to change their policies or courses of action. The increasing reliance on computers has opened new avenues for blackmail and political pressure. In 1984, a hacker penetrated TRW's credit report computers and obtained some incriminating information about a past small-claims court dispute involving hen incumbent Congressional candidate Tom Lantos of California. This information was passed to his opponent who further distributed the information to the press to discredit Lantos. In a second act of political computer crime, a hacker gained access to Representative Ed Zshau's computer system in Washington, D.C. and erased his data, including his correspondence and constituent database.

These events highlight the potentially selective nature of future cyberterrorism and crime. With a skilled computed operator, a terrorist group may be able to penetrate systems to manipulate a small number of people. Instead of attacking the public to affect a target audience, cyberterrorists may choose to affect the target audience to achieve their ends directly.

Environmental Groups

While "conventional" terrorist groups have targeted computer systems in the past, "eco-terror" groups, such as Earth First, have advocated attacking computer systems. In 1987, the group published a manual that advocated both physical destruction of computer equipment (conventional terrorism) and software and data manipulation/destruction (via cyberterrorism). the manual also included techniques to reduce the risk of being caught by using advance hacking techniques. The risk of cyberterrorism exists on all fronts. It is not merely limited to the "classic" conventional terrorist group. Any group with a strong interest or agenda will be able to attempt cyberterrorism.

Criminal Activity

Criminal activity directed at, or using, computers is receiving increasing attention in the press. The expansion of the Internet to include commercial ventures has sparked a debate over the correct level of security that should be afforded individuals in cyberspace. As terrorism is often crime with different intent, several criminal acts will be explored in this chapter. First, the case of a Russian hacker attempting to steal more than $10 million highlights the vast amounts of money being transferred in cyberspace. Second, the attempt to use computer viruses to hold computers hostage or attack a specific company will be examined. Finally, the possible physical risks to individuals as a result of criminal cyberspace activity are addressed in the case of a Texas professor.

Citibank. The use of computers and computer technology to perpetrate crimes has already occurred. Citibank recently "lost" $10.2 million electronically to a team of Russian hackers. A closer examination of the facts involved in this incident reveals some strengths and weaknesses of computer crime. First, the authorities can use the same technology employed by the cyberterrorist or criminal to track and capture him. Someone can, however, remain anonymous in cyberspace if they are not seeking financial gain, as virus writers have proven.

This incident, according to John Mohr, vice president of the New York Clearing House, is unique in that it utilized a personal computer. It appears that Vladimir L. Levin, a Russian computer expert employed by AO Saturn, a St. Petersburg trading company, broke into Citibank's computer system using stolen account identification numbers and passwords. With this information, he made 40 transfers from Citibank to accounts set up by accomplices in California and Israel.

These transfers occurred from June to October 1994 and were tracked by Citibank to determine who was responsible for the crime. While Citibank allowed the transfers to continue, the accounts into which he was transferring the money were frozen, While Levin attempted to transfer more than $10 million in this period, Citibank has recovered all but $400,000. Amy Dates of Citibank had the following answer when questioned about the level of security at Citibank: "We move half a trillion dollars a day through the payment system. Compare hat to the $400,000 they were able to withdraw. We think we have the right level of security." Despite these statements, Citibank implemented a new computer protocol to increase transaction security.

It is still unclear how Levin obtained the account numbers and their associated passwords, but an investigation is continuing into the possibility of inside help. Citibank, has implemented a new security system for its computer accounts that entails the use of "smart cards" that will generate a new password for each transaction.

This technology helps to defeat password "sniffer" programs that allow criminals to capture passwords as they are transmitted across the network for future use. This may have been how Levin obtained his passwords. He appears to have had access to the network for some time before attempting his crime as he was careful to follow the patterns of routine transactions and kept his individual transfers to below $300,000 to avoid "built-in" security programs that would have highlighted the transaction as abnormal.

While the adoption of the smart card security system and the employment of encryption technology has, Citibank hopes, corrected the security weakness exploited by Levin and his friends, the amount of money lost in this crime is relatively small. The high level of publicity afforded this incident is due to its extranormality, not its dollar value. Each year, according to the American Bankers Association, the following amounts are lost due to crime: Check fraud- $10 *Billion,* Credit Card fraud- $712 Million, ATM fraud- $18 Million, and Online fraud (as in the Citibank case)- $5 Milllion. While Citibank could use its computers to track and eventually catch Levin, computers and high technology aided in the success of a Vietnamese check fraud ring that operated undetected for seven months. The U.S. Secret Service investigated the crime under the name, "Operation Paper Dragon" and found that the ring took in $25 Million in just over half a year.These high technology money making schemes may appeal to terrorist organizations of the future who are unable to secure, or do not desire, state sponsorship. While attractive to terrorists, the security measures put in place by the banking industry to prevent criminals will likely defeat terrorists as well.

Viruses. In an apparent attempt to extort money, the computers of several universities were infected with a virus in an attempt to make them hostages. The virus demanded a ransom for the antidote to the virus.

Computer users who found the virus were told to send $2,000 to an address in Pakistan to obtain an immunity program that would rid the system of the virus. Investigation showed that the virus was written by two brothers in a computer store in Lahore, Pakistan-they had put their names, and address, and phone number in the virus! "It's like a fantasy of being a terrorist without the blood,: said Eric Corley, editor of a national hacker newsletter, 2600, whose electronic bulletin board was also infected.

The brothers' scheme did not pay well, and the virus was eradicated without their "immunity program." The "fantasy" of being a terrorist without the blood may become reality when an organization uses cyberterror weapons in an attack.

Recently, a virus was used to attack a specific business in Germany. A virus writer, known only as "The Wizard" created then released a virus that he called the "Media Market advertising virus." Media Markt is a German home-electronics group and was not involved in the virus writing or distribution. Media Markt's lawyer claims that "this is the first time that someone has distributed a virus and tied it to a company that has nothing to do with it" To stave off negative publicity, Media Markt has distributed an anti-virus program to disable the virus on affected computers.

While the true intention of the virus writer may never be known, the principle of indirect attack (attacking the general public to influence a target audience) normally utilized by terrorists was evidenced in these tactics. The virus writer, unleashed an attack on the "innocent" computer users to create negative publicity for Media Markt. In this case, Media Markt was clearly not involved in this activity. However, the anonymous and anarchic nature of cyberspace opens the possibility of creating chaos and making it appear as if someone else is responsible. While it appears that financial gain motivated the Russian hackers in the Citibank case, the possibility exists that terrorists or criminals could perpetrate electronic attacks in the future to weaken the target company, not make money. If a terrorist group could place someone "on the inside" of a software company and infect software with a virus *before* shipment, it may call the integrity of that software company into question. While there are no reported cases of terrorists staging a concerted information warfare attack on a business, the case of Citibank might be a benchmark. Despite news that it had lost more than $10 million, Citibank stock went *up* by 1/2 a point on the day that the Russian hacker story broke.

Personal Attacks. The potential exists for terrorists to single out individuals in cyberspace. In 1994, a hacker logged into a Texas A&M professor's E-mail account and used the account to send out 20,000 racist messages. To those receiving the messages, it appeared that they had come from the professor. As a result, the professor began to receive death threats.

CYBER-WARFARE TACTICS

Other cyber tactics are less sophisticated. The attack that temporarily brought down Estonian networks began with a flood of bogus messages targeting government servers, called a "denial of service" attack. The approach harnesses "botnets"—massive networks of interconnected computers—to bombard targeted networks with information requests while masking the location of the primary attacker. James Lewis, a security expert with the Center for Strategic and International Studies (CSIS), says hackers in the Estonia example likely took control of tens of thousands of computers around the world without the knowledge of their owners and directed them at the government's servers. The result, he says, was a relatively minor attack that was nearly impossible to trace.

Another technique is the use of "malware," "spyware," and other malicious programs imbedded into computer systems to steal information without user knowledge. The software is designed to hide undetected and siphon information from its host—everything from secrets stored on personal computers to Pentagon military mainframes.

A December 2007 analysis of U.S. Air Force cyber vulnerabilities notes much of the Pentagon's operating systems are off-the-shelf components manufactured overseas, due to cheaper costs. But pinching pennies has potentially opened U.S. military networks to intrusion. "Foreign countries could place hidden components inside the computers, making the computers vulnerable for attack and/or spying," the analysis concludes.

> *"Our ability to penetrate into enemy computer networks, our ability to exploit communication networks, to manipulate digital information, is real."*
> *–Defense Analyst William M. Arkin*

Less common but far more worrisome are cyber attacks aimed at critical infrastructure—like nuclear-power-plant control systems, banks, or subways. In March 2007 the Department of Energy's Idaho Lab conducted an experiment to determine whether a power plant could be compromised by hacking alone.

The result—a smoking, self-combusting diesel generator incapacitated by nothing more than keystrokes—sent shivers (CNN) through the private sector. The worries were apparently well-founded.

In January 2008 a CIA analyst told U.S. utilities that hackers had succeeded in infiltrating electric companies in undisclosed locations outside the United States and, it at least one instance, shut off power to multiple cities. The hackers then demanded money (AP). "The [U.S.] government is scrambling to try and protect its own systems, to try and check the Chinese from reading government email," says economist Scott Borg, director of the U.S. Cyber Consequences Unit, a nonprofit research institute that studies cyber threats. "But the focus probably needs to be critical infrastructure. That's what we need to defend."

Patching the Holes

On paper the U.S. government appears to agree. For over a decade government-sanctioned studies have delved into the subject; the Pentagon published a report on "Information Warfare-Defense" (PDF) in 1996, when public use of the Internet was still in its infancy. Saydjari says all of these studies reached the same conclusion: "The threat and vulnerabilities to our national infrastructure is serious, it's getting worse, and it's getting worse at an increasingly fast rate."

But only recently has the concern been a constant focus of attention for the security and intelligence communities. Part of the attention deficit lies with the difficulty in defining the cyber threat. A 2006 Air Force task force termed cyberspace "a warfighting domain bounded by the electromagnetic spectrum," but air force officials acknowledge "a full understanding of the domain is years away."

What is understood is how potentially devastating the loss of cyberspace dominance could be to U.S. interests. In his annual threat assessment to Congress delivered in February 2008, Director of National Intelligence Michael McConnell discussed "cyber threats" before talking about the war in Afghanistan.

"Our information infrastructure ...increasingly is being targeted for exploitation and potentially for disruption or destruction by a growing array of state and non-state adversaries," McConnell said. "We assess that nations, including Russia and China, have the technical capabilities to target and disrupt" the United States' information infrastructure.

"Chinese [cyber warfare] capabilities have evolved from defending networks from attack to offensive operations against adversary networks." –U.S. Deputy Under Secretary for Defense Richard P. Lawless

The Pentagon, too, has acknowledged the threat to its infrastructure. The Defense Department is considering banning nonofficial traffic (Federal Computer Week) from its servers, and the U.S. Air Force is creating a Cyber

Command to defend Pentagon networks. "When we talk about the speed range and flexibility of air power, the thing that enables this for us is the fact of our cyber-dominance," Air Force Gen. Robert Elder told United Press International.

The recent flurry of high-level pronouncements also comes amid a renewed funding commitment from Washington. In November 2007 the Bush administration called on the National Security Agency to coordinate with the Department of Homeland Security to protect government and civilian communication networks from hackers. The $144 million plan, unveiled quietly in White House budget documents (PDF), aims to enhance "civilian agency cybersecurity and strengthen defenses to combat terrorism."

In January 2008 President George W. Bush signed two presidential directives calling for the creation of a comprehensive national cybersecurity initiative. According to an article by the Wall Street Journal, the White House's 2009 budget request takes the program exponentially further, with an estimated $6 billion request to build a secretive system to protect U.S. communications networks. Details of the proposed program remain classified, angering some civil libertarians who fear monitoring of civilian networks could infringe on privacy rights. Rep. Bennie G. Thompson (D-MS), chairman of the House Homeland Security Committee, has called for the program to be put on hold (PDF) until Congress can adequately review it.

Measuring the Threat

Cyber experts don't dispute that electronic espionage is a vexing problem, or that the United States is a prime target. But they do disagree on how pervasive such attacks are, who is behind them, and how disruptive they may prove to be.

According to a tally by the Heritage Foundation, a conservative Washington think tank, the hackers may already be winning: In 2007 the Department of Homeland Security logged an estimated 37,000 attempted breaches of private and government computer systems, and over 80,000 attacks on Pentagon systems. Some hacks "reduced the U.S. military's operational capabilities," the report says. Economist Borg says the biggest threat from cyber attacks may be economic. He estimates a shutdown of electric power to any sizable region for more than ten days would stop over 70 percent of all economic activity in that region. "If you can do that with a pure cyber attack on only one critical infrastructure, why would you bother with any traditional military attack?" CSIS' Lewis takes a less alarmist view.

"The U.S. is a very big set of targets, and some of our important networks are very secure. So you could inflict damage on the U.S. but it wouldn't be crippling or decisive," he says. "I've seen people who say a cyber attack could turn the United States into a third-world nation in a matter of minutes. That's silly. We have to be realistic about this."

THE DAWN OF CHAOPLEXIC WARFARE

Cybernetic warfare experienced its first serious reversal with the Vietnam War, where its analytical techniques and military systems foundered in the conditions of a low-intensity conflict. James Gibson has written persuasively about the failure in the jungles of South-East Asia of 'technowar', an approach to military conflict in which war was viewed as 'a production system that can be rationally managed and warfare as a kind of activity that can be scientifically determined by constructing computer models'.

The conduct of the war was blighted by the attempts of the military and political hierarchy to micro-manage the conflict and by an obsession with statistical evaluation and information-gathering which frequently created assessments of the war that were completely at variance with the reality on the ground.

Despite the deployment of an unprecedented telecommunications network in the field of operations, command and control technologies failed to perform as expected, with saturation and bottlenecks preventing information on Vietcong positions and movements from arriving in time to be actionable.

Perhaps most seriously, a misguided faith in the powers of technoscience to grant military omnipotence led policy-makers to embrace armed force more willingly as the means to solve complex strategic problems. Such hubris was perfectly encapsulated by Henry Kissinger's claim in 1968 that 'a scientific revolution has, for all practical purposes, removed technical limits from the exercise of power in foreign policy'.

The debacle in Vietnam provoked some soul-searching among strategists and military men but did not result in an immediate abandonment of the central principles of cybernetic warfare, which continued to dominate military thinking through the 1980s. All the early contributions to the debate on the revolution in military affairs were premised on the idea that computers, telecommunication links and precision-guided munitions would finally deliver the frictionless, automated battlefield promised by Westmoreland. However, new thinking drawing on the emerging non-linear sciences did begin to penetrate military theory, at first espoused only by isolated individuals but entering the mainstream at the turn of the century.

The late US air force colonel John Boyd is perhaps the most prominent pioneer of chaoplexic warfare, and increasingly is considered to be one of the most important military thinkers of recent times. Boyd is best known for his formulation of the OODA loop (observe–orient–decide–act), describing the decision-making process of the warfighter engaged in combat. Although this is at first sight reminiscent of a typical cybernetic feedback loop, whereby a system adjusts its behaviour to incoming information from its environment in order to meet a desired objective, Boyd was insistent on the need for the analytical frameworks used during the orientation phase to be continually challenged and reinvented through a perpetual process of 'destruction and creation'.

No predetermined automated response can prevail for long in a world that is 'uncertain, everchanging, unpredictable'. Boyd went on to contribute to US Marine Corps doctrine, which displays clear signs of the influence of chaoplexity in asserting that 'the best we can hope for is to impose a general framework of order on the disorder, to prescribe the general flow of action rather than to try to control each event', and that 'like a living organism, a military organization is never in a state of stable equilibrium but is instead in a continuous state of flux—continuously adjusting to its surroundings'.

If the earlier proclamations of an imminent revolution in military affairs remained firmly tributary to cybernetic conceptions, the ascent of network-centric warfare (NCW) marked the onset of a shift towards chaoplexic notions on the centre ground of debates over military doctrine. With its ideas couched in the language and concepts of the non-linear sciences, NCW first appeared on the scene within the US navy in the late 1990s before rapidly rising to become the new official Pentagon gospel under the agenda of 'Transformation' with the founding of the Office of Force Transformation in 2001 under the stewardship of its original formulator Vice Admiral Arthur Cebrowski.

According to Cebrowski, networkcentric warfare views war as a 'complex, adaptive system where non-linear variables continuously interact'. Since 'coordination from the top down inevitably results in delays and errors in force dispositions', the military should seek to acquire 'the ability of a well-informed force to organize and coordinate complex warfare activities from the bottom up'. For Cebrowski, what is being proposed is nothing less than a 'new theory of war'.

Such a new theory can emerge only by breaking with the command and control principles that governed cybernetic warfare during the Cold War, as suggested by Alberts and Hayes: Control Theory requires both prediction and the existence of an adequate set of levers of control ... [But] having effective, centrally managed levers that can control or even predictably influence a complex, adaptive system is far from guaranteed ... In the Information Age, control needs to be thought about and approached differently.

Control is not something that can be imposed on a complex adaptive system, particularly when there are many independent actors. Control, that is, ensuring that behavior stays within or moving to within acceptable bounds, can only be achieved indirectly.

The most promising approach involves establishing, to the extent possible, a set of initial conditions that will *result* in the desired behavior. In other words, control is not achieved by imposing a parallel process, but rather emerges from influencing the behaviors of independent agents. NCW theorists claim that through the distribution of information across the battlefield and the constitution of a common operational picture via an overarching 'Global Information Grid', command and control will be decentralized and individual troops will be freed to act on their own initiative, leading to self-synchronization, a clear nod to the chaoplexic notion of self-organization.

New tactical schemes denied to their hierarchical counterparts are seen as the emergent properties that will be unlocked by fully networked self-synchronizing forces. Drawing further from the writings of complexity theorists and deploying biological metaphors, military theorists appeal to the 'swarm', the networks of distributed intelligence that enable bees, ants and termites to evolve complex forms of collective behaviour on the basis of the simple rules of interaction of their individual members.

Of particular interest are the resilience and flexibility of these swarms as amorphous ensembles whose continued existence and successful operation is not critically dependent on any single individual. Military swarms promise not only more adaptable and survivable forces but also new offensive and defensive tactics better suited to the contemporary battlespace. According to Alberts and Hayes, decentralization and information-sharing will permit military platforms to 'evolve from being networked entities to being nodes in the network, to organizing efforts resembling "packs" and "swarms"'. The ensembles of different entities making up fighting forces, whether human or robotic, will 'ultimately become dynamically reconfigurable packs, swarms, or other organizations of highly specialized components that work together like the cells of our bodies' and will be 'less mechanical and more organic, less engineered and more "grown"'.

Beyond the flexibility and evolutionary capability that are attributed to military swarms, it is also claimed that they will be able to bring force to bear in a new manner.

Rather than throwing themselves onto the enemy in 'waves', forces will be able to converge on their target from all directions in offensive bursts, thereby maximizing the shock effect.

For Arquilla and Ronfeldt, the full effects of swarming are achieved when the dispersed nodes of a network of small (and also perhaps some large) forces can converge on an enemy from multiple directions, through either fire or maneuver. The overall aim should be *sustainable pulsing*—swarm networks must be able to coalesce rapidly and stealthily on a target, then dissever and redisperse, immediately ready to recombine for a new pulse. A swarm network should have little to no mass as a rule (except perhaps during a pulse), but it should have a high energy potential—like a swarm of bees that can fell a mighty beast, or a network of antibodies that can attack a spreading virus.

Troops that can disperse swiftly after an attack or 'pulse' also have the advantage of being less vulnerable to enemy attacks, particularly in the context of the high lethality and precision characteristic of contemporary and future battlefields. The promises of network-centric warfare are bold and, for all its deployment of chaoplexic language, the doctrine suffers from a number of potentially critical weaknesses. In several respects it has not significantly broken with cybernetic warfare and therefore may not in fact implement all the features of a truly chaoplexic way of warfare.

While 'decentralization' is the order-word of the day, the networking of troops may in fact provide the technological infrastructure for greater micro-management than ever by a military brass which will have access to data feeds from anywhere in the battlespace.

Second, dependence on a unified 'Global Information Grid' could both create a critical vulnerability likely to be targeted by competent adversaries and deprive troops of the skills required to respond creatively to situations in which only limited local information is available (as most of the complex adaptive systems studied are found to do).

Furthermore, NCW advocates fall back all too often on impoverished conceptions of Boyd's OODA loop which substitute speed of execution of predetermined responses for creative thinking and adaptability to the unforeseen. Finally, there persists a tendency to see information technology as the panacea which will permanently lift the friction and fog of war which has plagued all past militaries, when in fact chaoplexity points to the irreducible contingency and unpredictability of war and the need to organize so as to tolerate and even take advantage of this uncertainty.

Ultimately chaoplexic warfare will depend more on doctrinal and organizational commitments than on any particular information technologies, which are liable to be employed to quite contrary purposes. The full arrival of chaoplexic warfare may therefore still lie ahead; but the debates around network-centric warfare clearly show an impetus towards greater decentralization and the use of the network form of organization within armed forces. NCW now has its counterparts in most major western militaries, including Network Enabled Capabilities (NEC) in the United Kingdom, NATO Network Enabled Capabilities (NNEC), and Network Enabled Operations (NEOps) in Canada. Where such militaries have encountered recent setbacks, for example in Iraq, Afghanistan or Lebanon, it has been against opponents that have employed decentralized networks to good effect against better-equipped forces, thereby further stimulating discussion about their merits and underlining the limitations of established modes of operation. Just as the ideas of mechanism, thermodynamics and cybernetics inspired past military thought and practice in association with their respective paradigmatic technologies, a new set of scientific theories are now occupying a central role within the doctrinal and organizational changes of the armies of the early twenty-first century. Our network age is therefore also that of chaoplexity.

INTELLIGENCE FOR CYBER-SPACE

Although many of the intelligence methodologies and principles remain the same, new ways of thinking appropriate to the cyber-domain are essential. The lack of borders in cyber-space is a critical difference from the more familiar domains of intelligence. Indeed, geography and political borders often aided traditional military intelligence analysis-it is a simple thing to develop threat scenarios if the potential enemy can only use certain terrain or sea lines of communication and then, only at certain times of the year-while simple factors of physics such as time and distance also provided opportunities for warning. Within the Internet, however, these limiting factors are absent, (although other limiting factors, such as geometry of network connectivity, might exist in a form useful to be incorporated into intelligence analysis), contributing to what can appear to be "instantaneous threats".

Assessment of cyber-space threats requires not only a merger of old methodologies and new modes of thinking but also analysts willing and able to approach the art of threat assessment and warning from new perspectives. Only with a distinctive blend of the traditional and the new will it be possible to obtain real understanding of threats and vulnerabilities, to differentiate among types of intrusions and to forecast or anticipate specific incidents or clusters of incidents in ways that lengthen warning time. Enhancing the ability to identify perpetrators is also highly desirable: removing the cloak of anonymity would make perpetrators more concerned about the potential costs and risks of their actions and could have an important deterrent effect. In short, there are several fundamental questions at the heart of the intelligence process. They consist of variations on the who, what, when, where, why and how questions that are familiar parts of most research and analysis.

Security Challenging

Efforts to identify intruders are critical both to the assessment of the challenge and the nature of the response. Potential intruders run the gamut from young hobbyists engaged in the equivalent of joy riding to terrorist organizations and nations that are intent on maximizing damage to the target. The problem of identification is particularly difficult in a domain where maintaining anonymity is easy and there are sometimes time lapses between the intruder action, the intrusion itself, and the actual disruptive effects. Moreover, the consequences are not always commensurate with the objectives, in some cases falling short of what the intruders hoped to achieve, and in others going well beyond what they had envisaged.

There is a broad spectrum of potential intruders on the Internet and an almost equal number of motives for intrusions against organizations. Not surprisingly, this includes perpetrators conducting operations against other perpetrators. As enticing as this prospect is, it does not mitigate the effects of such internecine rivalry. New and more sophisticated tools are often the result of such interplay. This sort of jousting can also provide valuable insights to analysts once it is recognized, but does not simplify the analytic task and puts an incredible strain on limited analytic/warning resources. With the continuing proliferation of sophisticated computer technologies into the mainstream population, attribution for an intrusion becomes more difficult by the day.

The dynamism of the intruder population is itself a problem. On the one hand, success breeds imitation and the sophistication of readily available tools means that even those with limited skills can become intruders.

On the one hand, there is a certain degree of attrition in the intruder community. Indeed, there are many reasons why intruders might cease their activity, including increased maturity, a need to find gainful employment, and a perception of the rewards of working to increase network security rather than attack it. The implication, of course, is that the mix of agents threatening network security is changing as the nature of the Internet changes.

The vast majority of the intrusions are probably being conducted by nuisance hackers or "ankle-biters" who have limited objectives and are usually satisfied with the actual penetration of the system or conduct relatively harmless cyber-vandalism such as the defacement or alteration of web-sites. While aggravating to the target, no significant or lasting damage occurs. The more serious problem occurs when an intrusion is carried out by a more sophisticated intruder (either an individual or a group) whose objective is better defined and involves malicious intent. Motives for these sorts of intrusions are also as varied as the persons carrying them out. They range from greed to defined military strategy and doctrine, and all that falls in between. Four of the more dangerous, and less well defined categories of intruder are governments conducting operations against other sovereign states, the organized terrorist group, insurgency or revolutionary groups, and organized crime.

All these entities are beginning to appreciate the potential power, anonymity, and effectiveness of the Internet. There are myriad examples of governments instituting programmes for Computer Network Warfare. In the case of Russia, policy-makers consider the security of their information infrastructure so critical that–rhetorically at least-they equate an attack against it with a strategic nuclear strike (and have promised an appropriate response). As a result of the realization of the criticality of information infrastructures, computer warfare is now a part of the formal Russian Military Strategy and Doctrine. The same is true of organized terrorist groups. In fact, "most of the 30 top terrorist organizations identified by the U.S. government have web pages and use e-mail, and are ``fairly well developed'' at using the Internet."[Casciano] In many cases, dependence on technology is viewed as an Achilles Heel to be exploited by terrorist organizations.

Within the U.S., many of the more militant indigenous groups have discovered the power of the Internet and have well designed and effective Web sites. Indeed, militia and supremacist groups have had significant increases in membership since developing their Web pages. It is a natural progression from using the Internet for propaganda and recruiting to exploiting its potential as a weapon. There is also growing evidence that some of the active insurgency groups around the world are discovering the potential of the computer. It is just a matter of time until they discover the effect of a computer-generated attack against the infrastructure of the government they are fighting. Once that realization is made, cyber-attacks will likely become a weapon of choice for organizations intent on overthrowing an existing government. Disturbingly, Aum Shinrikyo, the group responsible for the Sarin gas attack on the Japanese subway, has increasingly been involved in the Japanese software industry!

Organized crime probably was the first of the sophisticated intruder threats to realize the power and value of the computer. In 1995, it was discovered that the Cali cartel had sophisticated state-of-the-art equipment for electronic eavesdropping, while smaller drug trafficking organizations in Colombia are using the Internet to pressure the Colombian government to change the policy of extraditing traffickers to the United States. Furthermore, the use of computers by organized crime organizations to garner illicit profits is well documented. However, some criminal efforts have gone beyond simple siphoning of funds and money laundering. Extortion of money from financial institutions by threatening to destroy or modify their computer databases is also evident. It is probable that at least some of these extortion operations are conducted by transnational criminal groups. Some of the extortion efforts go wrong–as did the effort to extort Bloomberg. In other cases, however, large payoffs are almost certainly made to the extortionist. It seems likely, therefore, that larger and potentially more dangerous operations should be anticipated.

The obvious challenge is to develop a capacity to identify and track the activities of these potential intruders with the goal of being able to provide predictive analysis and warning of intrusions. Some of the traditional intelligence techniques should apply to these threats, but new methodologies and the ability to contemplate new and complex concepts have to be developed concurrently. This will become even more important (and difficult) as perpetrators of increasing sophistication operate on the Internet. As motivations vary, so will the efforts of the individuals behind malicious operations to either conceal or reveal their responsibility. All of this complicates efforts to track responsible parties determine attribution. Nations and transnational criminal organizations, by their nature, will be diligent in their efforts to maintain anonymity. In some of these cases, identifying the intended victim may give valuable insight into tracking the intruder. Sometimes the target of an intrusion allows the analyst to rule out certain possible perpetrators. A multi-million dollar extortion plot against a major financial institution is probably not the work of a 13-year-old hacker working out of his bedroom. At the same time, however, many victims, especially within government or sensitive industries such as banking or insurance, often complicate the effort to track intruders because of their reluctance to report the incident. In other cases, such as politically motivated attacks, the perpetrators may want their identity known, but not their location. As such operations become more sophisticated, tracking the attack back to its point of origin will be a major challenge to the intelligence analysts involved. What is clear from all of this is that tracking intruders and gaining attribution is much more than just a technical challenge.

One difficulty, of course, is that there are legal constraints on intelligence collection, especially by the military and the national security establishment. Traditionally the focus of intelligence has been on foreign threats, and there are restrictions on intelligence activities directed against individuals or groups that are domestic in nature. Insofar as these groups are the focus of government attention, it is from the law enforcement community. This points to yet another problem: that of coordination and information sharing between the traditional national security agencies and the law enforcement community. Generally law enforcement focuses on individual cases and wants evidence that stands up in court; intelligence agencies in contrast are concerned with protecting the sources of their information so that they can continue to use them. The problem with cyber-threats is that they fall in the gray area where crime and national security merge into one another.

Forms of Intrusion are Occurring

It is tempting to see intrusions in terms of a pyramid that goes from transient vulnerability probing and defacing web-sites at the base to large scale efforts to undermine the critical missions of an organization or the critical functions of a nation at the top-and to suggest that there is an inverse relationship between frequency and significance, with many trivial incidents and comparatively few of the more serious incidents. There are several difficulties with this however. The first is that probes that appear relatively insignificant could be a harbinger of more serious intrusions. The second is that there is sometimes a gap between intent and consequences–the effects and impact of an incident can either fall far short of what was intended, or far exceed what the perpetrator initially envisaged. This lack of congruence between limited intent and far-reaching consequences stems from the capacity of worms and viruses for infinite replication and multiplication combined with the seamless inter-connectivity of systems. Incidents such as the Love Bug cross the public-private divide and have an indiscriminate impact on corporations, governments, and private individuals irrespective of the initial target. In cases such as this, the consequences have less to do with targeting than with the ubiquity of a particular programme such as Microsoft Outlook that is used as the vector of transmission. In effect, the incident takes on its own momentum.

When the consequences are widespread, of course, the incident becomes very public and is the subject of much media and official commentary. In many other cases, however, there is far greater reticence about the scale, type and targets of attack. The analytic effort must successfully build a trust relationship for the collection of data across a broad variety of organizations. This trust relationship allows for observation of incidents from early probing and experimentation through widespread deployment of automated forms of intrusion. For example, in recent months (June and July 2000) CERTÒ/CC has received reports of intrusions involving a wide variety of automated tools, ranging from simple viruses and system corruption toolkits through complex viruses designed to attack relatively hardened sites with low probability of detection and distributed tools designed to crash network infrastructure. Roughly 10%-25% of the CERT/CC reports involve viruses. Roughly 20%-40% are intrusions where the victim site cannot discern the type of the intrusion from available data. The remaining intrusions are a large number of other forms of intrusion, including compromise of system administration accounts, web defacements, reconnaissance attempts and misuse of computing resources.

Being intruded Upon

Determining who are the victims of intrusions is, in some respects, an enormously significant part of the intelligence process. It is important-at least in those cases where attacks are not indiscriminate-to differentiate between public and private targets, to distinguish infrastructure targets from individual targets, to distinguish between intrusions that focus on targets of convenience and those that are much more precise and calculated. For example, existing analysis has shown a link between port scanning and certain types of later intrusions, but this needs to be more fully explored to provide for effective warnings.

Profiling victims can sometimes play a critical role in determining the nature of the intrusion and the nature of the intruders. For this to be done, understanding is needed of the level of "background noise", probes and intrusion attempts occurring across the Internet. Once understood, it may be possible to isolate this activity from the more significant activity directed at a particular victim.

Victim profiles will be just as important, in terms of strategic intelligence analysis of the Internet, as profiling potential intruders. The more serious the intrusion, the more critical this sort of profiling will be. One of the potential hurdles to this effort, however, will be the natural tendency of the victim, whether private or public, to withhold sensitive or proprietary information. A few examples of this kind of reticence would be financial institutions withholding information about loses due to intrusions; companies failing to divulge the nature of an intrusion due to proprietary corporate data; or a government agency protecting information that is sensitive or even classified. Beyond simply protecting proprietary or sensitive data, there are also serious legal questions that have not yet been resolved in the courts or in the legislature. These include constitutional guarantees of privacy; contradictory national laws (or lack of laws) as perpetrators use the global network; laws limiting various governmental agency's efforts to track down the source of an intrusion, and the need to determine what is domestic and what is foreign.

If these barriers can be overcome, critical information will become available. Details of the victim's infrastructure, the nature of the intrusion, identity clues left by the intruder, network traffic flow as observed by the victim site, and intrusion tools left as artifacts on the victim hosts can all provide indispensable clues. Without such information, motivation becomes more difficult to define and profiling efforts will be seriously flawed. Some work has already been accomplished in this area by organizations involved in incident monitoring, including the members of the Forum of Incident Response and Security Teams (FIRST) community.

Much more remains to be accomplished, however, as new cooperative agreements are forged and additional analytic efforts and methodologies are developed. Furthermore, while it is true that some of the legal restrictions are avoided by the voluntary nature of the cooperative relationships, they are by no means completely overcome.

The keys to success seem to be twofold. First, the analytic organization has to prove itself to be a highly secure confidant, never disclosing victim identities while working to assist victims in recovering from intrusions. Second, it must return information that is of value to the victims, including information that might place the intrusion in a larger context as well as providing assistance in dealing with vendors or other sites.

More simply put, the exchange of information must be in both directions. Experience with other organizations has shown that neither trustworthiness nor returned value alone is sufficient, but both appear to be required for effective information gathering with victims.

Beyond their reticence, victim organizations are often unaware of critical parts of their security stance. Available data suggests that victims are often not aware that their networks have been intruded upon. The effectiveness of installed security measures is often overestimated. Levels of trust given to users by computing practices are often unwarranted. All of this hampers both analysis and defence.

One of the reasons that profiling the victims is so critical is that it provides insights in to motivations that can greatly assist analysts in predicting future intrusions under similar circumstances.

This insight will need to incorporate identification of circumstances that facilitate or hamper intrusion. For example, K-12 educational institutions might offer a significant opportunity for intruders to stage their attacks, since many such institutions lack knowledgeable system administrators. However, such hosts may be removed from the network during summer break and other times when school is not in session. During the Year 2000 rollover, conditions for system intrusion were relatively poor not only because of the active presence of a large number of system administrators, carefully monitoring their systems, but also the significant number of alternative activities available to potential intruders. These examples serve to identify that there exist time-varying circumstances; further analysis is required to delineate these factors more fully.

THE NEED TO BE PREPARED FOR CYBER WAR

The growing threat of cyber warfare has not been well appreciated or sufficiently understood. Cyber warfare is a term that has been loosely used to describe almost all events in cyberspace, irrespective of perpetrator, motive or scale. Cyber warfare forms a part of Information War (IW), which extends to every form of media, and inter alia includes aspects of propaganda and perception management. Cyberspace, though technically restricted to the Internet, is now increasingly linked by convergence to every communication device. With greater connectivity, this divide is narrowing and every citizen or aspect of life is vulnerable. It is also an important constituent of NCW.

The cyber realm, like the universe, is expanding and it is estimated that by 2015 there will be almost double the number of devices connected to the Internet as there are people. The scope for exploitation by inimical elements, ranging from mischievous hackers, to criminals, terrorists, non-state actors as also nation states, is thus unlimited. The damage could be immense and many countries are pressing ahead and taking steps to build capabilities and capacities for defending themselves, as also taking offensive action in cyberspace.

The United States was the first country to formally declare this as the fifth domain warfare after land, sea, air and space. It has also formally classified the use of cyberspace as a "force", a euphemism for offensive capability.

The Chinese adopted the concept of "informationalisation" in the mid-1990s and have relentlessly built up structures and operations in this domain. Consequent to the raising of the US Cyber Command (USCYBERCOM), South Korea followed with the creation of a Cyber Warfare Command in December 2009.

This was also in response to North Korea's creation of cyber warfare units. The British Government Communications Headquarters (GCHQ) has begun preparing a cyber force, as also France. The Russians have actively been pursuing cyber warfare. In 2010 China overtly introduced its first department dedicated to defensive cyber warfare and information security in response to the creation of USCYBERCOM.

The race is thus on. India is a target. There have been numerous incidents of sensitive government and military computers being attacked by unknown entities and information being stolen. A group, which called itself the Pakistan Cyber Army, hacked the Central Bureau of Investigation website in December 2010. Further mocking India's cyber security the same group of hackers raided the Bharat Sanchar Nigam Limited website a few months later. Earlier this year, Pakistan-based hacker groups hacked 112 Indian websites in a span of three months leaving India red-faced. The panic that spread after the Assam violence because of images uploaded from Pakistan that caused thousands of people from the northeast to flee Bengaluru is a matter of grave concern. However, little has been done to put the national cyber security policy in place.

Union Home Secretary has accused websites in Pakistan of spreading false rumors and that investigators had found that most of the websites used images of people killed in cyclones and earthquakes and passed them off as Muslims killed in violence earlier this year to spread fear of revenge attacks. This clearly is the biggest instance of cyber warfare on India in recent times and the threat continues not only from Pakistan but also from China. While China looks to snoop into important defence information, Pakistan on the other hand defaces Indian websites and uses Indian networks to spread hatred via cyber space.

The greatest threat comes from the Pakistan Cyber Army and from a group called the Team_H4tr!ck, which have been largely responsible for hacking Indian websites. Both these groups in the past have hacked the BSNL website and claimed to have gained access to users' information, which included names, e-mail addresses, phone numbers and location details. Investigators had pointed out then that the database that they managed to collect could have been used for subversive activities. Pakistan has engaged in a cyber war since 1998 and since then created many groups to hack into websites of developing nations especially India. There have been several attempts by Pakistani hackers to hack into the Bhabha Atomic Research Centre website. Groups such as the armyinkashmir, Pakistan G Force, Pakistan Cyber Army, Pakistan Hackers Club have targeted nearly 500 websites while Indian hacker groups have made 40 such attempts. Moreover, social media today is a favourite tool of terror groups to spread jihad.

Recently, investigations into the Indian Mujahideen and its activities revealed that encrypted messages have been passed on through social media. The IM during the Delhi blasts used networking sites to create fake accounts. Not only did they share information between each other but also managed to conduct a recruitment drive. During this investigation, it was also found that the IM had been using lesser-known websites to communicate. According to experts, the National Cyber Security Policy is not fully in place. In addition to this, our servers are vulnerable. Moreover, Pakistan-based hackers are completely funded by its intelligence and unlike their counterparts in India they are fully protected. There has been a lot of intelligence regarding Pakistan groups using the social media and other websites to create panic. It was in this context that the Rs 800-crore National Cyber Coordination Committee was mooted. The NCCC will monitor content on social media and pass on information to intelligence agencies. Experts however feel that these are organisations are controlled by the government and this would lead to red-tapism. Although India does have a cyber army, many feel that they need more patronage from the government.

The frequency and intensity of such episodes is increasing. There is enough evidence to suggest that this is the action of nation states either directly or through proxies. There have also been cases of offensive action such as reports of shutting down of power systems. Such attacks on critical infrastructure either singly or in multiples are of serious concern, especially with respect to national security. The draft National Cyber Security Policy (NCSP) mainly covers defensive and response measures and makes no mention of the need to develop offensive capacity. This is a must if we are to ensure capability for self-defence granted under Article 51 of the UN Charter.

CYBER WAR: FIFTH DOMAIN OF WARFARE

The cyber warfare that this chapter addresses is that which is practised mainly by nation states or their proxies. The potency of this threat has compelled almost every country to develop capabilities in the cyber domain, as is the case for land, air, sea and space. According to Spy Ops, by the end of 2008 nearly 140 countries possessed varying degrees of cyber attack capabilities. In addition, an unknown number of extremist groups and non-state actors have developed or acquired cyber weapons.

Some commercially available products are flexible enough to be classified as dual purpose – security testing tools and weapons of attack. Thus some organisations have or are developing cyber weapons and cloaking them as security testing tools. All this is classified information and each nation works on its own. An assessment of cyber warfare threat matrix by the USA, which covered over 175 countries and organisations, made a watchlist in which the top ten in order of priority were: China; Russian business network; Iran; Russia tied with France; extremist/terrorist groups; Israel; North Korea; Japan; Turkey; and Pakistan. India on its growth path is vulnerable. Located in an unstable region where the larger neighbours possess this capacity, it is logical to assume that the country is under serious threat and constant attack. The impact on national security is thus serious and such that all institutions and organs of the state must jointly work to counter this challenge. In order to understand the challenge, the following issues need to be addressed:

Coordination

It is appreciated that in keeping with current needs, the Defence forces, DRDO (Defence Research and Development Organisation), NTRO (National

Technical Research Organisation), CERT-In (Computer Emergency Response Team India), RAW (Research and Analysis Wing), IB (Intelligence Bureau), C-DAC (Centre for Development of Advanced Computing), Ministries, NIC (National Informatics Centre), NASSCOM (National Association of Software and Services Companies), private industry et al. have to work in concert.

The impact of this on every aspect of electronic media requires a coordinated and integrated approach. Given its all encompassing nature, it also follows that control of all cyber and IW (Information Warfare) activities at the national level must fall under the purview of the NSC and controlled by its Secretariat i.e. the NSCS. Within this lead agencies for executing offensive cyber operations interalia could be the NTRO, CIDS (Chief of Integrated Defence Staff) and the DRDO.

Defining Objectives and Doctrine Application

Defining Objectives and Doctrine Application of such measures must be in accordance with clearly defined objectives that would be in keeping with customary international law and practice.

The primary objective would be to garner knowledge to find how systems are breached and thus provide the ability for defensive measures to be developed and put in place. There is a further argument that it must be visible as an armour of selfdefence so as to deter an attack. While this capability will be ambiguous, subtle signals and clear definition of objectives will lend credibility. Moral arguments stand thin in the face of realities. There is therefore a need to lay down the objectives and include them in the draft NCSP (National Cyber Security Policy) or issue a doctrine in this regard.

Proactive Cyber Defence

This comprises actions taken in anticipation to prevent an attack against computers and NWs. As opposed to the current practice of passive defence, it provides a via media between purely offensive and defensive action: interdicting and disrupting an attack, or an adversary's preparation to attack, either pre-emptively or in self-defence.

Proactive cyber defence will most often require operationalising upstream security mechanisms of the telecommunications or Internet providers. The most compelling reasons for a proactive defence can be couched in terms of cost and choice. Decision-makers will have few choices after an impact, and all of them are costly to start with. Proactive defence is thus the key to mitigating operational risk. The USA had set up a Proactive Pre-emptive Operations Group (P2OG) in 2002. Such actions thus find international acceptability.

Critical Infrastructure

There is a need to prioritise and protect critical infrastructure. In the USA 18 sectors have been identified. In India's case, the sectors of power, water supply, communications, transportation, defence and finance are vital constituents of national security. These need to be defined and suitable protection measures ensured as laid down in the IT Act. Steps to guard against threats, i.e. destructive actions or cyber exploitation will constitute a basis for research on offensive action.

The electric power system merits top priority. While the risk of an attack can be reduced, it would be unrealistic to assume that an attack can be prevented. This leads to the conclusion that containment, isolation, minimising the impact, backup systems and reactivation are areas of capacity building. The debate on which agency will undertake this in India rages and begs immediate resolution. As critical infrastructure spans both the public and private domains, the organisation to ensure its protection has to be in the public realm and, in a manner, accountable.

Legal Provisions

The IT Act of 2008 covers all actions in this domain. Sections 69, 69A and 69B contain provisions for intercepting, monitoring or blocking traffic where, amongst other reasons, there is a threat to national security. Section 70A covers protection of critical infrastructure.

There is a need to work within these provisions. LOAC (Laws of Armed Conflict) provide the primary legal framework within which one can analyse constraints for offensive cyber operations. Immunity for actions taken against another nation, institutions, hostile group or individual is possible if taken under LOAC or for selfdefence under Article 51 of the UN Charter. The cyber realm, with scope of non-attributable actions as also ease of deniability, provides immense scope for exploitation. The fact that there are no international cyber laws or treaties at present is also used to advantage. Offensive cyber operations by their very nature have to remain in the grey realm and restricted. Each nation would thus determine the structure best suited to its needs. However, the necessity to clearly enunciate such measures or self-defence actions in a doctrine as also the NCSP is essential for steps in this regard; it also acts as an element for deterrence. The emphasis must remain on protecting NWs, systems and users.

Controversy over terms

There is debate on whether the term "cyberwarfare" is accurate. In October 2011, for instance, the Journal of Strategic Studies, a leading journal in that field, published an article by Thomas Rid, "Cyber War Will Not Take Place." An act of cyber war would have to be potentially lethal, instrumental, and political. Then not one single cyber offense on record constitutes an act of war on its own. Instead, all politically motivated cyber attacks, Rid argued, are merely sophisticated versions of three activities that are as old as warfare itself: sabotage, espionage, and subversion.Howard Schmidt, an American cybersecurity expert, argued in March 2010 that "there is no cyberwar... I think that is a terrible metaphor and I think that is a terrible concept.

There are no winners in that environment." Other experts, however, believe that this type of activity already constitutes a war. The warfare analogy is often seen intended to motivate a militaristic response when that is not necessarily appropriate.

Ron Deibert, of Canada's Citizen Lab, has warned of a "militarization of cyberspace." The European cybersecurity expert Sandro Gaycken argued for a middle position. He considers cyberwar from a legal perspective an unlikely scenario, due to the reasons lined out by Rid (and, before him, Sommer), but the situation looks different from a strategic point of view.

States have to consider military-led cyber operations an attractive activity, within and without war, as they offer a large variety of cheap and risk-free options to weaken other countries and strengthen their own positions. Considered from a long-term, geostrategic perspective, cyber offensive operations can cripple whole economies, change political views, agitate conflicts within or among states, reduce their military efficiency and equalize the capacities of high-tech nations to that of low-tech nations, and use access to their critical infrastructures to blackmail them.

MEETING THE CYBER WARFARE CHALLENGE

Cyber warfare encompasses government and public and private domains. As clarified earlier, this must be coordinated by the NSCS (National Security Council Secretariat). In the USA it comes directly under the White House.

Thus the need to create a Directorate or Special Wing in the NSCS for this. It would oversee and coordinate both defensive and offensive cyber operations. There is also a requirement for intimate involvement of the private sector, as they are equal, if not larger, stakeholders. Regular meetings must be held and, if needed, working groups created. Current organisations which could be tasked to take on the cyber warfare challenge include the NTRO, HQ IDS (Headquarter Integrated Defence Services), DRDO, RAW and IB. Representatives of CERT, NASSCOM, etc. will invariably be involved. Each would have to function under guidelines and through proxies. This includes:

Raising of Cyber Command

While cyber warfare is ongoing activity during peacetime, there is a dire need to develop this capacity for a warlike situation. Cyber warfare in a manner is NCW and will form an essential part of preparation of the battlefield in any future conflict. Such attacks may also precede the kinetic war. Building this capability will take time and must remain covert and ambiguous. It could also form part of the strategic deception process. This should be the responsibility of the Armed Forces (HQIDS) along with the DRDO and other experts. Detailed discussions and consultations in this regard require to be initiated. India must raise a Cyber Command. This will comprise not only the three services but personnel from the DRDO and scientific and technological community. It could work with the space command because many aspects overlap and would economise on resources. It will oversee all activities undertaken during peacetime, as also plan for offensive cyber operations as required, to include preparation of the battlefield. It must work in close concert with the NTRO. To determine the structure it would be prudent to study the mission and objectives of USCYBERCOM (US Cyber Command) as a guide. USCYBERCOM plans, coordinates, integrates, synchronises and conducts activities to: "direct the operations and defense of specified Department of Defense information NWs and; prepare to, and when directed, conduct full spectrum military cyberspace operations in order to enable actions in all domains, ensure US/Allied freedom of action in cyberspace and deny the same to our adversaries." The Command is charged with pulling together existing cyberspace resources, creating synergy and synchronising war-fighting effects to defend the information security environment. It comes under the Strategic Command, which also has the Space Command as a constituent. A similar structure for India could be considered, especially as the US has evolved its structure based on experience and also because it functions as an open democracy. India already has the Strategic Forces Command, which could be augmented with both Space and Cyberspace Wings. These may be of smaller size to start with, and will develop in accordance with threats and needs. Each service has its own requirements. The structure therefore has to be need-based and flexible. The various elements of this could be:

Army, Navy and Air Force CERTs

These would monitor traffic, disseminate information, ensure remedial measures to ensure ongoing security to networks and systems. They would also in a manner be charged with protection of critical infrastructure of each service, i.e. communication backbone, power systems, high-priority networks. The structure thus envisages a Defence CERT which works in concert with each service CERT.

ARTIFICIAL INTELLIGENCE & CYBER WARFARE

In light of the convergence process that is now taking place between AI and cyber warfare systems and their corresponding areas of responsibility relating to military space systems and space warfare technologies internationally, their sections have been merged to reflect this evolution.

Human-machine interactions and interfaces are radically changing many aspects of the military space command and control structure. In many cases, specific combat operations are now being conducted by human and artificial operators working together in a virtual environment, which delivers a real-time view of the target area with semi-autonomous and autonomous attack options just a blink or a voice-command away. In 2020, AI-driven systems are now supplying consolidated information and refined military options to high-level decision makers, who are now unable to decipher and analyse vast data flows alone. The role of the war planner is now found to be most critical during the process of selecting war fighting strategies generated and provided by AI systems.

The entire sphere of global military operations in 2020 has the potential to be fully interconnected for those with the means and the desire to do so, as successful military operations are decided by this complex network of systems.

Vast protection measures have been taken to guard these systems, including actions to greatly reduce the number of network access points into military and national security systems and to centralize individual architectures in an attempt to prevent unauthorized access and lessen the probability of cyber attacks. This will prove to be a critical decision for many advanced military powers.

As governmental network access points are reduced and their decentralized layout is eventually integrated, the potential for security breaches is greatly decreased.

However, should a cyber denial of service or brute force attack prove successful, a full or near-full spectrum catastrophic failure could result. Scenarios such as these must be considered before the complete consolidation of information architectures is achieved. Decentralized systems lead to an increased potential for vulnerabilities; however they defuse the effects of successful attacks, thus minimizing the potential for significantly debilitating operational effects. Threats posed to computer networks that support critical military satellite systems are in 2020 becoming increasingly complex and are occurring more frequently. Specifically, attacks targeting ground stations and command centres threaten military connectivity and the seamlessness of the

Command, Control, Communications, Computer, Intelligence, Surveillance, and Reconnaissance systems (C4ISR).

Such attacks have the potential to effectively induce a systems blackout. A military's ability to adequately secure C4ISR systems and protect ground segments ensures success not only in space, but in all dimensions of warfare. Advances in cryptology, quantum cryptology, and related technologies such as ciphers and crypto-keys for performing encryption and decryption of these data streams are vital to space-systems security. Specifically, the preservation of secure crosslink/uplink/downlink data transmissions will require constant enhancement efforts due to the availability of advanced computer processing capabilities and the adaptive nature of highly skilled adversaries.

As with all military space-supporting computer systems, threat sources are not limited to code breakers and hackers trying to exploit weaknesses from outside government facilities in faraway lands, but from within the host government as well. In an environment where trust is everything, a weakness in the human element of security could jump all other protection measures.

Additionally, if an attack were to succeed against the C4ISR supporting space systems, a self-healing capability or Self-Regenerative Systems (SRS) solution must be executed immediately in order to repair and secure the effected network. Such abilities to survive a debilitating space systems attack will be made possible by advances in AI.

Nanotechnology

In 2020 it is nearly impossible to find nanotechnology detractors as universal applications are benefiting countless industries in this multidisciplinary field.

Up to this point, nanotechnology discoveries that improved space warfare capabilities had appeared mostly in the form of materials improvements, which enhanced solar power generation, survivability, and structural integrity. Now, micro-electro-mechanical systems (MEMS) and micro-opto-electro-mechanical systems (MOEMS) are beginning to lead to further improvements in sensors, such as Attitude Determination and Control (ADCS) and other components, such as actuators.

Meaningful research into the materials sciences has now been underway for nearly twenty-five years and novel applications are currently appearing and addressing key challenges. Specifically, developments made in the areas of carbon nanotubes (CNT) are resulting in materials capable of thermal and electrical conduction. Additionally, CNT in the proper configurations have led to the creation of materials with unprecedented ballistic protection and heat-shielding and load-bearing strength, including the ability to defuse and insulate against the effects of high-energy lasers. For example, 3D aerogels and xerogels are in 2020 capable of withstanding load-bearing pressures as extreme as 75,000psi. One can imagine numerous applications for such materials, especially when we factor in advances in oxide options. Nanocomposite materials such as those utilizing silica or polystyrene even demonstrate an ability to shield against the effects of high-power microwaves (HPM) and radio frequency (RF). This field of science is also delivering applications that provide the ability to blend an asset's thermal, visual, and radar appearance into its background. Through this research, advanced photovoltaics and power generation methods are evolving as well.

More elaborate, yet feasible, concepts are being pursued such as a Faraday Cage built on a nanoscale level, which would require doped and multi-walled carbon nanotubes (MWCNT). This concept uses carbon nanotubes to develop an enclosure for satellite subsystems and smaller satellite classes such as picosats and nanosats and would provide insulation against various DE threats. Such an enclosure could deter the effects of an electromagnetic pulse (EMP), electrostatic discharges and various other directed energy threats.

Also, self-healing materials are being researched by universities, industry, and militaries to develop self-repairing technologies to address damages such as those that could be sustained in space as a result of space debris or destructive space-asset attacks. Such impacts could lead to a satellite failure, and so a technology like this reaching the development stage would prove invaluable. These materials would use composite structures that contain nanoscale spheres, which encapsulate an unhardened polymer resin. When a satellite is hit, the resin would spread and then fill the cracks to prevent further damage. Such systems could also provide shielding.

Flexible nanoelectronic devices that are as thin as paper and mounted to a thin flexible substrate such a as a plastic would provide a flexible, conductive, and multiuse material, which could then be integrated into countless space systems. A very attractive manifestation of this application would be in the form of a substrate on which electronic circuits could be printed on demand. Such a nanomaterial would also be durable and could be rolled up and stored.

Flexible substrates and the use of various conductors could lead to thin-film solar cells for space applications or thin-film semiconductors. The next level: Molecular nanotechnology (MNT) promises to revolutionize countless products by engineering mechanical and electronic systems, including advanced materials, at the molecular scale. Such a capacity for discovery will touch upon every aspect of military technology in the realm of space warfare.

5

Future Network Centric Warfare Technology

BACKGROUND AND HISTORY

Network centric warfare can trace its immediate origins to 1996 when Admiral William Owens introduced the concept of a 'system of systems' in a paper of the same name published by the Institute National Security Studies. Owens described the serendipitous evolution of a system of intelligence sensors, command and control systems, and precision weapons that enabled enhanced situational awareness, rapid target assessment, and distributed weapon assignment.

Also in 1996, the Joint Chiefs of Staff released Joint Vision 2010, which introduced the military concept of full-spectrum dominance. Full Spectrum Dominance described the ability of the US military to dominate the battlespace from peace operations through to the outright application of military power that stemmed from the advantages of information superiority.

Network Centric Warfare

The term "network-centric warfare" and associated concepts first appeared in the Department of Navy's publication, "Copernicus: C4ISR for the 21st Century." The ideas of networking sensors, commanders, and shooters to flatten the hierarchy, reduce the operational pause, enhance precision, and increase speed of command were captured in this document. As a distinct concept, however, network-centric warfare first appeared publicly in a 1998 US Naval Institute Proceedings article by Vice Admiral Arthur K. Cebrowski and John Garstka. However, the first complete articulation of the idea was contained in the book Network Centric Warfare: Developing and Leveraging

Information Superiority by Alberts, Garstka and Stein published by the Command and Control Research Program (CCRP), This book derived a new theory of warfare from a series of case studies on how business was using information and communication technologies to improve situation analysis, accurately control inventory and production, as well as monitor customer relations.

Understanding Information Age Warfare

Network-centric warfare was followed in 2001 by *Understanding Information Age Warfare* (UIAW), jointly authored by Alberts, Garstka, Richard Hayes of Evidence Based Research and David S. Signori of RAND. UIAW pushed the implications of the shifts identified by network-centric warfare in order to derive an operational theory of warfare.

Starting with a series of premises on how the environment is sensed, UIAW posits a structure of three domains. The *physical domain* is where events take place and are perceived by sensors and individuals. Data emerging from the physical domain is transmitted through an *information domain.*

Data is subsequently received and processed by a *cognitive domain* where it is assessed and acted upon. The process replicates the "observe, orient, decide, act" loop first described by Col. John Boyd of the USAF.

Power to the Edge

The last publication dealing with the developing theory of network centric warfare appeared in 2003 with *Power to the Edge*, also published by the CCRP. *Power to the Edge* is a speculative work suggesting that modern military environments are far too complex to be understood by any one individual, organisation, or even military service.

Modern information technology permits the rapid and effective sharing of information to such a degree that "edge entities" or those that are essentially conducting military missions themselves, should be able to "pull" information from ubiquitous repositories, rather than having centralised agencies attempt to anticipate their information needs and "push" it to them. This would imply a major flattening of traditional military hierarchies, however.

Power To The Edge's radical ideas had been under investigation by the Pentagon since at least 2001. In *UIAW*, the concept of peer-to-peeractivity combined with more traditional hierarchical flow of data in the network had been introduced.

Shortly thereafter, the Pentagon began investing in peer-to-peer research, telling software engineers at a November 2001 peer-to-peer conference that there were advantages to be gained in the redundancy and robustness of a peer-to-peer network topology on the battlefield.

Network-centric warfare/operations is a cornerstone of the ongoing transformation effort at the Department of Defence initiated by former Secretary of Defence Donald Rumsfeld. It is also one of the five goals of the Office of Force Transformation, Office of the Secretary of Defence.

Related Technologies and Programs

The US DOD has mandated that the Global Information Grid (GIG) will be the primary technical framework to support US network-centric warfare/ network-centric operations. Under this directive, all advanced weapons platforms, sensor systems, and command and control centers are eventually to be linked via the GIG. The term system of systems is often used to describe the results of these types of massive integration efforts.

The topic Net-Centric Enterprise Services addresses the applications context of the GIG.

A number of significant U.S. military programs are taking technical steps towards supporting network-centric warfare. These include the Cooperative Engagement Capability (CEC) of the United States Navy and the BCT Network of the United States Army.

Net-Centric Enterprise Solutions for Interoperability (NESI) provides, for all phases of the acquisition of net-centric solutions, actionable guidance that meets network-centric warfare goals of the United States Department of Defence.

The guidance in NESI is derived from the higher level, more abstract concepts provided in various directives, policies and mandates such as the Net-Centric Operations and Warfare Reference Model (NCOW RM) and the ASD(NII) Net-Centric Checklist.

Doctrinal tenets in United States

The doctrine of network-centric warfare for the United States armed forces draws its highest level of guidance from the concept of "team warfare", meaning the integration and synchronization of all appropriate capabilities across the various services, ranging from Army to Air Force to Coast Guard. This is part of the principle of joint warfare.

The tenets of network-centric warfare are:

- Tenet 1: A robustly networked force improves information sharing.
- Tenet 2: Information sharing and collaboration enhance the quality of information and shared situational awareness.
- Tenet 3: Shared situational awareness enables self-synchronization.
- Tenet 4: These, in turn, dramatically increase mission effectiveness.

Net-Centric operations are compatible with Mission Command doctrine, which theoretically allows considerable freedom of action for combat troops, and with more decentralized approaches to Command and Control (C2).

Some architectural and design challenges

- The complexity of the Joint Tactical Radio System (JTRS) offers insight into the challenges of integrating numerous different communications systems into a unified whole. It is intended to be a software-defined radio for battlefield communications that will be backwards compatible with a very large number of other military and civilian radio systems.
- An April 10, 2008 GAO report (GAO FCS report) highlighted the scalability of the network as a major risk factor to the Network Centric FCS program. The proposed system will be unable to network all the units into one self-forming, self-healing network.
- The problem of coordinating bandwidth usage in a battlespace is a significant challenge, when every piece of mobile equipment and human participant becomes a potential source or relay of RF emissions.
- It is difficult to efficiently transfer information between networks having different levels of security classification. Although multi-level security systems provide part of the solution, human intervention and decision-making is still needed to determine what specific data can and cannot be transferred.
- Accurate locational awareness is limited when maneuvering in areas where Global Positioning System (GPS) coverage is weak or non-existent. These areas include the inside of buildings, caves, etc. as well as built-up areas and urban canyons, which are also settings for many modern military operations. Much work on reliable fusion of positional data from multiple sensors remains to be done.
- Providing secure communications in network-centric warfare/network-centric operations is difficult, since successful key managementfor encryption is typically the most difficult aspect of cryptography, especially with mobile systems. The problem is exacerbated with the need for speedy deployment and nimble reconfiguration of military teams, to respond to rapidly changing conditions in the modern battlespace.

International activities

There is significant need to harmonize the technical and operational aspects of net-centric warfare and net-centric operations among multiple nations, in order to support coalition activities, joint operations, etc. *Standard*

Agreement is the coordinating vehicle for establishing shared technical standards among NATO nations.

Supporting Comments

"With less than half of the ground forces and two-thirds of the military aircraft used 12 years ago in Desert Storm, we have achieved a far more difficult objective... In Desert Storm, it usually took up to two days for target planners to get a photo of a target, confirm its coordinates, plan the mission, and deliver it to the bomber crew. Now we have near real-time imaging of targets with photos and coordinates transmitted by e-mail to aircraft already in flight. In Desert Storm, battalion, brigade, and division commanders had to rely on maps, grease pencils, and radio reports to track the movements of our forces. Today, our commanders have a real-time display of our armed forces on their computer screen." —former Vice President Richard Cheney.

"Net-centric warfare's effectiveness has greatly improved in 12 years. Desert Storm forces, involving more than 500,000 troops, were supported with 100 Mbit/s of bandwidth. Today, OIF forces, with about 350,000 warfighters, had more than 3,000 Mbit/s of satellite bandwidth, which is 30 times more bandwidth for a force 45 percent smaller. U.S. troops essentially used the same weapon platforms used in Operation Desert Storm with significantly increased effectiveness." —Lieutenant general Harry D. Raduege Jr, director, Defence Information Systems Agency.

Contradictory views

"Our incipient NCW plans may suffer defeat by [adversaries] using primitive but cagey techniques, inspired by an ideology we can neither match nor understand; or by an enemy who can knock out our vulnerable Global Positioning System or use electromagnetic pulse weapons on a limited scale, removing intelligence as we have construed it and have come to depend upon. Fighting forces accustomed to relying upon downlinks for information and commands would have little to fall back upon." *—Charles Perrow, Information Assurance, National Defence University, May 2003*

The aspiration of the Australian Defence Force (ADF) to embrace network-centric warfare is outlined in the document *ADF Force 2020*. This vision has been criticized by Aldo Borgu, director of the Australian Strategic Policy Institute (ASPI). By developing interoperability with U.S. systems, in his view, the three arms of the Australian Defence Force could end up operating better with their sister United States services than with each other.

Network centric warfare is criticized by proponents of Fourth Generation Warfare (4GW) doctrine. Also, since Network-centric warfare focuses so much on distributing information, one has to be wary of the effect of false, misleading, or misinterpreted information entering the system, be it through enemy deception or simple error. Just as the usefulness of correct information can be amplified, so too can the repercussions of incorrect data entering the system achieve much greater non-positive outcomes.

One way that this can happen is through errors in initial conditions in an uncorrected, closed system that subsequently skew result-sets; the result-sets are then reused, amplifying the initial error by orders of magnitude in subsequent generations of result-sets; see chaos theory.

Other possible failure modes or problem areas in network-centric warfare include the occurrence of the Byzantine generals' problem in peer-to-peer systems; problems caused by an inadequate or a shallow understanding of (or general disregard for) self-regulation, self-organization, systems theory, emergent behaviour and cybernetics; in addition to this, there are potential issues arising from the very nature of any complex, rapidly developed artificial system arising from complexity theory, which implies the possibility of failure modes such as congestion collapse or cascading failure.

NET-CENTRICITY IN MODERN WARFARE

The advent of Revolution in Military Affairs (RMA) and its enabling features in prosecution of warfare in the modern era has generated considerable interest among the global military fraternity. Thus the terms 'information operations', 'digitisation' and 'net-centric warfare' have become part of routine glossary of military terminologies under the overall ambit of Information Warfare (IW). We are aware that the idea of harnessing the information-specific technology in conduct of warfare was conceived in the Russian military theology. Subsequently, it found formal fruition through strategic confabulations in the United States (US) before being propagated among other advanced militaries. Indian Army too responded to the concept of IW as early as 1990s. Since then, it has made considerable efforts to harness the advantages of 'information', 'digitisation' and 'net-centricity' in its operational, logistic and management functions. There are studies carried out, goals set, resources committed, projects undertaken and military exercises conducted under the unique parameters that these terms signify. In practice however, the stage when these parameters might instil confidence among the military fraternity, for them to depend on these under conditions of war, is far away yet.

India's strategic concerns are limited as compared to the western powers. It may therefore be logical to define the aforementioned aspects of IW to own understanding and purpose.

ANATOMY OF NETWORK-CENTRIC WARFARE

Ubiquitous Connectivity may have Hidden Consequences

As momentum grows for network centricity in military operations, architects of the plans may find themselves closely examining sciences such as sociology or biology to preview where network-centric activity can lead. When command, control, communications, computers and intelligence systems become more highly networked, the need for sophistication in the products and platforms that sit at the edges diminishes. In some cases, too much capability at the edge may actually inhibit self-organizing behaviour and negatively impact the mission of the networked whole.

The term network-centric is an oxymoron. Networks themselves are inherently centerless—it is all about the edges. The promise of networks is in the dynamic interactions of the nodes at the edges. When these nodes become highly connected, interesting things start to happen.

The fundamental principle that underlies today's thinking about network-centric warfare is Metcalfe's Law, named after Robert Metcalfe, the inventor of Ethernet and founder of 3Com Corporation. It was a phenomenon first observed in commercial communications as Metcalfe sought to address the problem of creating larger networks out of many smaller ones. The law contends that the power of a network increases with the square of the number of nodes connected to the network. Network-centric warfare advocates build on this law by asserting that maximizing the number of nodes increases the chances of realizing the promise of networks through ubiquitous connectivity and interoperability.

Pursuit of ubiquitous connectivity may have hidden consequences, however. Carried to its logical conclusion, such connectivity may give rise to an environment that becomes increasingly "biological" over time and begins to exhibit behaviour similar to that of living systems. However, living pathways represent everything that the traditional business of defence is not. The implications of biological constructs in defence are both surprising and scary.

Albert-László Barabási and Eric Bonabeau outlined recent discoveries regarding highly networked systems in an article in *Scientific American* magazine. Chief among these discoveries is the existence of power laws that underlie networks such as the World Wide Web or the relationships between people in society. The power law behind these networks means that they are inherently scale-free—there is no typical node and no peak in the distribution curve. In networks of this type, the vast majority of nodes have a small number of links but are juxtaposed with a tiny number of nodes that have an extraordinarily large number of connections. The latter are known as hubs.

Hubs are evident in everyday life. In society, a few people operate in a huge circle of acquaintances amidst a world where only a limited number of relationships are nurtured. This also is evident in the disproportional popularity of certain Web sites such as Amazon or Yahoo when compared with nearly every other Web page. Interestingly, these hubs also are present in the command and control (C^2) hierarchy and constructs that are currently employed in the business of defence.

Complex networks operate through the dynamic interaction of nodes and hubs that resemble an unfolding drama more than an engineered system. Perhaps the most conspicuous characteristic of these networks is that they continuously grow. In the push toward connectivity growth in network-centric warfare, the U.S. military may be unwittingly marching down a path that conforms to the logic of scale-free networks. The question is whether this is good or bad.

Barabási and Bonabeau ominously warn that while scale-free networks are quite survivable against random failure, they also are highly vulnerable to a focused attack because of the critical role of hubs in the network. Their research has shown that up to 80 percent of the nodes in a scale-free network can be randomly removed without compromising the functionality of the networked whole. However, a coordinated attack that disables 5 percent to 15 percent of the hubs simultaneously is all that is needed to mortally wound such a system.

Ubiquitous connectivity of a scale-free variety encourages a dangerous centrality of interaction focused on C^2 hubs. Dynamic tension exists between hierarchical C^2 models and the push for maximizing the number of nodes. While maintaining a hierarchical C^2 model, maximizing the number of nodes is a risky proposition because it amplifies the network's vulnerabilities. However, if maximizing the number of nodes is the overarching imperative, then new models of C^2 may emerge. These frameworks may be more efficacious in monitoring, pre-empting and combating threats of an asymmetric and fluid nature.

But these new C^2 models will likely have to dispense with traditional notions of control and efficiency to accentuate flexibility and adaptability. When networked information flow is nonexistent, hierarchy rules.

When it is abundant and dynamic, the traditional C^2 pyramid gets flipped upside down and the edges become primary. Command intent gradually diminishes in importance in comparison to emergent intent that arises spontaneously through the interaction of autonomous agents at the edge.

A scale-free philosophy also implies nodal expendability—by design. Small failures are bred into the system so that fatal breakdowns are avoided.

In today's ethos of casualty avoidance, how does this notion get initiated in battle planning wherein up to 80 percent of the nodes are potentially expendable without mission degradation? When such odds are possible, creation of operational concepts that leverage such odds in favor of overall mission accomplishment will naturally emerge to the benefit of hubs and to the potential detriment of most nodes.

From an operational perspective, the needs of the few outweigh the needs of the many if the overarching good of all is to be achieved. The likely consequence of such a construct is the increasing substitution of machines for humans at the nodes. Machines are expendable. Humans are not. This trade-off is already starting to occur in earnest.

The interaction of highly networked systems is not governed by mechanisms that traditional systems engineering techniques can necessarily discern or manage. Their nonlinear characteristics can frustrate the drive for precision, optimization and predictability—the hallmarks of military products, platforms and systems. The messy redundancy of networks has a recursive nature that manifests itself in curious ways.

Author Kevin Kelly, co-founder of *Wired* magazine, talks about simulations that illustrate the dynamics of networked interaction. They reveal a fragile balance between nodal intelligence and range of capability versus networked outcomes. In one simulation, the autonomous, self-organizing actions of thousands at a computer conference enable them to fly and land an airplane effectively without any direction from a coordinator. The key to mission accomplishment, however, was the limited range of behaviour accorded to each participant in the form of a joystick that enabled only up/down and left/right movement.

A follow-on simulation that took place several years later involved a submarine in search of targets. This time, the results were not initially successful. The primary difference was that participants were accorded a much higher level of sophistication and control. The increased range of behaviour resulted in chaos as individuals and groups of individuals nullified each other's actions in the exercise of their autonomy. Success was achieved only after the simulation director stepped up to the microphone and provided some explicit directions to the entire group, which then enabled swarm behaviour to be unleashed effectively. That direction was the visible hand of command and control.

The lessons of these simulations are interesting. For example, a highly networked environment provides the means for less capable legacy assets to be reborn with new purpose and meaning. Kelly has quipped that "dumb parts properly connected can yield smart results." Under certain conditions, ever increasing quantities of "dumber" nodes linked to the network are likely to enhance mission effectiveness as much if not more than adding more sophisticated ones.

However, achieving synergy among intelligence, quantity and control is a tricky proposition. In a network-centric warfare environment, C^2 becomes more of a coaxing and tweaking phenomenon. C^2 will gradually look more like the Federal Reserve chairman's attempts to influence the economy through soft levers like interest rate adjustments rather than through concrete orders and actions.

Biological constructs, much like world economies, however, sometimes give rise to wild-card factors that are not anticipated. The emergent characteristics are often rooted in the profusion of organic systems exerting influence laterally. These systems operate in a peering arrangement involving hundreds of thousands and even millions or billions of nodes. Where is the cross-over point in which unexpected effects begin to appear as the world of big numbers and horizontal causation unfolds? As military operations begin to make greater use of swarm systems in the form of networked microsensors, robots and unmanned vehicles in concert with humans, an understanding of thresholds separating discrete control versus unpredictability is critical.

NETWORKED SWARMING WARFARE

The concept of networked swarming warfare was first proposed by Dajun Huo in 2003. The key feature of the information age is the networking of organizational structure. The rising networked organization will overcome the limitation of traditional geography and link the operational resources distributed widely to form a military action network which combine strike range, speed and lethality, three elements of originally different developing, fundamentally transforming our idea of battle space. With the trend of decentralization of forces, we need to develop more small units with independent combat functions; meanwhile we can join these small units into a whole network as the technology's development. The warfare based on this network is called networked swarming warfare.

Definition

Networked swarming warfare is a wide area maneuver warfare to attack dynamically the enemy in parallel by flexible "concentration" and "dispersion", which integrates the multiple forces distributed widely into the operational network of flows in a multi-dimensional space.

Connotations

- In the organization of forces, it can integrate multiple operational resources distributed widely into an intact force network to realize information interaction, functional coupling and convergent ability, which is based on the information network and follows the networking logic of the organizational structure.

- In the deployment of troops, it is nonlinear, widely dispersed, irregular and mobile in a multi-dimensional space, emphasizing the combination of deployment and strike, and dominating the development of the battlespace situation by flexible maneuver, dispersal and concentration.
- In the distribution of space, it is mobile and dispersed in the wide space.
- In the distribution of time, it is non sequential to attack a target or a series of related targets in parallel.
- In the pattern of action, it is a nonlinear attack dynamic of multiple dispersed operations by the unity of small combat units, similar to the "long-range raid" operational pattern.

Features

Networked swarming warfare has three essential features: flowing of organization; objective-centered; multidirectional mobile attack.

TECHNOLOGY IN NETWORK-CENTRIC WARFARE

The technology supporting NCW is inherently complex, but not significantly moreso than the technology used to digitise and network the civilian world. It must however be more resilient physically, thermally, electrically and be better resistent to hostile penetration, and in wireless systems, hostile jamming.

The prerequisite for an NCW capability is the digitisation of combat platforms. A combat aircraft with a digital weapon system can be seamlessly integrated in an NCW environment by providing digital wireless connections to other platforms.

Without the digital weapon system, and its internal computers, NCW is not implementable. The growing gap between the US military and the EU military largely reflects the Europeans' reluctance to heavily invest in digitising their combat platforms.

Provision of digital wireless connectivity between combat platforms is a major technical challenge which cannot be understated. While civilian networking of computers can largely rely on cabled links, be they copper or optical fibres, with wireless connectivity as an adjunct, in a military environment centred in moving platforms and field deployed basing, wireless connectivity is the central means of carrying information.

The problems faced in providing military networking are generally well understood, but often push the boundaries of available technology. Key issues can be summarised thus:

1. Security of transmission. Since everybody does their best to eavesdrop, digital links have to be difficult to eavesdrop, and robustly encrypted to defeat any eavesdropping which might succeed. Even if a signal cannot be successfully decrypted, its detection provides an opponent with valuable information on the presence, position and often activity of the platform or unit in question.
2. Robustness of transmission. In the face of transmission impairments such as solar flares, bad weather and hostile jamming, networks must continue to function. If a signal cannot penetrate a rainshower or is blotted out by an opponent's barrage jammer, the link is broken and the NCW model also breaks.
3. Transmission capacity. How fast data can be transmitted is vital, especially where digitised imagery must be sent. If a 10 Megabyte recce image must be sent, or a 2 Megabit/sec digitised video feed observed, a 9600 bit/sec channel will be nearly useless. A popular misconception is that digital data compression solves this problem - the reality of Shannon's communication theory is very much at odds with this popular (in some Canberra circles) fantasy. Robustness against jamming and the overheads of encryption both function at the expense of transmission channel capacity for a given radio communications link - the robust the link, the more capacity is soaked up with overheads to protect it.
4. Message and signal routing. Platforms must be able to specifically address and access other platforms or systems in an NCW environment. Just as email on a civilian network must have an address, so must a military messaging scheme. Such addressing must be able to cope with a fluid network topology, as platforms entre and leave an area of operations.
5. Signal format and communications protocol compatibility. It is essential that dissimilar platforms and systems can communicate in an NCW environment. This problem extends not only to the use of disparate signal modulations and digital protocols, but to the use of partially incompatible implementations of what is ostensibly the same signal modulation or communications protocol. The mutual incompatibility headaches we see in commercial computing are often more traumatic in the challenging military environment.

At the time of writing nearly all military datalinks used in NCW operate at speeds which would be considered intolerable in the civilian/commercial world, reflecting the realities of wireless communications. Moreover, the military world lives with a veritable Tower of Babel in both signal modulations, operating frequencies and digital communications protocols, and variations of nominally standard protocols.

To contextualise this, Western armed forces currently deploy systems using a wide range of current and legacy signal formats and protocols, examples being:

1. Link 1 at 1200/2400 bits per second used for air defence systems, devised in the 1950s.
2. TADIL A / Link-11/11B at 1364 bits per second used for naval links and ground based SAM systems, using original CLEW DQPSK modulation, or newer FTBCB convolutional coding at 1800 bits per second. It is 1960s technology.
3. TADIL C / Link-4 at 5,000 bits per second in the UHF band, used for naval aviation, AEW&C to fighter links, and fighter to fighter links on the F-14 series. It is also 1960s technology.
4. Link-14 used for HF transmission between naval combatants at low data rates.
5. TADIL J / MIDS/JTIDS / Link-16 which is a jam resistant L-band time division Spread Spectrum Multiple Access (SSMA)system based on 1970s technology. While its time slot model permits some allocation of capacity, in practical terms it is limited to kilobits/sec data rates, over distances of about 250 nautical miles. JTIDS is multi-platform and multi-service and widely used for transmitting tactical position data, directives, advisories, and for defacto Identification Friend Foe. Its limitation is that it is ill suited to sending reconnaissance imagery and inherently tied to master stations which generate its timebase - reflecting its origins of three decades ago. Satellite link and higher data rate derivatives exist but retain the basic limitations of its time division technique.
6. CDL/TCDL/HIDL/ABIT which are US high speed datalinks design primarily for satellite and UAV transmission of imagery. CDL family links are typically assymetric, using a 200 kilobit/s uplink for control and management, and a 10.71, 45, 137 or 234 Megabit/s high speed uplink, and a specialised for the control of satellite/UAVs and receipt of gathered data. ABIT is a development of CDL operating at 548 Megabits/s with low probability of intercept capabilities.

7. Improved Data Modem (IDM) is used over Have Quick II spread spectrum radios to provide low data rate but secure transmission of targeting coordinates and imagery. It has been used widely for transmission of targeting data to F-15E/F-16C strike fighters and F-16CJ Wild Weasels. It is essentially an analogue to commercial voiceband modems.
8. Army Tactical Data Link 1 - ATDL 1 used for US Army Hawk and Patriot SAM batteries.
9. PATRIOT Digital Information Link - PADIL used by Patriot SAM batteries.
10. Tactical Information Broadcast System - TIBS used for theatre missile defence systems.
11. PLRS/EPLRS/SADL are a family of US Army/Marine Corps datalinks used for tracking ground force units, and providing defacto Identification Friend Foe of ground units. EPRLs is also used for data transmission between ground units.
12. TCP/IP (Internet) protocol implementations running over other channels, to provide connectivity between platforms and remote ground facilities.
13. Joint Tactical Radio System (JTRS), intended to supplant most legacy protocols with networking equipment which can communicate both in legacy prototols and modulations, and its own JTRS protocols and modulations. The JTRS Wideband Netwroking Waveform (WNW) is to provide multi-Megabit/s throughput.

This veritable menagerie of datalink modulations/protocols is by no means exhaustive, but reflects the realities observed in the computer industry in the decades predating the Internet.

New protocols like the Joint Tactical Radio System (JTRS) are in part intended to incorporate mechanisms for translating such legacy protocols into formats which can be sent over a common channel.

Separate from these multi-platform protocols and modulations are the type specific datalinks, such as the intra- and interflight datalinks used on the F/A-22A and later the JSF.

As yet there has been little effort to capitalise on the new technology of ad hoc network protocols, designed for self organising networks of mobile platforms, although the JTRS WNW effort looks promising. The DARPA GLOMO program in the late 1980s saw considerable seed money invested, but did not yield any publicised dramatic breakthroughs. Ad hoc networking remains a yet to be fully explored frontier in the networking domain, one which is apt to provide a decisive technology breakthrough for NCW. The technological issues in NCW often dominate the debate at the expense of the deeper philosophical and functional issues which is unfortunate, since both domains matter and getting either wrong results in an equally disfunctional end result.

NCW and Australia

In Australia networking has been very much in the limelight of the defence debate. Sadly, it has also been used to justify a great many dubious decisions, all predicated on premises which do not hold.

Like most intellectually demanding and complex systems problems, NCW must be properly understood before it can be used as a basis for strategic planning decisions. Clearly this has not been the case in many key areas of the DoD, resulting in public statements which would be comical were not the circumstances so dire. Perhaps the best exposition of this problem lies in the package of submissions presented earlier this year to the JSCFADT committee of Federal Parliament, especially the Air Combat Capability paper.

In this document we learn that networking can substitute for combat fleet numbers, despite the contrary experience in Afghanistan and Iraq, where aircraft size became the pivotal issue. We also learn that the combat effect of the system should exceed the sum of its parts despite the contrary mathematics underpinning this problem. Limitations in the F/A-18A and JSF we learn do not matter, since Australia will evidently have an asymmetric advantage in networking and AEW&C, despite regional buys of Russian/Israeli A-50 AWACS, and Russian marketing of TKS-2 digital datalinks on Su-30 fighters. We also learn in this document that AEW&C aircraft and networks will not be challenged, as evidently Russian R-172, Kh-31 and R-37 missiles, or high power jammers, will never be used in the region - regional buys notwithstanding. No differently, Australia need not invest in high power jamming aircraft since other nations will never use their AEW&C and networking systems. We also learn that five A330-200 tankers will improve the RAAF's combat persistence, since evidently the fuel carried in F-111s need not be counted. No less surprisingly we also discover that the mere AU$20M to 30M required to put networking into the F-111s is unusually expensive and not worth doing - evidently it is better to kill off the aircraft than invest into networking it.

The ugly reality is that networking has become a cure all panacea in the DoD bureacratic machine, one which can magically offset all force structure limitations, and one which magically only Australia can possess and use properly in the Pacrim.

The analytical perspective is very different, however. Most regional nations are now operating, deploying or shopping for AEW&C aircraft. Russia is actively marketing digital datalinks, like the TKS-2 and older APD-518, and marketing counter-ISR weapons like the Novator R-172 (KS-172) or Kh-31 series missiles. Russia is also marketing high power jamming equipment, especially pods using Digital RF Memory (DRFM) technology, and there is a good prospect of a Growler-ski based on the Su-32 materialising before the end of the decade.

In practical terms, by 2010-2015 regional opponents without AEW&C, long range counter-ISR missiles and jamming pods are likely to be the obliging exception to the rule. US thinking is not surprisingly centred in using F/A-22As to sanitise airspace permitting unhindered use of ISR platforms and networks, and the program to replace the lost capabilities of the EF-111A Raven with the B-52J or EB-52, equipped with high power stand-off jamming equipment to disrupt opposing networks and ISR sensors. The reality we observe regionally and globally is, like the physics and mathematics which apply to the network problem, very different to the interpretation of these issues which we observe in the confines of Russell Offices. The Departmental leadership have effectively committed Australia to major strategic decisions, like the JSF program and F-111 retirement, on the basis of beliefs which are simply not supportable by fact. That a major fraction of virtually every public document dealing with the JSF and F-111 issues is dedicated to extolling the virtues of NCW is evidence in its own right.

The sad conclusion is that this emotive rather than rational approach to NCW amounts to little more than a doctrinal and strategic heresy, one which will no doubt vanish into oblivion no differently than the enthusiasm for the 'Revolution in Military Affairs' did some years ago. Until that much awaited day comes, damage will continue to be done to Australia's basic capabilities.

THE NETWORK IS THE STRATEGIC FABRIC

An intelligent network allows an organization to more closely align its network with its processes, making the network more responsive, more flexible, and more effective at addressing everyday operations, as well as high-tempo operations experienced during contingencies and emergency responses. And it enables an organization to embed security deep within its infrastructure, to protect military assets and respond quickly to threats.

Since the network can be a hacker's target, it must include appropriate security mechanisms that will allow the military to use the efficiencies and effectiveness gained by moving to a networked environment, without placing their operations at risk.

An intelligent network is the strategic fabric that streamlines and synthesizes the flow of information, integrating the complex array of proprietary networks, systems, and applications that provide support for military operations. Under an NCO model, military resources can be simply considered nodes on the network. Each of these resources or "networked vehicles" in the field of operation can enjoy complete access to voice, data, video, and command and control—to and from headquarters.

Leading military organizations are moving away from traditional centralized thinking and planning, and toward an edge-centered approach to information sharing and availability. An intelligent network provides the foundational elements, such as collaborative tools, storage, security, messaging, and mediation, creating a common platform that supports the full array of services and applications used by military forces. These services can be used across service or agency boundaries—transparently to the user. An intelligent network is also central to an environment where users can pull the information they require, without relying on a top-down, "push" approach to intelligence and decision making. This ability to "reach back" also reduces the forward footprint necessary for military operations, dramatically reducing costs and risks to personnel.

To deliver mission-critical information, the network must meet stringent requirements. It must be resilient enough to ensure that information is always available, protected from network outages, service spikes, and security breaches. And it must be responsive enough to serve up multiple types of information—including voice, video, and data—from multiple sources, to provide the highest degree of shared situational awareness.

In a defence environment, mission critical information is essential to command and control and other logistics, and can come in the form of intelligence, surveillance, or reconnaissance. Consider the advantages this information could provide if it were simultaneously broadcast from a single network across the chain of command down to battlefield operating systems.

Overcoming Challenges

Today's defence agencies must contend with a disparate communications environment. Their communications infrastructures likely include legacy equipment and systems that have accumulated over several years. Some of this equipment may be proprietary, making connectivity with other systems difficult. Or the communications infrastructure may be a collection of different systems that have been pieced together. In demanding situations, the disparity in capabilities of the networked elements can dramatically reduce the effectiveness of operations. All too often, current infrastructures are:

- Inaccessible—Legacy systems and networks offer limited capability, information accessibility, and scalability. They do not provide the necessary network intelligence to support advanced communications, security, and wireless capabilities.
- Incomplete—Because the military information domain is scattered between disparate systems, it is difficult for decision makers to obtain a complete picture. Insight and planning are hampered by proprietary enterprise systems; Command, Control, Communications, Computers, Intelligence, Surveillance, Target Acquisition, and Reconnaissance (C4ISTAR) Systems; weapons and sensor systems; and service provisioning or logistics systems—each focusing on only limited areas.
- Irrelevant—Different lines of service and coalitions use systems that are deliberately segmented, due to security constraints. Sharing relevant information between these systems in a timely manner is difficult or impossible.

Inability to provide shared situational awareness can have catastrophic results. Defence establishments need to achieve the highest degree of situational awareness to facilitate fast, accurate decisions, and promote self-synchronized action across the entire chain of command.

Seizing The Information Domain

Defence agencies recognize that immediate information is vital to mission effectiveness in military operations, and are looking to networking technology to increase the real-time availability of information. An intelligent network provides the foundation to integrate surveillance, reconnaissance, military intelligence, weapon and IT systems, and applications required to run successful command and control operations.

For example, the Royal Netherlands Army faced the challenge of replacing its European Command (EUROCOM)1-based mobile communications network with a solution that allows fully integrated services. This new solution, the Theatre-Independent Tactical Army and Air Force Network (TITAAN), uses a Cisco IP infrastructure as support for integrated voice, data, and video services. A revolutionary network solution, TITAAN is one of the first tactical military networks almost completely based on commercial off-the-shelf software and hardware components.

The U.S. Department of Defence is also actively transforming itself to take advantage of the benefits of NCO. Its "Network-Centric Warfare" report cites four main tenets:

- A robustly networked force improves information sharing

- Information sharing enhances the quality of information and shared situational awareness
- Shared situational awareness facilitates collaboration and self-synchronization, and enhances sustainability and speed of command
- These, in turn, dramatically increase mission effectiveness

NCO is changing the institutional culture of the military by enabling defence establishments to respond quickly to the changing landscape. The following benefits facilitate these changes.

Shared Situational Awareness

An intelligent network enables defence forces to deliver mission-critical information throughout the chain of command. Organizations can share situational awareness, regardless of the location or time of day.

An intelligent network enables the protection of sensitive information, helping to ensure that sensitive communications and data are available only to authorized personnel. And it streamlines the delivery of information, even from multiple sources and locations. By offering support for data, voice, and video transmissions, an intelligent network gives forces a complete picture of a combat situation.

Because it is based on standards-compliant components and technologies, an intelligent network can interoperate smoothly with existing systems. And it can scale to support thousands of users on the network at the same time.

In its report to Congress, the U.S. Department of Defence underscored the ability of NCO to provide unique advantages to armed forces:

"Network-centric operations provide a force with access to a new, previously unreachable region of the information domain. The ability to operate in this region provides warfighters with a new type of information advantage. This advantage is enabled by the dramatic improvements in information sharing made possible by networking. With this information advantage, a warfighting force can achieve dramatically improved shared situational awareness and knowledge."

Whether at peace, at war, or engaged in a humanitarian effort, forces need information in a timely and secure fashion to make proactive decisions and successfully achieve their missions.

Greater Mission Effectiveness

An intelligent network boosts mission effectiveness. It gives defence forces the ability to understand a situation more fully, and allows dispersed personnel to simultaneously and accurately evaluate and respond to each situation. The network improves communications, coordination, and collaboration, to create greater operational efficiencies. And it boosts the effectiveness of military personnel in achieving goals or targets, enabling them to do things they couldn't do before in the field.

For example, the Royal Netherlands Army's new TITAAN system enables the organization to carry its phone traffic and several information systems over a single IP network infrastructure. According to Lieutenant Colonel Bertil Sundquest, Chief Current Ops, "With TITAAN, we can run, on any workstation, command-and-control information, planning, and support systems such as ADAMS, BICES, JOIIS, or LOCE. We can also display digital maps and aerial photos, if required, overlaid on each other, using the 3M projector systems mounted overhead in our headquarters."

Support for Ad-Hoc Operations

A network-centric strategy gives military agencies an unprecedented capability to address high-risk situations, wherever they occur. For example, a secure, ubiquitous network infrastructure can support instantaneous collaboration between military branches of service and coalition partners. Standards-based networking also allows that network to extend out to forces that are on the move, freeing them from dependence on a static location. The network's support for mobile operations can provide a tactical commander with new levels of field visibility.

Because an intelligent network integrates a broad range of networks, advanced systems, and applications, defence forces can collaborate more effectively and share information as an operation unfolds.

Continuity of Operations

Continuity of operations (COOP) is a critical requirement for any defence agency. The interruption of communication, at any level, can jeopardize a mission. An NCO strategy provides the advanced technologies and best practices necessary to protect the network and information assets from unplanned outages and security threats. It also provides the critical emergency response systems to handle new threats and unforeseen situations.

Reduced Operational and Capital Costs

NCO lowers operational and capital costs by converging multiple networks together on a single intelligent network. And, because it consolidates multiple communications systems onto a common infrastructure, it enables military organizations to reduce the costs of provisioning, installing, integrating, and managing the network.

An NCO strategy also allows military organizations to more easily upgrade and support intelligent network services such as converged voice and data applications—which can dramatically improve operational efficiency. With careful planning, the strategy can also reduce the costs of performing incremental upgrades, with network downtime and consumption of IT resources. One example of standards-based networks helping to reduce costs is in applying wireless in the field environment. By connecting field operations through wireless networking, field operations can save significant time and money in airlift, sealift, and excavation costs, compared to laying cable.

NCO enhances reliability and reduces troubleshooting costs, using embedded technologies and services such as integrated security, telephony, management, caching, and content management. These technologies, found on Cisco integrated services routers, protect the network from unplanned network outages, slow service, and security breaches. Training and administrative costs—a significant portion of network cost of ownership—are reduced, because network administrative staff can use a common interface to manage and administer the network. By employing open standards-based technologies, organizations can also avoid the costly pitfalls and limited interoperability associated with proprietary systems.

For example, Cisco and Scientific Research Corporation (SRC) collaborated to deliver a "push to talk" system to soldiers. The system requires minimal configuration, is self-healing, and provides ample bandwidth for military applications. By using standards-based, off-the-shelf components in the design, partners were able to create a valuable, innovative solution that cost significantly less than proprietary systems.

It also improves interoperability across different vendor systems, and enables faster rollout of new capabilities. Using an open standards-based architecture gives military organizations unprecedented flexibility, enabling them to more closely attune their infrastructures to highly specific needs—and quickly adjust when those needs change.

POWERFUL, INTEROPERABLE NETWORK SOLUTIONS

Cisco Systems, the emerging leader in defence networking, offers a range of integrated solutions that securely and automatically provide the entire chain of command with access to mission-critical information. Cisco network solutions help ensure that the information that captures and communicates a complete picture built around converged data, voice, and video is delivered securely and immediately. And Cisco products offer the resilience necessary to help ensure that mission-critical information is available and timely—even in crisis situations. Cisco augments its technologies with a consulting organization that has extensive experience in the design, operations, management, and support required to transform the way the military conducts missions. Its multidisciplined team is a seasoned organization specializing in providing customized, collaborative assistance through each stage of deployment.

Cisco also provides a comprehensive set of best practices, including its High-Availability Networking Capabilities, which includes deployment blueprints, advanced technical capabilities, case studies, and workshops that are designed to align the network with the operations and to maintain those operations through disruption.

Cisco's expertise in NCO is not limited to its own organization. Cisco also collaborates with best-of-breed partners in the networking industry to deliver additional networking capabilities. These partners offer added expertise for specialized applications, and can accelerate the performance and improve the effectiveness of a wide range of defence operations. For example, Cisco is a founding member of the Network-Centric Operations Industry Consortium (NCOIC), which focuses on industry working together to provide customers with network-centric

environments, where all classes of information systems interoperate by integrating open standards into a common evolving global framework. The mission of the consortium is to help accelerate the achievement of increased interoperability within and between all levels of government in the United States and its allies involved in joint, interagency, and multinational (JIM) operations.

Cisco network solutions and partnerships with the worldwide defence establishment provide an intelligent information network that serves as a technical foundation for defence organizations that are transforming into network-centric operations. The solutions provide the entire chain of command with secure access to mission-critical information from any point on the network, without the barriers of time or location. Combatant and noncombatant personnel around the world—including troops on the move—can accomplish their tasks better, faster, and more securely.

Cisco IP Communications Foster Collaboration

Defence agencies are already replacing legacy telephone systems with IP systems. These converged platforms enable organizations to take advantage of sophisticated and streamlined communications, as well as collaborative tools that dramatically improve the effectiveness of personnel across the chain of command. Cisco IP Communications solutions consist of a U.S. Department of Defence-certified set of mission- grade capabilities, including advanced IP telephony, IP Communications PBX, unified communications, IP video- and audioconferencing, and surveillance and critical emergency response solutions.

Designed for mission-critical applications, Cisco IP Communications solutions conform to demanding government and industry standards, such as Federal Information Processing Standards (FIPS), Common Criteria standards, and IPv6. Together, Cisco IP Communications solutions provide sophisticated and streamlined communications.

For example, governments are replacing antiquated and proprietary emergency conferencing systems with Cisco advanced IP Communication solutions that provide more sophisticated and streamlined communications and collaboration capabilities to prepare forces for any kind of emergency or disaster, including acts of terrorism. Cisco MeetingPlace, a Defence Collaboration Tool Suite (DCTS)-certified solution that is part of the Cisco IP Communications portfolio, enables critical emergency response through rich media conferencing capabilities that create a virtual command and control center for handling crisis communications, crisis team management, and crisis monitoring. It empowers military commanders with a more collaborative environment to precisely and securely dispatch mission-critical information instantaneously across the chain of command when a crisis occurs. Cisco MeetingPlace enables military organizations to provide a far more effective response in handling emergency situations, including a single point of accountability.

Cisco Mobile and Wireless Solutions Enable Ad-Hoc Operations

Combatant and noncombatant operations depend on personnel on the move. Cisco Mobile and Wireless solutions consist of a wireless intelligent information network infrastructure that includes high-performance LAN/Wi-Fi and WAN services. Cisco Mobile and Wireless solutions offer an expanding suite of mobile services to extend network access beyond the limits of wires. Mobile solutions are an efficient and flexible way to empower troops and other military personnel with vital communications, regardless of location. These solutions offer military forces more flexibility and maneuverability while providing greater access to communications and information.

For example, as part of its collaborative project with SRC, Cisco has begun testing its Scalable Mobile Architecture for Tactical Communications at Ft. Bragg, North Carolina, and at the National Training Center in Ft. Irwin, California.

Using standards-based 802.11 technology, military units can roam freely and securely between wireless coverage areas. These roaming models can support tactical communications as complex as a vehicle on the move with a wireless bridge, associating and disassociating as it moves through the battlefield. Depending on the combination of output power and antenna gain, distances up to 14 kilometers can be achieved with omnidirectional antennas, and even longer distances can be achieved with directional antennas. In the past, similar tactical communications often required a direct line of sight back to a communications node, which imposed limits on maneuverability and mobility.

Cisco Security Solutions Safeguard Vital Assets

Defence establishments have put the highest priority on protecting and securing communications and other important military assets. Cisco offers a wide range of highly reinforced, tightly integrated security solutions, including secure connectivity, threat defence, and trust and identity management. Cisco solutions provide a multilayered approach in securing assets from external and internal threats, providing rapid response to both known and unknown security issues. Cisco security solutions prevent unauthorized network access, mitigate worm attacks, and circumvent denial of service attacks. They conform to government regulations and include commercial-grade encryption technology that has been certified for use in government and military applications. This comprehensive safeguarding of network assets enables military organizations to maximize network uptime and productivity, while minimizing threat impact.

As part of its security portfolio, Cisco also supports Network Admission Control (NAC), a Cisco Systems-sponsored industry initiative that uses the network infrastructure to enforce security policy compliance on all devices seeking to access network resources. This strict policy enforcement initiative is designed to limit damage from viruses and worms. Using NAC, the military can provide network access to endpoint devices, such as PCs, PDAs, and servers that are verified to be fully compliant with established security policy. NAC can also identify noncompliant devices and deny them access, place them in a quarantined area, or give them restricted access to computing resources. When combined with Cisco's broad array of security technologies, NAC can actually respond to threats so quickly that the network becomes self-defending. When combined with other standards-based technologies like 802.1X (also supported in Cisco network switches and router switch modules) that restrict access to network resources to authorized endpoints, NAC demonstrates Cisco's multilevel, integrated approach to security.

Cisco Solutions for COOP

Cisco Solutions for COOP are an offensive measure that helps ensure continued optimal performance of military operations in the event of disruptions, including natural disasters or other unexpected events that can sever vital communications.

Defence organizations recognize that continuity of operations planning is crucial in ensuring that the military can function at full capacity, even in the event of a catastrophe.

Cisco Solutions for COOP are based on four components: high-availability networking to ensure the highest degree of network uptime; data center and storage networking, including solid back and recovery of operational assets and interconnections for backup data centers; Cisco VirtualCOOP for field personnel to protect remote connections; and crisis management to notify first responders in the event of a crisis.

Together, these components offer a heavily fortified infrastructure that provides mission-critical information that is accessible from alternative offices and other remote locations.

HIGH-AVAILABILITY NETWORKING

A highly available network is at the core of Cisco Solutions for COOP. Studies have shown that most network failures are traced back to factors outside of network components, including inadequate policies and procedures, or power disruptions.

Cisco High-Availability Networking is a preventive network outage blueprint, including best practice guidelines and resources for fortifying military grade networks. Cisco offers the most cohesive, collaborative approach for helping to ensure the nonstop delivery of advanced applications throughout the lifecycle of the network—even as new users, technologies, and network services are added to the network. This increases the operational efficiency of the military and transforms the network from an IT component to a strategic asset for combatant and noncombatant operations.

Data Center and Storage Networking

To keep their operations up and running, defence organizations require a fortified data center, including robust storage with strong backup and recovery capabilities. Cisco Data Center Networking consists of a highly adaptable data center network architecture that optimizes the performance and resilience of networked applications. A suite of integrated data center solutions includes a sound network infrastructure, powerful storage networking, reinforced data center security, application optimization, and business continuance networking. This enables a highly resilient, responsive data center environment that can securely support millions of users simultaneously. Because business continuance is designed into Cisco data and storage networking solutions, defence organizations can quickly and efficiently transfer operations to a resilient data center in the event of an emergency.

Cisco VirtualCOOP for Resource Dispersion

To achieve maximum mission effectiveness, military, intelligence, and relief personnel operating in remote locations require secure, continuous access to mission-critical information. Cisco VirtualCOOP is an IT-managed COOP system designed for personnel working in the field.

It provides a highly available, highly secure solution that provides access to NCO systems, maximizing situational awareness. This improves continuity and increases effectiveness by providing defence personnel with mission-critical information, even during network disruptions or when resources are unable to reach their intended destinations. Additionally, Cisco VirtualCOOP can disperse resources to minimize the impact of a single geographic event.

Crisis Management

The Cisco Crisis Management Application gives defence organizations a single architecture for converged conferencing of voice, data, and video for emergency communications and collaboration. This conferencing solution employs traditional TDM and IP telephony converged architectures, together with highly scalable features, to give military personnel greater situational awareness over a crisis environment.

The system provides quadruple levels of redundancy for maximum reliability in the event of an emergency. It provides extensive conferencing features that give organizations greater flexibility in dispatching information instantaneously. For example, organizations can use broadcast dial features to quickly disseminate information and facilitate field agent emergency response. And the system supports IP videoconferencing for training, coordination, and conferencing to military personnel across the globe.

The Cisco Crisis Management Application lets military organizations expand the reach of their responses, increase their communications frequency, and reduce the limitations of location and time—saving lives in a crisis situation.

NETWORK CENTRIC OPERATIONS INDUSTRY CONSORTIUM

The Network Centric Operations Industry Consortium (NCOIC) is an international not-for-profit, chartered in the United States, whose goal is to facilitate the adoption of existing and emerging cross-domain interoperability standards. Formed in September 2004, the organization is composed of more than 50 authoritative member companies, government organizations and academic institutions within aerospace, defence, information technology andcommunication entities openly working in the forefront. NCO is the application of the fundamental tenets of network-centric warfare to aspects of national security, especially industry support for the missions of both the United States Department of Defence and the Department of Homeland Security (DHS).

The NCOIC does not only subscribe to the military ends of this theory, applying NCO to emergency first responders, health care providers, law enforcement, and corporations.

Network Centric Warfare defined

NCW is the embodiment of an "Information Age" transformation of the United States Department of Defence and all the elements that support it. NCW represents a set of war fighting concepts and associated military capabilities that allow warfighters to take full advantage of all available information and bring all available assets to bear in a rapid and flexible manner. NCW is based on the following tenets:

- A robustly networked force improves information sharing,
- Information sharing enhances the quality of information and shared situational awareness,
- Shared situational awareness enables collaboration and self-synchronization, and enhances sustainability and speed of command,

Interoperability Frameworks

NCOIC streamlines systems for the elimination of interoperability issues to reduce operating costs for more effective direction of organizational resources.

Key deliverables

Systems, Capabilities, Operations, Programs, & Enterprises (SCOPE) Model

- The SCOPE interoperability assessment model is designed to characterize interoperability-relevant aspects or capabilities of a system or set of systems over a network in terms of a set of dimensions and values along those dimensions.

NCOIC Interoperability Framework (NIF)

- The NIF is a development framework that helps system architects and system engineers to embed interoperability elements throughout the life cycle of programs, beginning with requirements. Whenever possible, those resources are based upon standards.

Net Centric Patterns

- NCOIC Net Centric Patterns contain prescriptive recommendations on approaches and standards in specific interoperability domains.

Network Centric Analysis Tool (NCAT)

- NCAT is a collaborative, web-enabled questionnaire-based tool developed to assist NCOIC teams and member companies to enhance the likelihood and reduce the time and effort of member companies developing interoperable systems consistent with customers' policies and guidelines, reference models and architectures. It is also available in an excel format.

NCOIC Lexicon

- The Lexicon defines terms and expressions that are relevant to texts published by the NCOIC. This material is offered for dynamic debate, discussion and additional submissions in this online wiki. NCOIC Lexicon Custodian Working Group periodically reviews the wiki, and publishes updates of the consensed catalogue, including comments for entries that have been deleted.

NCOIC internal structure

Functional teams

Functional Teams (FTs) implement the technical roadmap of the Consortium by focusing on specific technical elements that lead to netcentricity.

The teams and their associated working groups are coordinated through a Technical Council, composed of the leaders of each Functional Team.

NIF Architecture Concepts FT

- Manages the development of the NCOIC's Interoperability Framework (NIF) and champions its use within the consortium. The NIF provides the framework through which the NCOIC will publish its prescribed use of standards and patterns in specific domains and describes the relationships between the individual Specialized Frameworks.

Specialized Frameworks FT

- Hosts and encourages the development, approval, and publication of specialized Frameworks and Patterns that contain guidelines and standards recommendations for the broad range of domains that are of interest to NCOIC members and their customers.

Building Blocks FT

- Provides a catalog of products for use by government and commercial systems engineers, which meet NCOIC criteria for the support of network centric operations requirements, network centric environments and industry standards.

Netcentric Assessment FT

- Defines, identifies, establishes and assembles the necessary criteria for measuring and assessing network centricity and network enablement in all the relevant forms.

System Engineering & Integration FT

- Helps to integrate the efforts and promote the deliverables of NCOIC Functional Teams for the accomplishment of NCOIC goals.

Integrated Project Teams

Integrated Project Teams (IPTs) serve as domain specific customer teams, who work with global NCO stakeholders in solving their interoperability problems. The IPTs harness the expertise of the Technical Functional Teams in utilizing NCOIC tools and best practices to provide customers with the appropriate guidance to achieve their netcentric missions. The IPTs thereby validate and refine NCOIC approaches in collaboration with customers.

Net Enabled Emergency Response IPT (NEER)

- The NEER IPT will recommend net-enabled solutions needed to bridge the gaps among the diverse organizations that need to come together to provide emergency response for day-to-day emergencies as well as for complex humanitarian disasters (CHD).

C3 Interoperability IPT

- Facilitates inter-operation and overarching coordination of the military, civil-military and civil C2-environment", promoting interoperability to achieve Situational Awareness and effective decision-making based on standards and best practices.

Sense & Respond Logistics IPT

- Provides a forum for defence and commercial stakeholders of Logistics Communities of Interest (COIs) to identify and coordinate solutions to obstacles to achieving net-centric interoperability by leveraging NCOIC solutions.

Aviation IPT

- Advocates global aviation transformation through net-centric solutions. The IPT supports this mission through industry best practices and tools to advise the use of existing and emerging standards and their patterns in support of global aviation needs.

Maritime Awareness IPT

- Establishes shared understanding of the net-centric aspects of Maritime Awareness. Advocates the enhancement of Maritime Awareness through application of net-centric concepts and technologies.

THE ADF'S NCW CONCEPT

In December 2003, the final NCW Concept Paper was produced by the Policy Guidance and Analysis Division, within the Strategy Group. The Concept Paper argued that NCW involved the linkage of engagement systems to sensors through networks and the sharing of information between force elements. Information is only useful if it allows people to act more effectively: this makes the human dimension fundamental to NCW. NCW thus has two closely related and mutually reinforcing dimensions—the human dimension and the network dimension. The NCW Concept argues that the human dimension is based on professional mastery and mission command, and requires high standards of training, education, doctrine, organisation and leadership. This dimension is about the way people collaborate to share their awareness of the situation, so that they can fight more effectively. It requires trust between warfighters across different levels, and trust between warfighters and their supporting agencies.

The Concept continues: The second dimension, the network, connects major military systems, including engagement, sensor and command systems. The network dimension was the initial focus of development, but change here was always expected to have a profound influence on the human dimension.

NCW is seen by the ADF as a 'means to realising a more effective warfighting ability. New technology will change the character of conflict, but war's enduring nature—its friction, fog and chaotic features—will persist'. The Australian NCW Concept accepts this enduring nature of war, but does seek to reduce the effects of fog and friction.

The purpose of the NCW Concept was to provide a starting point for the identification and exploitation of the opportunities of NCW. It would inform and shape the conduct of Defence's NCW-related research and experimentation programs, which would further crystalise an understanding of the opportunities and risks associated with NCW. The ADF would continually revisit the concept in order to confirm its validity based on the lessons learned through research, experimentation and operational experience.

The ADF's NCW Concept is based on the following premises, which will be tested through experimentation:

- Professional mastery is essential to NCW.
- Mission command will remain an effective command philosophy into the future.
- Information and intelligence will be shared if a network is built by connecting engagement systems, sensor systems, and C2 systems.

- Robust networks will allow the ADF, and supporting agencies, to collaborate more effectively and achieve shared situational awareness.
- Shared situational awareness will enable self-synchronisation, which helps warfighters to adapt to changing circumstances and allows them to apply MDM more effectively.

The last two are fundamental in transforming the way in which information is managed, used and exploited. These are expanded on below.

Networks

Robust networks involve sharing information and intelligence through a connected network that also includes engagement, sensor and command systems. While we might look at these systems separately, many of the ADF's platforms perform across all four grids. There is an expectation that NCW will offer an ability to explore alternatives, whereby sensors may be separated from the engagement system, or the ADF might be able to reduce the size of its deployed force.

The ADF aims to develop and integrate an advanced sensor system, ranging from space-based assets to humans, to gather widely disparate information. In doing this, the ADF expects a certain amount of redundancy (without wasteful duplication) to ensure persistent battlespace awareness. That said, the integration of information from sensors will not provide complete understanding of the battlespace, although greater analytic capacity to produce intelligence is anticipated. In the end, commanders will still have to decide whether to fight for more information or to work with the information and intelligence available.

Advanced command support systems will bring together information about the adversary, own and friendly forces, other parties, and the environment into a Common Relevant Operating Picture (CROP). In addition, these systems will allow different levels of the ADF, relevant government agencies, and coalition partners to work together. Through these advanced command support systems, the ADF would expect to enhance its capacity for mission rehearsal, wargaming and development, and analysis of possible courses of action. Essential logistic information between the warfighters and support bases should also be able to be exchanged more effectively. In terms of its engagement systems, the ADF will aim for its decision-makers to have timely access to the most useful engagement systems for the mission, noting that different systems have different levels of mobility, firepower and self-protection. The intent will be to shorten the time between detection, identification, engagement and assessment. The network dimension of NCW assists forces to:

- *collect* relevant information;
- *connect* units and platforms through networking, doctrine, training and organisation;
- *use* the information and intelligence in a timely manner to achieve the commander's intent; and
- *protect* the network from external interference or technical failure.

The *collect-connect-use-protect* framework is the means through which the ADF can organise its effort to develop the network. This framework, which underpins the IS&S Concept, is discussed in more detail later.

The ADF will need to monitor carefully the way networks are progressing in the commercial sector, where developments will have a strong influence on what is available, noting that Defence will move increasingly to commercial off-the-shelf (COTS) solutions for its hardware and software.

As networks and people come together and the notions of trust and information sharing become integral to making decisions, the ADF will need to be aware of interactions across the information, cognitive and physical domains:

- In the *information domain*, connectivity allows people to share, access and protect information.
- In the *cognitive domain*, connectivity allows people to develop a shared understanding of the commander's intent, and to identify opportunities in the situation and vulnerabilities in the adversary.
- In the *physical domain*, selected elements of a force are equipped to achieve secure and seamless connectivity and interoperability. This connectivity will allow some sensor systems to pass target acquisition information directly to engagement systems. Based on the shared understanding developed in the other domains, forces are able to synchronise actions in the physical domain.

These domains also apply to an adversary; hence, the NCW Concept also seeks to influence an adversary by disrupting their ability to function effectively within, and across, each of these domains.

Shared situational awareness

Shared situational awareness develops as people absorb information, collaborate to understand its implications, and then acquire a shared view of the situation at hand. Thus, shared situational awareness brings together both the network and human dimensions of NCW.

Collaboration is essential to shared situational awareness because it allows widely dispersed forces to use their battlespace awareness for mutual advantage in terms of analysis, decision-making, and application of force. The challenge for the ADF will be to cope with a shift from sequential planning activities through a hierarchy to an ongoing interaction between different levels, which will save time and provide opportunities for simultaneous action. Again, both the network (technical means) and human dimensions (ability of people) are important for collaboration.

Collaboration requires a high degree of trust throughout the chain of command. Hence, training and personnel development must provide opportunities for different elements of the ADF to become familiar with one another, the Defence organisation more broadly, and with other agencies.

Self-synchronisation

Another challenge of NCW will be for the ADF to evolve from its top-down way of synchronising forces and actions. People will need to use their shared situational awareness to recognise changes and opportunities themselves, and to act without direction to meet the commander's intent. Self-synchronisation will thus lead to speedier decision-to-action cycles by capitalising on the shared understanding and collective initiative of lower-level commanders and staffs.

THE *NCW ROADMAP*

The 2020 networked force will be an exceptionally complex organisation with a range of different relationships (machine and human) which will require careful and thorough integration. Conducting rapid prototyping and development (RPD) activities will allow Defence to mitigate the risks that are inherent in this integration. It will support experimentation and provide the ability to simulate future capabilities to aid in determining the optimum level of integration between engagement, sensor and C2 systems. RPD will reduce the risk of implementing NCW and help accelerate change.

The capacity to concurrently 'learn by doing' is also important for implementing NCW. Hence, the way ahead, or the *NCW Roadmap*, centres on a 'learn by doing' strategy. A draft *NCW Roadmap* was also produced in December 2003, to plan and coordinate the implementation of NCW, but was not formally released until October 2005. This document set out the future requirement for NCW, the current level of networked capability, and the steps needed to realise a future networked force. Defence also released a short document explaining NCW.

The first step in 'learn by doing' involves constructing the foundation for enhanced collaboration and shared situational awareness. This foundation will, in the main, comprise the information infrastructure and the governance measures needed to improve connectivity for selected force elements. As this underlying infrastructure improves; so too will the collaborative ability of elements within the ADF.

As stated earlier, the long-term aspiration is to link all ADF elements into a 'single virtual network', where information is assembled and passed through a series of interlinked grids: sensor grids gather data; information grids fuse and process it; and engagement grids (overlaid by an appropriate C2 grid) allow warfighters to generate the desired battlespace effects.

NCW has the potential to facilitate the collaboration required for the ADF to employ MDM more effectively. It will assist the force to generate the tempo, agility and ultimately the warfighting advantage needed to prevail against a wide variety of adversaries. However, the ADF will also need to enhance the capacities of its people and its platforms for the future, ensuring they are networked to better exploit the chaotic conditions of the battlespace. The fog, friction and ambiguity will remain; the ADF must ensure that it is better able to exploit this than an adversary.

The 2005 *NCW Roadmap* provides the direction, and initial steps, to implement the NCW Concept. It is Defence's guide to discovering and exploiting the opportunities of NCW; and identifies four key actions:

- set the NCW-related targets for Defence to achieve;
- establish the Network to provide the underlying information infrastructure upon which the networked force will be developed;
- explore the human dimensions of the networked force and initiate changes in doctrine, education and training with appropriate support mechanisms; and
- accelerate the process of change and innovation through the establishment of a RPD capability in partnership with Industry.

Subsequent to publication of the 2005 *NCW Roadmap*, Defence released a publication entitled *Explaining NCW*. Defence argues in this document that 'NCW is a means of organising the force by using modern information technology (IT) to link sensors, decision-makers and weapon systems to help people work more effectively together to achieve the commander's intent'. Furthermore, NCW can 'contribute significantly to producing a warfighting advantage'. The information network sits at the centre, linking the C2 systems, sensor systems, and engagement systems. Defence identified the key capability development projects that would deliver the desired network capability and packaged them as a system, which also provided a model for future systems planning and capability integration. This included projects associated with communications in the maritime, land and air environments; a wide area communications network; network management and defence; satellite communications (SATCOM); tactical information exchange; information exchange in a coalition environment; and other information protection measures.

Indeed, General Peter Cosgrove had already presaged some of these projects when he said, in May 2003, that Defence would look at how it could harmonise sophisticated technology with people in networked systems, noting that the future maritime surveillance and response project and the Joint Command Support System showed great promise here. He also referred to other behind-the-scenes changes, such as the adoption of a standardised 'J series' message format (supporting tactical information exchange) as being critical pieces of the NCW puzzle. He also foreshadowed that Defence would place key links, such as Airborne Early Warning and Control (AEW&C) aircraft, into the network over the next few years. And the recent move into space, through the Optus satellite, provides another part of an increasingly pervasive network. These systems, said Cosgrove, will magnify the pay-off from our network-centric approach.

A governance system for the Defence Information Environment was implemented in 2003, led by the newly-created Office of the Chief Information Officer, to ensure that activity across the Department was aligned and enforced. This governance framework encapsulated the interrelationships and interdependencies in the development, management and operation of Defence's supporting information environment.

Network protection was to be designed through the use of an Information Security Architecture, which is an integral component of a Defence-wide Information Architecture. The architecture would address the design of information systems, access control, data management and accountability frameworks.

The Human Dimension

The examination of NCW's human dimension was to focus on the following areas:

- the nature of C2;
- transitioning to a new way of operating;
- nurturing innovation; and
- Defence culture.

As General Cosgrove had remarked in May 2003, 'it is vital that we keep people in our focus as we implement NCW. Anybody can buy technology. Anybody can copy concepts. But nobody can duplicate the advantage we get from our smart, dedicated and adaptable people'.

The 2005 *NCW Roadmap* developed this human dimension further, with a focus on doctrine, education, training and development. It argued the need to raise NCW awareness, educate the senior leaders, prepare the future leaders, understand the future workforce, produce the NCW tools and plan for doctrine development, and develop a mechanism for evaluation and feedback of lessons learnt.

Accelerating change and innovation

In terms of accelerating change and innovation, Defence was to establish a RPD program by July 2004 to fulfill three functions:

- identify and test new technologies, concepts, procedures and organisations that could be implemented in the near term (6–18 months) to improve the ADF's networked warfighting capabilities;
- identify early problems with the implementation of NCW and use RPD as an intervention activity to redress the problem or mitigate risk; and
- provide for the rapid delivery of capability to warfighters to meet or anticipate emerging security challenges.

A Rapid Prototyping, Development and Evaluation (RPDE) capability was set up in 2005, with the mission of enhancing 'ADF warfighting capacity through accelerated capability change in the NCW environment'. Importantly, RPDE allows collaboration across a wide range of organisations, more rapid fielding of capability improvements, and a focus on all fundamental inputs to capability—personnel, organisation, collective training, major systems, supplies, facilities, support, and command and management.

DEFENCE'S INFORMATION SUPERIORITY AND SUPPORT CONCEPT

In August 2004 Defence released its IS&S Concept, which articulated the key components of the concept, described the architectural approach to be taken, identified the target states for the future and posed a key set of questions to be addressed.

The key components of the concept (focused on connecting, collecting, using and protecting information) are outlined below:

- *Ubiquitous network or information distribution (Connect)* enables effective sharing of information by people, systems, applications and sensors, whether it is by voice, data or video. It involves coordinating the infrastructure including fixed and mobile communications, computers, processes, systems and tools that enable the sharing of information throughout the force to achieve information and decision superiority.

When the network is threatened, it must allow for a graceful degradation of service availability and access to information that ensures continuity of operations. Once the threat has been resolved, access to information and original service availability levels must be rapidly reconstituted.

- *Persistent awareness (Collect)* enhances situational awareness that allows better perception of battlespace elements in terms of time and space, the comprehension of their meaning and projected intent. Persistent awareness tools and systems help collect, collate and fuse disparate data and information, which requires greater attention to content management. Persistence does not mean continuous; it means sufficient awareness to enable the ADF to act in a way that is operationally responsive and appropriate.
- *Smart use or decision support (Use)* focuses on achievable intent. It involves planning and the provision of information and common processes and collaboration tools to facilitate timely and effective decision-making throughout the various levels of command.
- *Pervasive Security (Protect)* provides a secure information environment that offers a trusted and reliable flow of information to continuously support operations and business activities.

Networking issues

The IS&S Concept emerged from the observation that networking improves efficiency and effectiveness of operations. It depends on computers and communications to link people through information flows, which in turn depends on interoperability across all systems. Networking involves collaboration and sharing of information to ensure that all appropriate assets can be quickly brought to bear by commanders during combat operations. In a 2004 report by the US Congress, a number of key networking issues were identified, the most relevant of which, for the purposes of this discussion, was network architectures.

Because NCW is so highly dependent on the interoperability of communications equipment, data, and software to enable the networking of people, sensors, and platforms (both manned and unmanned), network architectures are very important.

Architectures are needed to bring together all the elements of NCW technology that rely on line-of-sight radio transmission for microwave or infra-red signals, or laser beams; as well as other technologies that aggregate information for transmission through larger network trunks for global distribution via fibre-optic cables, microwave towers, or both low-altitude and high-altitude satellites.

The ADF architecture must enable rapid communications between individuals in all three Services, as well as rapid sharing of data and information between mobile platforms and sensors used across the ADF. As the ADF comes to depend on networking, the network itself must be able to re-form when any communications node is interrupted (the United States refers to this as dynamically self-healing).

THE ADF'S CAPABILITY PLANNING FOR NCW

The ADF's concept is less about warfighting and more about how net-centric capability will enable future warfighting. Defence has been moving steadily along the net-centric path for several years now in terms of developing the capability to provide the ability for data to be exchanged across linked networks. Some ships and aircraft as well as fixed and deployable communications systems have already achieved a degree of data connectivity.

The ADF can deliver secure C2 to small-scale deployments around the world. It can use its 'Secret' and 'Restricted' fixed networks, as well as data-links (Link 11) and radios (*Parakeet*) to provide certain levels of connectivity.

It can draw information from multiple sources such as the over-the-horizon *Jindalee* Operational Radar Network (JORN) and radars on Royal Australian Navy (RAN) ships to generate a basic level of situational awareness. Major combat units are linked by voice communications, with some aircraft and ships data-linked. Secure SATCOM are available to select elements of the ADF, such as Special Forces, and secure satellite data-link provides connectivity between ground-based air defence systems and the Royal Australian Air Force (RAAF)'s Regional Operations Centre. Defence has argued that it is developing its networked force by:

- creating new doctrine, better training and a more agile organisation, all of which leads to people operating more effectively as a network;
- guiding force development through the release of the 2005 *NCW Roadmap* and Integration Plan (the latter is not available publicly);
- connecting broad areas of Defence so that information can be shared and used more cooperatively; and
- fast-tracking the introduction of new technology through its RPDE program.

The Chief of Capability Development Group is responsible for implementing NCW across Defence, which reinforces the earlier point that the ADF's network-centric focus is on developing capability to enhance future warfighting effectiveness.

The major network projects that have been identified for implementation thus far include:

- A joint command support environment, which will link the air, maritime, land and special operations elements into the one single ADF command system.
- A similar project, which will integrate intelligence systems.
- Military SATCOM that will provide the ADF with coverage throughout the region.
- Tactical information exchange that will facilitate movement of information from sensors to weapon systems, starting with *ANZAC* frigates and *Hornet* fighters.
- Battlespace communications for air, land and maritime forces, which will provide the information backbone and tactical data distribution for deployed forces.
- A Defence wide-area communications network, which will provide the next-generation fixed infrastructure for secure computers and telephones. Linkages will be established between the fixed and deployable communications networks.
- A Defence network operations centre, which will enhance current computer network defence capabilities.
- Combined information exchanges with the United States, United Kingdom, Canada and New Zealand, which will provide a permanent system for exchanging information and enabling collaboration.
- A number of major systems that will connect to the 'network', such as the New Air Combat Capability, high-altitude long-endurance UAVs, the Air Warfare Destroyer (AWD), and a suite of other projects that will 'harden' and 'network' the Australian Army.

By 2020, a networked ADF should be able to generate a range of lethal and non-lethal effects that are timely, appropriate and synchronised. It will have continuous information connectivity to link fighting units, sensors and decision-makers that sees an ADF with increased situational awareness and the capacity to act decisively. The Defence C2 system will promote collaboration. Defence will be capable of rapidly deploying and protecting an optimised force. A pervasive network of active and passive sensors will improve awareness for force protection purposes. Key logistics networks will be linked and offer connectivity and collaboration.

NET-CENTRIC ENTERPRISE SERVICES

Net-Centric Enterprise Services (NCES) is a Department of Defence program, managed by the Defence Information Systems Agency, to develop information technology infrastructure services for future systems used by the

United States military. Technically, the program is based on the concept of 'enterprise integration' from the sub discipline enterprise engineering of systems engineering, which enables the transmission of right information at the right place and at the right time and thereby enable communication between people, machines and computers and their efficient co-operation and co-ordination.

There are nine core enterprise services defined in the Network Centric Operations and Warfare - Reference Model (NCOW-RM):

1. storage
2. mediation
3. user assist
4. IA (Information Assurance)
5. ESM (Enterprise Service Management)
6. messaging
7. discovery & delivery
8. application
9. collaboration

NCES maps these nine services to four product areas:

1. Enterprise service-oriented architecture (SOA) foundation
2. Content discovery and delivery
3. Enterprise collaboration
4. Defence on-line portal

NETWORK-CENTRIC ORGANIZATION

A network-centric organization is a network governance pattern emerging in many progressive 21st century enterprises. This implies new ways of working, with consequences for the enterprise's infrastructure, processes, people and culture.

Overview

With a network-centric configuration, knowledge workers are able to create and leverage information to increase competitive advantage through the collaboration of small and agile self-directed teams. For this, the organizational culture needs to change from one solely determined by a single form of organizing (e.g., hierarchy) to an adaptive hybrid enabling multiple forms of organizing within the same organization. The nature of the work, in an area, determines best the way its conduct is organized and the networked mediation of work activities affords interoperability among differentially-organized areas of work.

A network-centric organization is both a sensible response to a complex environment and an enactor of sensibility on that environment. The business climate of the new millennium is characterized by profound and continuous changes due to globalization, exponential leaps in technological capabilities, and other market forces. Rapid developments of ICT are driving and supporting the change from the industrial to the information age.

In this world of rapid change and uncertainty, organizations need to continually renew, reinvent and reinvigorate themselves in order to respond creatively. The network-centric approach aims to tap into the hidden resources of knowledge workers supported and enabled by ICT, in particular the social technologies associated with Web 2.0 and Enterprise 2.0. Essentially though, a network-centric organization is more about people and culture than technology. A useful survey of network organization theory appears in Van Alstyne (1997)

Network-centric organization topics

Knowledge Work

There is a synthesis of thinking, learning and doing at the core of creative human activity that underpins the concept of knowledge work. Knowledge workers collaborate on tasks that are cognitively demanding, involving complex technical judgements, a high degree of professional and individual expertise and experience. The knowledge worker is astutely aware, not only of the means and purpose of their work, but also its political and social dimensions. Much of this knowledge is tacit and shared among the work group becoming embedded in its culture.

There is a broad expanse of uncharted territory between the real knowledge work that occurs in an organization and the formal organizational structure and espoused practices. The concentration on formal organizational programs aimed at the individual workers ignored the real nature of work practices that reside in a space between the organization and individual perspectives. This space often remain hidden from the organizational landscape, unappreciated and undervalued. Revealing the nature of this hidden space holds the key to understanding knowledge work and is critical to successful organizational outcomes and learning.

Hybrid enterprises

Many enterprises are hybrids of hierarchical bureaucracies, heterarchic work groups distributed across organizational and spatial boundaries, and responsibly autonomous individuals where competition and cooperation coexist due to a strict division of work activities. Network-centric organizations locate the partitioning of work activities in the self-direction of individuals and work groups, rather than in the hierarchy.

Enterprises which have complex hybrid structures consisting of hierarchies and networks are more like organic eco-systems than machines.

The latter are likely to be exploitative and bureaucratic while the former can be networked and innovative. This reflects the tension between the natural tendency for disorder to increase while humans strive to impose order by developing ever more complex rigid structures and systems. It is quite a natural state of affairs that organizations can be part mechanistic and part organic with continual transformations among these forms. Network-centric organizations enact governance systems that manage these ongoing transformations.

Sensible organization

A complex environment presents an enterprise with too large a range and diversity of inputs to comprehend logically so the sensible response is not to try.

Attempts to deal with complexity are unsuccessful if they aim to either simplify or assert control over complex situations. It makes more sense to maintain and support the natural creative energies of complex environments, encouraging the emergence of innovative new forms of working.

Sensible enterprises will become agile, flexible and adaptable by incorporating more creativity and diversity into their structures, processes and human resources. The informality, interactivity and adaptability of small teams of people retains a space for what we traditionally call 'common sense' for both understanding and action amid the accountability and constraints of the formal enterprise. Sensible managers will relinquish some of their traditional control to knowledge workers in small self-directed teams. A network-centric organization will also have an increased need and reliance on data sensing, analysis, and closed-loop action driven by repeated application of "sense-and-respond" cycle.

Social technologies

At the current time, a new civil digital culture has taken hold, in which so-called 'social' and/or 'conversational' technologies or social software are providing unprecedented opportunities for everyday user activities. The term Web 2.0 has entered the vocabulary to reflect the ongoing transition of the World Wide Web from a collection of websites to a full-fledged computing platform serving social web applications such as email, discussion forums, chatrooms, Weblogs and Wikis to end users. Constructivist learning theorists explained that the process of expressing knowledge aids its creation and conversations benefits the refinement of knowledge. Cheung et al. (2005) maintains that conversational knowledge management fulfils this purpose because conversations, e.g. questions and answers, become the source of relevant knowledge.

Social technologies facilitate processes where knowledge creation and storage is carried out through a discussion forum where participants contribute to the discussion with questions and answers, or through a Weblog which is typified by a process of storytelling or through a Wiki using collaborative writing (Hasan and Pfaff 2006). In the corporate setting, the term Enterprise 2.0 is emerging to reflect the use of freeform social software within companies to support work units and the individual knowledge worker. Gordon and Ganesan (2005) advocates a different vision for knowledge management systems to one that is specifically targeted to the capture and use of the stories told in communities and organizations in the context of normal, spoken conversations.

Conversation and other types of human-human communication must be exploited in today's knowledge management systems so as harness the value of conversation in packaging and transmitting tacit knowledge. The attraction of these social technologies is their low cost, intuitive functionality and connectivity. Social technologies support new forms of network-centric interaction and activity between people, allowing and enhancing informal access to create and distribute information. These technologies empower ordinary people to have a global presence for business, political and social purposes. The new social technologies at the focus of this project are tools of a rising digital democracy.

One of the newest approaches on the horizon is worknetting. A worknet is a form of organization where stakeholders, individuals or institutions or both, can come together around a shared purpose. Whereas a network centres around the relationships between partners, a worknet centres around each partner's relationship with the shared purpose. In this way, the unique strengths and contributions of each partner can be optimized and enhanced, as they are situated in the context of the worknets common interest.

Power shift in traditional organizations

Traditional organizations that favor a rigid hierarchical structure and ego-centric methods still employ the outmoded concept where the decision-making authority lies solely in the domain of its corporate headquarters. Changes resulting from developments in ICT and the growth of the Internet, have made it increasingly difficult to provide a platform for effective and efficient management and operations. As observed by De Vulpian (2005), "we are in the process of moving from a pyramidal, hierarchical society to a single-story society whereheterarchical relationships dominate".

There is a tension between ego-centric thinking and network-centric thinking – the tension between the institutional power that emanates from an organization and the transactional power that inheres in its members' daily interactions. Progressive organizations are tending to refocus on supporting teams in community-style networks. There is a growing realization that if "decisions are allowed to move out of the corporate headquarters to individual business units, business units will in turn distribute power and decision-making to self-managed teams and profit centers (Allee 2003)." This is the basis of the concept of knowledge work where workers have control over their own activities through knowledge acquired in the course of both training and experience.

Links to Network Centric Warfare

Network-centric warfare is a simple concept that involves the linkage of engagement systems to sensors through networks and the sharing of information between force elements. The early development of the concept evolved by connecting information systems and creating software applications that allow people to use the available data. McKenna, Moon, Davis and Warne (2006) emphasise on the human dimension of NCW which is based on the idea that information is only useful if it allows people to act more effectively.

NETWORK CENTRIC PRODUCT SUPPORT

Network Centric Product Support (NCPS) is an emerging computer architecture that was developed to leverage new information technology and global networks to assist in managing maintenance, support and supply chain of mobile complex products made up of one or more systems, such as an aircraft or fleet. This is accomplished by embedding intelligence through micro-web servers that also function as a computer workstation with the aircraft Engine control unit or other subsystem, and enabling 2-way communications using existingInternet technologies and communications networks. NCPS can be considered to be the support flip side of Network-centric warfare, as this approach goes beyond traditional performance based logistics initiatives by taking a complex adaptive system management approach and integrating field maintenance and logistics in a unified factory and field environment. Its evolution began out of insights gained by CDR Dave Loda (USNR) from Network Centric Warfare-based fleet battle experimentation at the US Naval Warfare Development Command (NWDC) in the late 1990s, with initial commercial applications in commercial aviation through United Technologies Corporation beginning in 2001.

Purpose

Simply put, this architecture extends the existing World Wide Web infrastructure of networked web servers down into the product at its system's controller level. Its core is an embedded dual function webserver/computer workstation connected to the controller's test ports (in retrofit applications) or can be integrated directly into the controller, hence providing access to controller cycles and sensor information in a clustered, internet addressable node that allows for local or remote access, and the ability to host reconfigurable software that can collect and process data from its mated subsystem controller on board. It creates a localized wireless World Wide Web in and around the aircraft that can be securely connected to by a mechanic with any web browser-equipped handheld, independent of the greater World Wide Web. Legacy systems usually require a human to manually connect a laptop to the system controller to collect data and carry it back to a location where it can be later transferred to the factory for analysis.

The architecture also enables communications with other micro-webservers in its Computer cluster (i.e. the aircraft), or to higher level clusters (such as an internet portal managed fleet and flight operations managers), thus enabling access to personnel and factory engineers at remote office computers through the World Wide Web. The system operates asynchronously, in that it does not have to be always connected to the World Wide Web to function; rather it simply operates locally, then synchronizes two-way information relevant to the subsystem, acting as a Gateway (telecommunications) on board that connects with other gateways within the network, which can be airborne or on the ground, on an as-needed basis when communications is available. This can be accomplished through a Wireless LAN Network, satellite, cellular network or other wireless or wired communications capabilities.

Typical Usage

The extension of the World Wide Web architecture into the product is important to understand, as all decisions for manufacturing of spare parts, scheduling for flights, and other factory OEM and airline operator functions, are driven primarily by what happens to the product in the field (rate of wear and impending failure, primarily). Predicting the rate of wear, and hence the impact on operations and forecasting for producing spare parts in the future, is critical for optimizing operations for all involved. Managing a complex system such as a fleet of aircraft or vehicles can be accomplished in this manner. For example, coupled with technologies such as RFID, the system could track parts from the factory to the aircraft on board, then continue to read the configuration of the subsystem's replaceable tagged parts, map their configuration to hours run and duty cycles, then process/communicate the projected wear rate through the World Wide Web back to the operator or factory. In this way mechanical wear rates and future failures can be predicted more accurately and the forecasting of spare parts manufacturing and shipment can be significantly improved. This is called Prognostics Health Monitoring (PHM), which has become possible in recent years with the advent of electronic controllers, and is a recent evolutionary step in aircraft support and maintenance management that began as individual processes prior to World War II and solidified into a manual tracking system to support aircraft fleets in the Korean War. Support for the mechanic comes in local wireless access to technical information stored and remotely updated on board the micro-webserver component relevant to that product, such as service bulletins, factory updates, fault code driven, intelligent 3D computer game-like maintenance procedures, and enabling 2-way voice, text and image communications.

Background and Other Examples

The original micro-webserver component of NCPS (network centric product support) was first developed and demonstrated in 2001 by David Loda, Enzo Macchia, Sam Quadri and Bjorn Stickling, and initially tested on board a Fairchild-Dornier 328 regional jet in January 2002. It was introduced to the public and demonstrated at the Farnborough Air Show in July 2002 and again in 2004 as a flight certified product offering by Altair Avionics, and is beginning to see service in a number of aircraft and helicopters.

A similar complex systems approach in a completely different application was successfully demonstrated in the Eisenhower Interstate Highway System, though what is transported in NCPS is information, not cars and trucks. Network Centric Product Support, or net-centric product support, is an architectural concept, and merely connects the major avenues already existing in global communications and the internet into the mobile product, extending maintenance and supply chain processes into a product centric system.

For example, to gain information about a particular engine on a mobile aircraft, it is most efficient to send the inquiry to the engine directly and host all information generated and relevant to that system, as well synchronize in a twin remote database for access and queuing when the engine system is not in communications.

Other examples where this can be applied include shipping containers, automobiles, spacecraft, appliances, human medical monitoring, or any other complex product with sensors and subsystems that require maintenance support and monitoring.

More and more organizations are beginning to see the value of a netcentric (also spelled "net-centric") approach to managing complex systems, including the Network Centric Operations Industry Consortium (NCOIC), which is an association of leading aerospace and defence contractors in the Network Centric Warfare arena. Network Centric thinking for aircraft operations, including Network Enabled Operations (NEO) demonstrations, also figure prominently in the commercial Next Generation Air Transportation System (NextGen) approach being made by the US Government to revamping air transportation management in the 21st Century.

TRADITIONAL METHODS OF WARFARE

The main instruments initially used by these agencies were the printed pamphlets, the radio and books. The CIA set up two radio stations in Munich, called Radio Free Europe and Radio Liberty, to broadcast to the communist countries. The Voice of America, which is controlled by the State Department and not by the CIA, worked in concert with the CIA stations of Munich. The MI6 continued to rely on the BBC. Another technique widely used during the Cold War was the co-opting of journalists, authors and publishing houses to help the intelligence agencies.

One would recall the large number of baseless reports regarding India granting base facilities to the Soviet Navy in Vizag and in the Andaman & Nicobar disseminated by the US and UK news agencies and newspapers during the prime ministership of Mrs.Indira Gandhi.

Another baseless report disseminated by Western journalists was that experts of the KGB, the intelligence agency of the erstwhile USSR, were attached as advisers to the late Gen.Sunderji during Operation Blue Star of 1984. These reports stopped circulating as mysteriously as they had started after her assassination in 1984.

Following disclosures in the media, the John Major Government of the UK admitted in 1995 that a number of British authors, whose anti-communist books had become best-sellers during the Cold War, had been co-operating with the External Publicity Division of the British Foreign Office. Their co-operation was, in fact, with the MI6. How did their books become best-sellers? The MI6 encouraged publishing houses under its influence to publish their books, persuaded book reviewers to review their books favourably, bought thousands of copies of these books and had them smuggled into the communist countries and gave them free of cost to book-sellers of Third World countries co-operating with the MI6.

This period also saw the mushrooming, with funds allegedly provided by the CIA, of a large number of private radio stations in South-East Asia.

Many of these radio stations, which were run by Christian organisations, were anti-communist and anti-socialist in the contents of their programmes.

Another technique, perfected during the Cold War and still used, was the co-opting of policy and decision makers as well as academics and other sections of the elite of the Third World countries by arranging invitations for travel to West Europe and the US, either for research or for participation in seminars, helping individuals in these countries to float think-tanks and non-governmental organisations (NGOs) and arranging funds for them.

The funds were arranged through cut-outs of Western universities, academics and NGOs. The indirect funding of the so-called Track 2 diplomacy gatherings is another psywar technique of recent origin. Amongst well-known NGOs, which in the past had allegedly been in receipt of funds from intelligence agencies, were the Amnesty International of the UK and the International Commission of Jurists (ICJ) of Geneva. The Amnesty International was allegedly in receipt of funds from the Harold Wilson Government in return for its playing down allegations of human rights violations by the British Security forces in Aden and Rhodesia (now Zimbabwe) and the ICJ was allegedly in receipt of funds from private lawyers' organisations in the US, whose contributions to the ICJ were re-imbursed to them by the CIA. Following disclosures to the British media by a secretary of the Amnesty, the Wilson Government had admitted its links with the organisation and the CIA's alleged contributions to the ICJ through private lawyers' organisations came to notice during the post-Watergate enquiries into the functioning of the CIA and the FBI.

Use of The TV

The TV came on its own as an instrument of perception-management in the 1960s. The role played by the visuals from Vietnam disseminated by the anti-war groups in the West in turning public opinion against the war brought home to the Western agencies the importance of manipulating this medium. TV Marti, the TV station of the CIA, started telecasting programmes to the Cuban people and the CIA helped a number of private businessmen to start TV stations for telecasting programmes to the communist countries from places such as West Berlin and Hong Kong. Instruments such as printed pamphlets, books, radio broadcasts, the telephone and the fax, the E-mail and the Internet are good for the hard aspects of psywar for alienating the people from their state and for discrediting the state in the eyes of its people and the world, but have only limited use for the soft aspect of projecting the power or group behind the psywar in an attractive light and creating a desire to emulate its culture, ways of life etc. It is here that the value of the TV as a medium comes. Through a sophisticated production and projection of programmes, one can create in the minds of the targeted audience, particularly the urban-based elite and youth, an uncritical admiration of the Western societies, soften their prejudices towards the West and evoke a desire to imitate them. Sections of the targeted audience lose faith in their own society and culture.

Writing in the "Washington Quarterly" of summer 1995, Gerald Segal, Senior Fellow, the International Institute For Strategic Studies, London, said: " It is only when Hong Kong-based consortia began satellite broadcasting of foreign and Chinese soap operas and international sports that the satellite broadcasts were watched by many millions of people on a regular basis. The fact that the BBC World Service TV was carried on the commercial satellite gave it greater penetration of the market, but persistent anecdotal evidence is clear that the viewers (in Asia) were picking up Western values mainly from the entertainment and only in passing from "talking heads" (talk shows) discussing human rights. It was "Baywatch", "Dallas", "Beavis and Butt-Head" or "Kung-Fu" episodes that were watched by most people and precisely because they were so much more attractive than more cerebral television, such programmes were more effective in undermining state retention of authority and control over values." He further said: " When Rupert Murdoch, well-known for his outspoken criticism of Asian and especially communist authoritarians, dropped BBCWSTV from his Hong Kong-based STAR TV because China warned that its presence put at risk the entire venture, many saw the move as an uncharacteristic pre-emptive kowtow to communists. But, by removing the overtly political message and continuing to provide soap operas about conspicuous consumption and loose morals, STAR was actually beginning to do far more damage to the authority of the Chinese Communist Party."

Writing of the CNN and the BBCWSTV, Segal further said: " CNN and, for a time, BBCWSTV added subversive images to the subversive voices that came from the likes of the Voice of America and a wide range of European shortwave broadcasters." As examples of such images, he cited the coverage of the demolition of the Berlin Wall, the popular uprising in Romania in 1989-90 and the student riots in Bangkok in 1992. India has bitter memories of how doctored TV images and stories were used to incite the Kashmiris against the Government of India. In 1989-90, before the advent of the satellite TV to the South Asian region, Pakistan TV bought large quantities of video clips of the Romanian uprising from Western TV companies and telecast them to the Valley, inciting the local people to emulate the Romanians and rise against their government. Concerned over this, the then V.P.Singh Government set up a special committee to counter the subversion of the Kashmiris through the TV. In October 1993, when the Kashmiri extremists occupied the Hazratbal shrine, the BBC telecast a report alleging that the Indian army had launched an operation Blue Star type raid of the shrine as a result of which it had caught fire. It never corrected this blatantly false report.

In May 1995, after the burning-down of the Charar-e-Sharif holy shrine in Kashmir by the extremists, the BBC, while telecasting the news, showed visuals of Russian-made tanks, apparently to create an impression in the minds of the Muslim viewers that the shrine probably caught fire because of the use of the tanks by the Indian army. When the Government of India protested and pointed out that the same visuals had some days earlier been shown while telecasting the fighting between Russian troops and Muslim extremists in Chechnya, the BBC telecast a correction only in its Asian service and not to the rest of the world. It admitted that the visuals were from Chechnya and not Kashmir and attributed the mistake to a technical mix-up. Digitalisation and Direct-To-Home (DTH) TV have added to the concerns of security experts. The Strategic Assessment for 1995 brought out by the Institute For National Strategic Studies of Washington, which functions under the National Defence University of the Pentagon, said: " Tomorrow's antennas can increasingly be blended into walls and other background, thus frustrating bans on their possession. Electronic focussing can frustrate terrestrial jamming. Video compression, which multiplies the number of channels that any satellite can host, enhances the economics of narrowcasting. A billion dollar investment can yield well over a hundred digital stations, which, in turn, could be profitably leased for perhaps US $ two million a year. At that price, any of several aggrieved national or political groups—Kurds, radical Shiites, Sikhs, Burmese mountain tribes—could afford to broadcast propaganda 24 hours a day to wide swaths of territory."

The DTHTV provides extremist elements, having large funds earned from narcotics, and foreign intelligence agencies with the opportunity of leasing channels under front companies from a DTH operator and using the channels to disseminate doctored images such as those of a Muslim killing Hindus or Christians or vice versa and rumours to the drawing rooms of individual viewers, thereby adding to social and communal tensions. Writing in the "Foreign Policy" (Fall 1997), John Deutch, Director of the CIA during Clinton's first term, referred to the dangers of morphed images and messages being introduced into a country's radio and TV systems, spreading lies and inciting people to violence.

Till recently, in the US, foreigners were not permitted to operate telephone and DTH services. Murdoch had to take up US nationality and permanent residence there before he could apply for a DTH licence. However, he has since abandoned his DTH project because of opposition from local cable operators. Now because of the stipulation of the World Trade Organisation on the opening-up of the telephone services to foreigners, the US Congress has been considering conditions under which foreigners would be issued a licence. One of the conditions seeks to lay down that a licence can be refused in public interest, that is, on grounds of national security. Similar conditions are expected to be imposed in respect of DTH services by foreigners too.

In South-East and East Asia, only Japan allows foreigners to have 25 per cent equity participation in companies offering DTH services. In other countries, including China, there is a ban on foreign participation in DTH services. Writing jointly in the "Foreign Affairs" journal of the US (March-April,1996), Joseph S.Nye, former Chairman of the US National Intelligence Council and former Assistant Secretary of Defence for International Affairs in the Clinton Administration, and Admiral William A.Owens, former Vice-Chairman of the Joint Chiefs of Staff in the Clinton Administration, said as follows: "Soft power is the ability to achieve desired outcomes in international affairs through attraction rather than coercion. It works by convincing others to follow, or getting them to agree to, norms and institutions that produce the desired behaviour. Soft power can rest on the appeal of one's ideas or the ability to set the agenda in ways that shape the preference of others. If a state can make its power legitimate in the perception of others and establish international institutions that encourage them to channel or limit their activities, it may not need to expend as many of its costly traditional economic or military resources." They also added: " The Voice of America has in the last few years become the primary news source for 60 per cent of the educated Chinese. America's increasing technical ability to communicate with the public in foreign countries literally over the heads of their rulers via satellite (TV), provides a great opportunity to foster democracy."

After the collapse of the communist regimes of Europe, the direction of the US psywar machine has turned to Asia. The set-up of Radio Free Europe has reportedly been shifted from Munich to Prague to broadcast anti-Saddam Hussein programmes to Iraq. Since September 1996, a new radio station called Radio Free Asia, ostensibly privately run, but funded by the Congress, has been broadcasting programmes in Chinese, Tibetan, Burmese, Vietnamese and Korean languages. China started jamming these broadcasts in Septembert, 1997.

'INFORMATION' AND 'KNOWLEDGE'

It is not that the domain of 'information' and its fallout, 'knowledge' are of recent advent, these had been before as well – Alexander had the information of the crossing places across the river Jhelum and used it to gain knowledge of a suitable one to outflank King Porus during the Battle of Hydaspes in 326 BCE. Thus 'information' is but an eternally existential phenomenon; the object of information - like terrain, enemy forces, deployment, etc., - exist naturally at any point of time, though they had not been so easily accessible as they may be today. The difference has been conditioned by proliferation of science and technology that has made it practicable to access the 'information' needed and analyse it to register the relevant 'knowledge', that in turn generates actionable 'intelligence' to make planning and execution of operations more comprehensive, coordinated, accurate and timely. It therefore may not be off the mark to state that these terms, as appropriated by western strategic thinkers, need to be translated to the Indian military lexicon. Indeed, in the context of contemporary Indian Army, it may be more meaningful to subsume the terms 'information' (data which have to be accessed, registered and then transmitted) and 'knowledge' (which have to be acquired by collation and analysis of the information) into the better understood overall definition of military 'intelligence'.

We may now delve further into the aspects of access, registration and transmission of existential 'information', for it to be processed into 'knowledge' that is relevant to the tactical and operational situation that the Indian Army might be confronted with.

Information access and registrationModern technology has advanced to an extent that many of the scientific expositions in theory have found practical materialisation. Thus, it is possible to sweep the environment to register information of natural, man-made and war-like attributes that exist at any point of time over vastly spread areas; besides, it is also possible to penetrate through man-made or natural camouflage to detect such attributes which might normally remain obscured. This is an operation that requires electro-magnetic devises to be coupled with mechanical linkages and electronic articulators, and packaged with requisite motive power to move and manipulate. Access to the object of information may be accomplished both in static mode (such as surveillance radars, geo-synchronous satellites, laser designators, aerostats, observers and 'moles') or in manoeuvrable format (such as orbital satellites, aircraft, balloons, reconnaissance radars, intelligence teams and 'agents'). Having gained access to the objects of 'information', the next step is to register the signatures emitted by these objects. This activity is programmed by activating various kinds of 'sensors' that might function on optical, acoustic, thermal, seismic or even visual mode. Registration of the input signatures is carried out in 'digital' rather than analogue mode for ease of processing into 'knowledge.' In short, modern technology enables creation of a 'system' of many components, to accomplish coverage of extensive areas as well as heretofore inaccessible objects, to register information remotely. Point to note is that the tactical decisions regarding areas of search, timings, objects of interest and informational queries continue to remain in the realm of military art – technology may assist but not elevate the application of military acumen.

At this stage, the 'information' accessed and registered is in raw form, besides being burdened with unnecessary details. These have to be transmitted to be filtered, collated and analysed to, as stated earlier, cull out the relevant 'knowledge'.

Digitisation and transmission of inputs

Here again, technological advancements play a pivotal role. Thus as aforestated, instead of registering the emission of photo-particles or other radiations from the objects in visual, acoustic, photographic, descriptive or analogue mode, this is done by electronically converting the emitted signatures into digital code - 'bits' and 'bytes' in millions of electronic chips, so to say. This is a simple process of primary 'digitisation,' built into the sensing devices, that renders the inputs extremely accurate, highly revealing and perfectly formatted for near-instantaneous 'transmission' over vast distances.

Thus the accessed and digitally registered information is 'transmitted' by means of carrier electromagnetic waves, to be recorded at the intelligence control centre. Digitisation of input data also facilitates near real-time user customisation, filtration and preferential formatting of information through application of mathematical algorithms (software), to convert it into 'knowledge'. This is the process of secondary digitisation whence the raw data is edited, trimmed, elaborated and formatted according to its usage. However, to reiterate, the decisions regarding focussing these processes to the required parameters of relevant knowledge remains an exercise of military art. Having filtered and marshalled the raw informational inputs according to the parameters of relevant knowledge by means of the task-dedicated 'systems' discussed above, the stage is now set for the 'system of systems' to generate actionable military 'intelligence'.

INTELLIGENCE PREPARATION OF BATTLE-SPACE (IPB)

This again is a vastly overarching strategic term devised by the western thinkers, which in India's limited operational context may be described as the process of 'intelligence appreciation' and implementation of 'intelligence plan'. In short, IPB is but a traditional exercise, firstly, of marshalling operational intelligence, and secondly, assimilation of that intelligence to strengthen the process of planning, deployment and control of operations. Of course, modern military technology has elevated that exercise to a near-perfect level. Further, modern networked transmission systems have rendered the intelligence inputs as highly transferable across vast distances in near real-time.

These advantages facilitate the best orchestrated conduct of battles in which each element of battle is deployed and employed to the optimal capability, thus achieving a force-multiplication effect.

IPB is highly relevant in the Indian context as it would permit the most effective exploitation of decisive weapons and equipments of war, limited as these are either in terms of availability – being imported at high costs – or in terms of sophistication in those which are indigenously produced.

Logistic intelligence

So far we have confined the discussion to operational intelligence. However, there is no gain saying that a similarly structured cycle of information collection, knowledge processing and intelligence gathering could elevate the Indian military logistics to a state of near-perfectness in terms of military force-projection, movements, supply-chain management and so on.

More, it would cut costs, for utilisation of savings elsewhere. We may term it as the 'Intelligence Preparation of Logistics', IPL in short.

Net-centricity

We have discussed as to how information is sensed, digitised and processed into knowledge and then converted to actionable intelligence, before being disseminated across the areas of operations. To affect these transfers, there are 'transmission' links connecting the highest, the lowest and parallel echelons of the military structure.

When seen in totality over an area, sector, zone or theatre, these links emerge in the form of complex 'networks' of multiple to-and-fro exchange of raw information, processed knowledge, and finally, actionable intelligence. Obviously, besides performing the role of 'information highways', net-centricity also extends to the exchange of command, control and management instructions as well as feedback. Simply illustrated, net-centricity might have prevented Marshal Grouchy from diverting from Napoleon's intended plan of preventing Marshal Blucher's Prussian Corps from joining up with Duke of Wellington at Waterloo; the European Alliance would then have been defeated and the world would have been different from what we find it today.

We may therefore observe that what is referred to by 'digitised battlefield', even 'digitised battle formations' and 'net-centric warfare' – described by Chinese strategists as 'warfare under conditions of informalisation' - implies the exercise of traditional art of war, with contemporary weapons and hardware, under vastly superior abilities of generation and dissemination of intelligence, command and control instructions and feedback.

'Net-centric warfare' therefore enhances manyfold the capabilities of surveillance, reconnaissance, target acquisition and analysis, best engagement of weapons and equipment, exchange of intelligence, passage of instructions and feedback. It therefore imparts the ability to marshal and commit various battle groups and its elements in as advantageous manner as the prevailing tactical situation might permit under the overall sobriquet of IW.

Information warfare

The features discussed so far, particularly that of net-centricity and IPB, all put together comes under the ambit of IW. Thus originates the concept of Information Operations (IO).

IO is a continuous process of building up 'Information Superiority' that would permit, at the time of war, the ability to dominate in manoeuvre, orchestrate successful engagements and target accurately, all duly backed up with optimal logistic support - prosecution of IW in nutshell. In larger context, IO also extends to political, social and economic regimes. That has led to formation of dedicated 'commands' or 'departments' in many advanced nations, but most purposefully by the US, China, NATO and Russia.

NETWORK-CENTRIC WARFARE IN ASIA

The USA pioneered network-centric warfare (NCW) doctrine, or network-centric operations, in the 1990s. But first we must define NCW, as it can be a nebulous thing. Indeed, it is a theory of war rather than a collection of hardware. A US Department of Defence release in 2005, entitled 'The Implementation of Network- Centric Warfare', defined NCW as "the combination of emerging tactics, techniques and procedures that a fully or even partially networked force can employ to create a decisive war-fighting advantage." The document highlighted three characteristics:

- NCW is first of all about human behaviour as opposed to information technology. The focus is on the verb 'to network' rather than on the noun 'network', which is just an enabler;
- NCW is a concept that, at the highest level, constitutes the military's response to the information age;
- NCW is an emerging theory of war because it identifies new sources of power (information sharing, information access, speed), how those sources relate to each other, how they are brought to bear to achieve the desired outcome, and how they link to political objectives.

The term 'network-centric warfare' first appeared in the US Department of Navy publication 'Copernicus: C4ISR for the 21st Century' in 1997. NCW is essentially 'team warfare', where all military services integrate and synchronise to achieve joint warfare. It has four major tenets:

1. A robustly networked force improves information sharing.
2. Information sharing provides a common tactical picture and enhances the quality of information and shared situational awareness.
3. Shared situational awareness enables collaboration and self-synchronisation, and enhances sustainability and speed of command.
4. These, in turn, dramatically increase overall mission effectiveness.

The USA is the world's undisputed proponent of NCW, turning its vast information-gathering apparatus into a competitive advantage through robust networking of interconnected forces across the globe. This article offers a quick précis of NCW developments in the Asia-Pacific region. NCW involves three domains: (1) Physical domain where events occur and reality is perceived by sensors and individuals; (2) Information domain where collected data is transmitted; and (3) Cognitive domain that receives information so it can be assessed and acted upon. Because NCW encompasses many intangibles that are difficult to gauge, much of the following content focuses on new hardware being employed. In theory, such acquisitions should reflect more deep-seated NCW changes occurring within militaries.

Singapore has made the most progress regionally as it transforms into a 'Third-Generation Force' thanks to high levels of investment and an advanced technological base. The Singapore Army's newest vehicles such as the Terrex carry a battlefield management system (BMS) from ST Electronics. Vehicles possess two BMS terminals, while the Command, Control and Information System (CCIS) synchronises dismounted infantrymen fitted with the Advanced Combat Man System (ACM) to higher headquarters. The CCIS interacts with other ground-based systems and aerial platforms too. Another element aboard the Terrex is a Blue Force Tracking and Red Force Marking (BFT/RFM) system. Singapore's network-enabled force is the region's most advanced user of unmanned aerial vehicles (UAV) like the Heron 1 and Hermes 450. The Republic of Singapore Air Force (RSAF) has four Gulfstream G550 airborne early warning and control (AEW&C) aircraft fitted with an Elta EL/W-2085 Phalcon radar, and data from such platforms feed into Singapore's tactical picture.

In Malaysia, Sapura has commenced Phase 1A of the nation's Network-Centric Operations (NCO) contract. The two-year programme is due for completion in early 2014 and aims to integrate existing command, control, communications, computers and intelligence (C4I) systems and to study future capabilities. Phase 1B will be more comprehensive, probably adding capabilities like a BMS and integrating the Soldier Advanced Kombat Technology Integrated (SAKTI) programme. Thales, based on existing cooperation with Sapura, seems a likely foreign partner. Thales is also involved in fitting the Open Information Communication System (OICS) onto the AV8 armoured vehicle to allow internal/external information exchange and serve as a BMS platform.

In 2010, Northrop Grumman UK won a contract to create a Joint Operations Centre (JOC) in Brunei. Its heart is the company's International-Joint Operational Command and Control System. The contract provides both a static headquarters and deployable JOC. Common core software allows interoperability with regional partners. Phase 2 is believed to be under way, and it should implement tactical components such as a BMS. The network encompasses Harris Corporation Falcon II radios, but wideband networking radios and high-capacity line-of-sight (HCLOS) radios are an obvious future purchase.

In Thailand the Directorate of Signals is in charge of NCW technical aspects. Thailand employs commercial off-the-shelf (COTS) solutions alongside military-specific C4I systems as this proves more economical. In recent times the Royal Thai Air Force (RTAF) has made significant gains owing to a package of Saab JAS 39 Gripen fighters and Saab S100B Argus AEW&C aircraft. An integral part of the Swedish deal was installation of the StriC network, whose data-links connect Gripen and AEW&C aircraft into a complete air defence system. StriC, which greatly enhances the RTAF's networkcentricity was delivered in March 2011. Saab was subsequently requested to expand Thailand's air defence C2 system with a contract running from 2011-13.

Since 2001, Taiwan has invested heavily in its Lockheed Martin-derived Po Sheng ('Broad Victory') C4ISR system. The high-level Po Sheng system can quickly plug into the Joint Tactical Information Distribution System (JTIDS) of the USA's Pacific Command (PACOM). In the worst case of Chinese espionage in 50 years, authorities conceded Taiwan's C4ISR platform may have been compromised by Major General Lo Hsien-che before his arrest in 2011. The military has been hardening its communication system that is primarily based on a fibre-optic cable backbone connecting bases. There is now a need to extend it into an agile tactical network, and to add ISR capabilities. Furthermore, work is required to integrate Taiwan's Surveillance Radar Programme (SRP), a mountain-top missile early-warning radar, with Patriot PAC-3 and Po Sheng networks. Cyber-warfare is a threat to NCW, with Taiwan's National Security Bureau (NSB) revealing that, in the first half of 2012, hackers launched more than one million attacks on the NSB.

Over the years the author has observed increasing digitisation in China's People's Liberation Army (PLA), primarily through equipment being fielded in the elite Hong Kong Garrison. New assets include the Z-9ZH helicopter, a C2 platform with forward-looking infrared (FLIR) system and cabin command console. In addition, the garrison received the Type 07 6x6 Armoured Command Vehicle accommodating the latest radio equipment that can transmit/receive real-time data.

These platforms illustrate PLA advances in its drive towards NCW. 'Informationisation' is a fundamental goal, and in one sense, because the PLA was a late starter, it can take advantage of leapfrog technologies. C4ISR is crucial to China's blue-water naval presence, anti-access/area denial and missile capability. China has procured both KJ-2000 and KJ-200 AEW&C aircraft. China still has much to learn about gaining maximum benefit from them, plus their practicality is stymied by the fact that older fighters do not have digital data-links.

South Korea is rolling out its Tactical Information Communication Network (TICN) to replace its SPIDER communications system.

The USD3.8 billion TICN deal involving Samsung Thales, Huneed and LIG Nex1 has five subsystems such as High-Capacity Trunk Radio, Tactical Multiband and Multirole Radio, and Network Management System. Other important C4ISR projects include: (1) Korea Joint Command and Control System (KJCCS) to connect the Joint Chiefs of Staff to each service; (2) Military Information Management System (MIMS) to enable tactical-level cross-service interoperability; and (3) Joint Tactical Data Link System (JTDLS) to allow dissemination of digitised tactical information between all services.

South Korea knows it needs to improve C4ISR capabilities before it takes over wartime operational control (OPCON) of military forces on the peninsula in December 2015. Four Boeing 737 "Peace Eye" AEW&C aircraft have been inducted, plus it is contemplating RQ-4 Global Hawk UAVs, despite blanching at the USD1.2 billion price last year. The government has delayed any decision by at least a year, and is investigating cheaper alternatives. Since 2006, South Korea has been developing its Korea Air and Missile Defence (KAMD) system due for completion in 2015. Key components include Aegis-equipped KDX-III destroyers, EL/M-2080 Super Green Pine early-warning radars and Patriot missiles.

Japan is greatly concerned at North Korea's missile arsenal, as well as maritime territorial disputes with China. The Japan Air Self-Defence Force (JASDF) operates four Boeing E-767 AEW&C aircraft with JTIDS and 13 E-2C Hawkeyes. Missile defence incorporates four FPS-5 and seven FPS-4 radar installations, six Aegis-equipped destroyers, plus a series of communications and imagery satellites. Money is being invested in a new X-band satellite network. Initiated in 2009, the USD935 million Japan Aerospace Defence Ground Environment (JADGE) system, centralised at Yokota, brings a wider upgrade to conventional air defence and ballistic-missile defence systems. JADGE is closely interlinked to US systems. A JSDF C4 Systems Command was established in 2008, while a far-reaching mobile communication network is promoting information sharing. However, the 2011 tsunami revealed communication capability gaps, leading to funding for the Next-Generation Field Communication System. The government stated the system "will enable the rapid creation of high-speed and wide-area communication networks and also be useful for disaster response."

Moving to a different continent, two years ago the author witnessed Elbit Systems' Battle Group and Below Command, Control and Communications (BGC3) system being trialled by Australia's 7th Brigade. This forms part of the $300 million LAND 75/125 programme awarded in 2010, with full operational capacity scheduled for late 2013. The Israeli system has two core software components: TORC2H and Tactical Intranet Geographic Dissemination in Real-time (TIGER). BGC3 was first installed on Bushmaster vehicles and used a layer of Harris radios. Australia has performed a lot of engineering to make it work with non-Israeli applications such as Raytheon's Advanced Field Artillery Tactical Data System (AFATDS) and Northrop Grumman's Force XXI Battle Command Brigade and Below (FBCB2) system aboard Abrams tanks.

The Royal Australian Air Force (RAAF) has six Boeing E-7A "Wedgetail" aircraft, and initial operational capability was declared last November. The RAAF instituted the Project Vigilare Network- Centric Command and Control System (NC3S) under AIR 5333, with new installations at RAAF Bases Tindal and Williamtown. Boeing helped develop NC3S along with an Air Defence System communications network integrating data from 45 different land, sea, air and space interfaces. It commenced operations on 2 September 2010.

Across the Tasman Sea, New Zealand is acquiring a Defence Command and Control System (DC2S) to support high-level decision-making as well as joint operations. Delivery is expected in 2015-16. The Network Enabled Army programme will deliver most of the tactical C4I capability from 2013-33, though it needs a new communications network and strategic links via the Strategic Bearer Network Project. India has high hopes for its Tactical Communications Systems (TCS) though, as usual, movement has bogged down. Two local companies – Bharat Electronics Limited (BEL), and an L&T, Tata Power and HCL Infosys consortium – were shortlisted. An important step is a BMS for the Indian Army, but its delivery to a combat group is unlikely before 2015. Phase 2 should offer wider fielding of BMS from 2017-21, and the third phase would see upgrades in 2022-26. Total cost will be at least INR2.3 billion. It will also align with the Futuristic Infantry Soldier As a System (F-INSAS) programme.

The Combined Information & Decision Support System (CIDSS) has been stymied by the failed appearance of TCS as its key bearer. Last May the military ordered an investigation into the substandard CIDSS programme, though BEL is still working on it. CIDSS is one element of the army's Tac C3I system, with other elements being the Battlefield Surveillance System (BSS), Artillery Combat Command and Control System (ACCCS), and Air Defence Control and Reporting System (ADC&RS). India is essentially pursuing a bottom-up approach because of a lack of tri-service cooperation.

Cisco Systems helped the Indian Air Force inaugurate its fibre optic-based Air Force Network (AFNet) in September 2010. Riding on its backbone is the Integrated Air Command and Control System (IACCS) that provides connectivity and real-time transfer of voice, data and images between aircraft, satellites, UAVs, aerostats and ground bases. It also offers a ballistic-missile defence capacity. The Israel-launched RISAT-2 satellite is crucial to India's NCW capabilities, and the first element of the seven-satellite Indian Regional Navigational Satellite System (IRNSS) was launched in July.

NEW BATTLEFIELD FOR WARFARE

The innovation of more advanced and autonomous ICTs has engendered a new revolution in military affairs, which encompasses nations' use of ICTs in both cyberspace and the physical battlefield to wage war against their adversaries. The three most prevalent revolutions in military affairs come in the form of cyber attacks, autonomous robots and communication management.

Within the realm of cyberspace, there are two primary weapons: network-centric warfare and C4ISR, which denotes integrated Command, Control, Communications, Computers, Intelligence, Surveillance and Reconnaissance. Furthermore, cyberspace attacks initiated by one nation against another nation have an underlying goal of gaining information superiority over the attacked party, which includes disrupting or denying the victimized party's ability to gather and distribute information. A real-world occurrence that illustrated the dangerous potential of cyber attacks transpired in 2007 when a strike from Israeli forces demolished a nuclear reactor in Syria that was being constructed via a collaborative effort between Syria and North Korea. Accompanied with the strike was a cyber attack on Syria's air defenses, which left them blind to the attack on the nuclear reactor and, ultimately allowed for the attack to occur (New York Times 2014). An example of a more basic attack on a nation within cyberspace is a Distributed Denial of Service (DDOS) attack, which is utilized to hinder networks or websites until they lose their primary functionality. As implied, cyber attacks do not just affect the military party being attacked, but rather the whole population of the victimized nation. Since more aspects of daily life are being integrated into networks in cyberspace, civilian populations can potentially be negatively affected during wartime. For example, if a nation chose to attack another nation's power grid servers in a specific area to disrupt communications, civilians and businesses in that area would also have to deal with power outages, which could potentially lead to economic disruptions as well.

Moreover, physical ICTs have also been implemented into the latest revolution in military affairs by deploying new, more autonomous robots (i.e. – unmanned drones) into the battlefield to carry out duties such as patrolling borders and attacking ground targets.

Humans from remote locations pilot many of the unmanned drones, however, some of the more advanced robots, such as the Northrop Grumman X-47B, are capable of autonomous decisions. Despite piloting the drones from remote locations, a proportion of drone pilots still suffer from stress factors of more traditional warfare. According to NPR, a study performed by the Pentagon in 2011 found that 29% of drone pilots are "burned out" and undergo high levels of stress. Furthermore, approximately 17% of the drone pilots surveyed in the study were labeled "clinically distressed" with some of those pilots also showing signs of post-traumatic stress disorder (National Public Radio 2011). Modern ICTs have also brought advancements to communications management among military forces. Communication is a vital aspect of war for any involved party and, through the implementation of new ICTs such as data-enabled devices, military forces are now able to disseminate information faster than ever before. For example, some militaries are now employing the use of iPhones to upload data and information gathered by drones in the same area.

Legal and Ethical Concerns

While information warfare has yielded many advances in the types of attack that a government can make, it has also raised concerns about the moral and legal ambiguities surrounding this particularly new brand of war. Traditionally, wars have been analyzed by moral scholars according to Just War Theory. However, with Information Warfare, Just War Theory fails because the theory is based on the traditional conception of war. Information Warfare has three main issues surrounding it compared to traditional warfare:

1) The risk for the party or nation initiating the cyber attack is substantially lower than the risk for a party or nation initiating a traditional attack. This makes it easier for governments, as well as potentially terrorist or criminal organizations, to make these attacks more frequently than they could with traditional war.
2) Information communication technologies are so immersed in the modern world that a very wide range of technologies are at risk of a cyber attack. Specifically, civilian technologies can be targeted for cyber attacks and attacks can even potentially be launched through civilian computers or websites. As such, it is harder to enforce control of civilian infrastructures than a physical space. Attempting to do so would also raise many ethical concerns about the right to privacy, making defending against such attacks even tougher.
3) The mass-integration of information communication technologies into our system of war makes it much harder to assess accountability for situations that may arise when using robotic and/or cyber attacks. For robotic weapons and automated systems, it's becoming increasing hard to determine who is responsible for any particular event that happens. This issue is exacerbated in the case of cyber attacks, as sometimes it is virtually impossible to trace who initiated the attack in the first place.

Recently, legal concerns have arisen centered around these issues, specifically the issue of the right to privacy in the United States of America. Lt. General Keith B. Alexander, the general who is the head of Cyber Command, noted that there was a "mismatch between our technical capabilities to conduct operations and the governing laws and policies" when writing to the Senate Armed Services Committee. A key point of concern was the targeting of civilian institutions for cyber attacks, to which the general promised to try and maintain a mindset similar to that of traditional war, in which they will seek to limit the impact on civilians.

6

Future Warfare Technique by Drones

The MQ-Ma generation will be supplanted by the MQ-Mb, theoretically capable of taking over even more roles once assigned to traditional fighter-bombers and spy planes, including the suppression of enemy air defenses, bombing and strafing of ground targets, and surveillance missions. These will fly more autonomously and be better linked-in to other drone platforms for cooperative missions involving many aircraft under the command of a single "pilot." Imagine, for instance, one human operator overseeing a single command drone that in turn holds sway over a small squadron of autonomous drones carrying out a coordinated air attacks.

The year 2047 is the U.S. Air Force's holy grail, "the capstone for its long term plan to turn the skies over to war-fighting drones." By then, the USAF plans to have MQ-Mc dominating the skies with futuristic hypersonic drones. It is possible that 30 to 40 years from now, the MQ-Mc will incorporate all of the advances of the current MQ-M generation while being equipped for mission platforms like aerial combat and missile defense.

Shaping the Future

Currently the United States has more or less a monopoly on drones, which will not likely last any longer than the American monopoly on nuclear weapons did after WWII. Drone technology is already proliferating, suggesting that the United States is not the only country that understands the future strategic significance of drones. Modern military powers such as Germany and India have announced plans to acquire combat drones, while several other countries have growing UAV capabilities, most notably the Chinese,

Iranians, and Russians. Of these three countries, China poses the most significant threat in terms of UAV capability.

China is fast developing tactical unmanned aerial vehicles capable of supporting ground, sea, and air forces with similar capabilities to American platforms. According to a 2013 report by the Project 2049 Institute: In a worrisome trend, China has ramped up research in recent years faster than any other country... It displayed its first unmanned system model at the [annual] Zhuhai air show five years ago, and now every major manufacturer for the Chinese military has a research centre devoted to unmanned systems.

The report, which said "the military significance of China's move into unmanned systems is alarming," suggested that China could "easily match or outpace U.S. spending on unmanned systems, rapidly close the technology gaps and become a formidable global competitor in unmanned systems." Two Chinese drones that closely resemble the American Reaper and Predator UAVs were unveiled at the Zhuhai air show in China in November of 2012. The Chinese arsenal also possesses a larger drone that Western experts say is modeled after the American RQ-4 Global Hawk. The proliferation of armed drones in other nations is indicative of the platform's increasing strategic significance as countries recognize UAVs as a valuable war fighting tool that will play a vital role in future conflicts.

Paralleling the proliferation of drone technology as well as the rapid pace of American drone capabilities is an organizational shift that symbolizes the growth of the UAV role within U.S. military force structure. The Air Force is beginning to recruit separately for drone programs since the type of individual operating a drone is extremely different from those piloting fighter jets both mentally and physically. A new talent pool is drawing on a generation that has grown up surrounded by technology and therefore has a greater aptitude for dealing with unmanned systems. The move to identify new skill sets represents a profound cultural change within the Air Force and U.S. military as a whole. The growth of the RPA community and its integration within the Air Force indicates a larger organizational shift within the military to embrace the rising RPA platform.

Further evidence of the drone's strategic evolution within the military is a growing tension between the Department of Defense and clandestine drone operators. In a *National Journal* article, journalist Michael Hirsh argues that current CIA Director John Brennan thinks that, "the drone program has run its course as a CIA operation" and that moving the a program to the Department of Defense (DoD) is the way of the future. A proposed transfer of the operational network to the DoD would unify the command and control structure of targeted killings and create a uniform set of rules and procedures. According to *The Daily Beast* reporter Daniel Klaidman, the move could potentially toughen the criteria for drone strikes, strengthen the program's accountability, and increase transparency, as the military would have operational control over targeting. Lethal missions would take place under Title 10 of the U.S. Code of Laws, which outlines the role of the armed forces, rather than Title 50, which outlines the legal authority for intelligence activities and covert operations. This possible organizational modification represents the growth of the program from a simple tool of counterterrorism to assuming a broader role within the U.S. military and defense community.

Will drones lead to more war in the future? Or a "space race" within drone technology, leading up to a world filled with drone warfare on all sides? It has been argued that virtual technologies make it easier for democracies to wage war because they eliminate the risk of blood sacrifice that once forced prudence. Indiana Congresswoman Susan Brooks wrote in *The Washington Post*:

Drones will not reduce conflict. Their very ease of use will tempt nations, our own very much included, to engage in automated conflict. The problem with automated conflict, however, is that it doesn't stay automated. People die in drone wars, just like they died from the automation of arrows when the crossbow was invented. War machinery has a terrible capacity to tempt us to think it's something else.

Proponents of this line of thought argue that technology disengages the public and instead turns war into something merely to be watched and not weighed with great seriousness. Without public debate or risking troops, the decision of war may reflect a nation that does not care due to the lack of lives invested in a conflict.

Others have dismissed the idea that drone weaponry by itself will subtract humanity from warfare. Human psychology and human emotions are still a primary driving force behind wars, and technological advances have not substantially curbed that element of warfare in the past. He argued:

Despite the nearly century-long prevalence of airpower, we have not become numb to war. Airpower, drones included, has not erased emotion from war because war is a complex mixture of irrational forces, chance, and rational policy. And as long as humans are involved in conflict, these forces will continue to exert themselves on the theory and practice of war.

Thus, rather than drones determining the frequency of future conflicts, they will likely define its characteristics. As unmanned systems become more prevalent, militaries will be more likely to use force, but also will be less willing to conduct operations that expose soldiers to danger. As a result, the experience of going to war is changing.

Humans are increasingly functioning "on the loop" of combat systems, overseeing the autonomous actions of vehicles rather than participating directly. Simultaneously, advances in artificial intelligence will enable systems to make combat decisions without necessarily requiring human input. Such weapons seem advanced, but represent just the beginning. "There has been a game change in weaponry over the last several years," Peter Singer and Thomas Wright say, "with a new generation of advanced technology that moves the point of critical human decision, both geographically off the battlefield and also, increasingly, chronologically away from the time of kinetic action."

New UAV technology will be like every other in initiating a new evolution in military platforms and doctrine. However, unlike previous military "revolutions," Peter Singer writes that "the introduction of unmanned systems to the battlefield doesn't change simply how we fight, but for the first time changes who fights at the most fundamental level. It transforms the very agent of war, rather than just its capabilities." He goes on to say, "In the dismaying history of war machinery, armed drones are a game-changing technology, akin to gunpowder, the steam engine, the atomic bomb, opening up possibilities that were fiction a generation earlier but also opening up perils that were unknown a generation ago."

Therefore, while drones currently present a narrow tactical benefit, they posses tremendous potential that could spur the U.S. military to an onset of a decades-long technological transformation in warfare that will be defined by the strategic use of unmanned aerial platforms. UAV technology could spur a paradigm shift in the nature of warfare, comparable to the introduction of mechanization and airpower in WWII.

DRONE STRIKES IN YEMEN

Six months after President Obama laid out US rules for using armed drones, a Bureau analysis shows that covert drone strikes in Yemen and Pakistan have killed more people than in the six months before the speech. Each drone strike kills more people on average in both countries. The number of strikes fell across the two countries in the six months after the speech compared with the six months before, yet the overall death toll increased.

'To say a military tactic is legal, or even effective, is not to say it is wise or moral in every instance.' – President Obama

This analysis will raise questions about how much Obama's new rules constrain the drone programme, as he claimed it would in his speech.

On May 23 Obama explained how a new policy will govern the use of drones. He said using drones for targeted killing is legal, but added: 'To say a military tactic is legal, or even effective, is not to say it is wise or moral in every instance.'

He said: 'The same human progress that gives us the technology to strike half a world away also demands the discipline to constrain that power – or risk abusing it.' The President's remarks, and a background briefing to the media by unnamed administration officials,led some to report the US was ending the controversial practice of signature strikes – strikes which target groups of unidentified individuals based on their behaviour. However in the weeks after the speech, analyst Micah Zenko wrote: 'There is no evidence that signature strikes will be reduced or ended based upon anything the Obama administration has recently stated.'

The speech and briefings fuelled reports that the US military – in the form of the Joint Special Operations Command (JSOC) – would soon be given responsibility for carrying out drone strikes outside Afghanistan. But six months later the CIA is reportedly still carrying out strikes in Pakistan and Yemen. It was reported this week that the administration is trying to find a way to merge the CIA and Pentagon drone programmes. According to the Washington Post the ambition is to allow the CIA to keep running a fleet of drones but put JSOC in charge of the final, lethal step in a strike sequence, known as the finish.

Get the data: Obama 2013 Pakistan drone strikes

Obama's speech addressed 'criticism about drone strikes', saying the US only carries out such attacks against individuals who pose 'a continuing and imminent threat' to US citizens, not 'to punish individuals'. He added: 'before any strike is taken, there must be near-certainty that no civilians will be killed or injured – the highest standard we can set'. Civilians have been killed in US strikes in the past, the President said. The day before the speech, Attorney General Eric Holder published a letter to Congress saying those killed included a 16-year-old US citizen, Abdulrahman al Awlaqi. In Yemen, civilians have reportedly been killed in drone strikes after the speech. Between six and seven civilians were reported killed, two of whom were said to be children. It also emerged this month that the US knew it had killed civilians in strikes after the speech. The LA Times reported that the CIA briefed Congress about civilian casualties, including a child aged 6-13 who had been riding in a car with his older brother, an alleged militant, when the drones attacked. The CIA reportedly did not know he was in the car at the time. Other reports have identified the child as Abdulaziz, younger brother of Hassan al-Saleh Huraydan, an alleged AQAP commander. Every confirmed US drone strike in the past six months came in a 15-day period in late July and August, when eight attacks took place. The bombardment was more intense than any period in Yemen since mid-2012 when the US was providing air support to Yemeni forces as they fought an al Qaeda insurgency. The group established its own 'Islamic emirate' in several towns and villages in southern Yemen, exploiting a security vacuum during popular unrest in 2011. Although other aerial attacks have been reported it is not clear whether they were carried out by drones or manned aircraft. The 2013 onslaught of strikes was a response to a perceived terror threat the US reportedly believed was coming from Yemen. Washington reacted to intelligence of an impending attack by closing over 20 embassies and consulates in Africa and the Middle East and launching a barrage of drone strikes. The attacks killed at least 29 people, many of them identified as al Qaeda members. But only three of them were described in reports as significant leaders in the group.

Against the prevailing trend

There were fewer drone strikes in Pakistan in the six months after May 23 compared to the previous six months – 13 between May and the present, compared with 18 in the previous six months. But each strike killed more people on average. This went against the prevailing trend: the average number of people killed in each strike has been falling since 2009 when over 11 people were killed on average in every strike. That was down to fewer than five people killed on average in each attack at the end of 2012. In the six months before the speech, an average of 3.5 people were killed in each strike. Since the speech this has risen to almost five. There were no confirmed reports of civilian deaths in the six months after the speech. However this could be a continuing trend rather than a direct consequence of the speech. Total civilian casualties have been falling since 2009, and the average number of civilian deaths in each strike has also been declining over the past four years. The attacks in Pakistan have killed some named high-profile members of the Haqqani Network and Pakistan Taliban, the TTP.

Hakimullah Mehsud, leader of the Pakistan Taliban, was the most high-profile target in the past six months. A CIA drone killed him on November 1. He became leader in 2009 when his predecessor,Baitullah Mehsud, was killed by US drones. Following this attack, Hakimullah sent a suicide bomber to attack a CIA base in Khost, on the border in Afghanistan. The attack killed seven CIA officers. He had been wrongly reported to have been killed on at least three previous occasions. Since Obama's speech, drones have also killed both Mullah Sangeen Zadran, the Taliban shadow governor of Paktika province in Afghanistan, and Ahmad Jan, the shadow finance minster in Paktika, both of the Haqqani Network.

DRONE OPERATIONS FOR WARFARE

For over a decade, America's drone campaign has been driven by short-term objectives: the degradation of al Qaeda and militant groups like the Taliban through the use of targeted killings on a tactical scale. The targeted strikes, which occur in both battlefield settings and countries where the United States does not have troops deployed, are possible due to the lethal precision of armed drones. With their unprecedented reconnaissance capabilities and ability to stalk a target for hours, drones have become the hallmark innovation in the U.S. "War on Terror." Unmanned aerial vehicles (UAVs) have proven themselves to be the asymmetric tactical response to the asymmetric threat of militant networks, insurgencies, and other non-conventional targets.

Both the U.S. military and Obama administration's embrace of drones, as well as drone development programs, signify that UAVs are outgrowing their tactical niche within the strategic framework of counterterrorism operations- instead they may soon become a common characteristic of modern militaries. In order to embrace the paradigm shift in the character of warfare brought about by drones, a UAV strategic framework is needed. However, growing public discourse regarding current drone use has obscured this larger military-technical development. Therefore, policymakers must look past the current drone debate in order to recognize the growing strategic role of future drone systems.

The following argument provides evidence for the evolution from the tactical to strategic nature of the platform. I will provide a history of drone technology and its development over the course of the 20th and early 21st century in order to create a foundation for discussing modern UAV deployment. Following the historical framework is an analysis of the turning point of drone use that occurred after the 9/11 attacks. I then turn to the contemporary drone debate and how it must be adjusted to fully capitalize on the emerging potential of the platform. Finally, I conclude with an outlook on the drones of the future, how they will change the nature of warfare, and the role of policy-makers in framing advances in military technology.

Historical Overview

While drones have only recently become a topic of public conversation, they have a lengthy history. UAVs claim a lineage as the progenitor of manned flight that dates back to the dawn of aerial warfare. The earliest cited example of the military application of UAVs dates back to the mid-19th century, when the Austrian military attacked the Italian city of Venice using balloons laden with explosives that were controlled by timed fuses. Although balloons do not generally meet today's definition of a UAV, the concept was strong enough that once winged aircraft had been invented, the effort to fly them unmanned for military purposes was not far behind.

The early years of unmanned flight were indistinguishable from missiles. Rather than debating single-use versus reusable vehicles, military planners were investigating whether pilotless aircraft had any military purpose at all. At the turn of the twentieth century, the American military was studying the idea of unmanned, automatically controlled "aerial torpedoes." Shortly before WWI, the U.S. Navy was involved in the development of the Navy-Sperry "Flying Bomb," the first technology that demonstrated the concept of an unmanned aircraft. In another case, the Navy hired Elmer Ambrose Sperry, the inventor of the gyroscope, to develop a fleet of unmanned Curtis biplanes designed to be launched by catapult and fly over enemy positions.

The "aerial torpedoes," an early version of today's cruise missiles, were filled with TNT and guided towards an enemy position using a predetermined distance. Upon reaching the known distance of the target, the craft would essentially fall out of the sky onto the target. Research and development continued from 1915 to 1922, when the program's lack of progress along with a lack of funds forced the Navy to cancel the effort.

While the Navy struggled with Sperry's invention, the U.S. Army developed a slightly more successful "flying bomb." The Army's Kettering Bug, the precursor to cruise missile technology, was a biplane that flew on a pre-set course using an on-board gyroscope and altimeter. Like the Navy, the Army cancelled the program soon after the end of WWI due to a lack of funding.

During the Second World War, UAVs participated in a similar fashion to their use during WWI- retrofitted aerial vehicles designed to carry high explosives. For example, in 1944 the U.S. Navy launched a UAV program designed to destroy German bunkers. It used refitted B-24 bombers filled to double capacity with explosives and guided by remote control devices, crashing them at selected targets in Germany and Nazi-controlled France.

The most infamous use of WWII UAVs was the German V-1 "flying bomb," which devastated London and other British cities. The V-1 is considered the first cruise missile, was cost-effective, and employed in large numbers by German forces.

In 1944 the United States reverse-engineered the V-1 from fragments of rockets that had landed in Britain to produce its own cruise missiles, almost identical to those of the Nazis. Due to his wartime encounters with the crude rockets, Commanding General of the Army Air Forces Hap Arnold predicted that the future emphasis in air power would shift from pilots to scientists and machinery.

Arnold's endorsement of replacing soldiers with machines was a distinct break from traditional military culture, as American missile and assault drone production was not allowed to interfere with any other elements of the war effort during WWII. Nonetheless, Arnold's forecast represents the early discerning of a tactical and technological system that would not achieve its potential for over half a century.

Two different examples of pilotless aircraft emerged after WWII. The first example was cruise missiles or proto-drones, miniature versions of what the U.S. military had attempted to manufacture as far back as 1917. These autonomous missiles could be fired at the enemy from a great distance and at high velocity, but could also be guided using cameras. However, cruise missiles could not linger over a battlefield in the manner of a holding pattern nor could they return to base. Their weapons delivery was the missile itself-blunt and inflexible. The second example of unmanned aircraft was assault drones, which were slower than cruise missiles and could not operate outside one's line-of-sight. They lent themselves to roles in surveillance where television capability was used to gather intelligence. Similar to the contemporary development of UAVs, drones at the onset of the Cold War were relegated to ancillary roles, since the destructive capacity of cruise missiles occupied the attention of modern militaries. Despite resistance to the nascent technology, the slow progression of both drone and cruise missile technology represent the universal evolution of a growing distancing between soldier and weapon, as well as a desire for a precision strike capability.

"Flying bombs" became officially known as drones during the early years of the Cold War, and were used as aerial targets to train fighter pilots. The word "drone" was used because it denoted the aircraft's limited abilities, giving it a connotation of being disposable. It was not until the Vietnam War in Southeast Asia that UAV technology had advanced to allow for a new combat role and a redefinition of the unmanned concept. Drones were given combat roles to replace manned reconnaissance flights due to concerns about American pilots being shot down over enemy territory. As a result, U.S. forces were estimated to have flown more than 5,000 surveillance missions using the plane-launched AQM-34 Ryan Firebee drone. The Firebee was controlled by a ground operator using a remote control camera and was able to launch air to ground missiles as well as conventional bombs. The jet-powered drone could fly at subsonic speeds and accommodate numerous modifications and a variety of payloads. In addition to their reconnaissance and bomb damage assessment roles, the Firebee was used to bait and reveal North Vietnamese anti-aircraft installations, and was later used by the CIA to develop electronic countermeasures for such defenses.

The new application of pilotless aircraft marked a shift in the American military's conception of the drone platform: UAVs were developed to fill a role previously occupied by manned aircraft. From this point forward, UAVs would operate in roles traditionally occupied by manned aircraft, and began to be referred to as "remotely piloted aircraft," or RPAs. This change in lexicon reflects a decisive shift from the general WWI and WWII label of "flying bombs" to a force-multiplying platform with the advantage of being able to take over functions of traditional manned aircraft. While UAVs were frequently deployed during the Vietnam War, they were not publicized nor recognized as a significant military platform worth developing. This was due to cultural resistances within the U.S. Air Force, which resulted in drone technology being largely abandoned until late in the 20th century.

In 1973 war broke out in the Middle East in what came to be known as the Yom Kippur War. Israel employed UAV systems similar to those the U.S. deployed in Vietnam, but with greater accentuation and unprecedented effectiveness. Israeli forces integrated UAVs in joint operations with piloted aircraft to provide reconnaissance that was vital in helping the Israeli Defense Force halt the Arab advance and eventually repel the invading armies. Impressed by Israel's success, general awareness and military-wide acceptance of UAV utility spread throughout the U.S. defense community. The United States quickly acquired a number of Israeli UAVs, which it used to develop the first modern American UAVs: the Hunter and the Pioneer. These drones underwent research and development in the late 1970s and 80s, making their combat debut during the Gulf War.

Modern American combat drones were first utilized during Desert Storm, or "the first UAV war." According to a May 1991 Department of the Navy report, at least one UAV was airborne at all times during Desert Storm. During military operations, with most of the U.S.'s manned tactical reconnaissance assets committed, UAVs emerged as a critical tool for gathering intelligence at the tactical level. These systems were employed for battlefield damage assessment, targeting, and surveillance missions, particularly in high-threat airspace. According to a 1993 congressional report from the House Oversight and Investigations Subcommittee, "The Pioneer unmanned aerial vehicle provided substantial imagery support to Marine, Army, and Navy units during Operation Desert Storm. They were so good many that more could have been used." The intelligence officer for a Marine Division that was "blessed" with more UAVs than any other unit in-theatre commented, "UAVs were great for target validation and battlefield damage assessment, but we could have used three times as many as we had." The war confirmed the military utility of drones, both as a force multiplier as well as its utility in previously manned aerial operations.

After the Gulf War successfully demonstrated the effectiveness of UAVs, modern militaries began to invest in the research and development of combat UAVs, perhaps none more so than the U.S. military. The U.S. Predator drone was developed in the early 1990s through a program called the Advanced Technology Demonstrator Program for reconnaissance and forward observation roles.

While the pace of development of UAVs had reflected the pace of technology in general, major improvements in computing and electronic controlling systems in the 1980s and '90s made modern-day drones like the Predator possible. The invention of Global Positioning System technology, along with advances in micro-computing, ushered in the possibility of greatly advanced and automated unmanned flight. Due to these developments, it was in the late '90s that the U.S. Air Force made great strides in the technical aspects of arming unmanned aircraft with guided missiles. Though the tactical usefulness of armed drones was still unknown, the emergence of network terrorism and their unconventional tactics soon predicated the need for a platform that could survey and strike select targets.

The Modern Drone Campaign

While U.S. drones were first used for battlefield reconnaissance, since the 9/11 attacks drones have evolved into America's preferred killing machines in the "War on Terror" as well as for locations where the U.S. military does not operate openly on the ground. Just months after 9/11, the first operational armed strike by an unmanned aerial vehicle took place in Afghanistan. Since that first attack, the use of armed drones has risen dramatically to the point where drone strikes are now a common occurrence not only in battlefield settings, but also in neighboring countries where militants have attempted to seek refuge. Though the evolution of UAVs has occurred rapidly over the past decade, scholars Leila Hudson, Matt Flannes, and Colin Owens divide the post-9/11 drone campaign's development into four phases.

Phase One

The first phase, coinciding with the invasion of Afghanistan, served as a testing period of limited strikes on high-value targets like members of al Qaeda and the Taliban. It was during this phase that the first use of remotely piloted drones for missile attacks outside identified warzones took place. This attack occurred in northeastern Yemen in 2002, killing al Qaeda member Salim Sinan al-Harethi, who was suspected of masterminding the 2000 *USS Cole* bombing in Aden. It also marked the beginning of the covert component of the drone war, which was kept out of view from the public and many government officials.

Phase Two

The second phase, coinciding with the 2007 surge in Iraq, consisted of a slight increase in strikes but retained the same target set: high-value terrorist suspects. With combat operations and resources focused on salvaging what was left of the war in Iraq, American forces were stretched thin in terms of combat capabilities in the expansive and difficult terrain of Afghanistan. Drones provided a highly valuable force multiplier that made up for resources that were transferred from the Afghan theatre to Iraqi battlefields. This phase is also characterized by the proliferation of attacks from warzones in Afghanistan to insurgent sanctuaries in the volatile tribal regions of Pakistan.

Phase Three

The third phase of the drone war took place during the end of the Bush Administration. It consisted of an acceleration of attack frequency: 37 drone strikes occurred during 2008, compared to a total of nine from 2001-2007. The success of the drone program during its first two phases gave the Bush Administration the impression that if limited drone strikes were successful in disrupting terrorist organizations, then increasing the use of unmanned precision strikes could play a pivotal role in combating the diffuse threat posed by militants on both sides of the Afghan-Pakistani border. Similar to the application of counterinsurgency doctrine in Iraq and subsequently Afghanistan to combat asymmetric insurgencies, drone warfare was seen as an emerging asymmetric tactical solution to asymmetric militant operations.

Phase Four

The most rapid proliferation of drone attacks occurred under the Obama Administration. Phase four of the drone program therefore consists of an expanded target list and attack frequency. The list expanded to include unidentified militants of dubious rank and other targets of opportunity like known militant safe houses. It has been calculated that the Obama Administration has conducted roughly 370 drone strikes in Yemen and Pakistan (undeclared combat zones) since 2009. This is compared to close to 50 similar strikes during the Bush Administration.

The Current Campaign

The growth in drone use has culminated in what Micah Zenko of the Council on Foreign Relations calls "America's third war." This war, consisting of targeted killings in non-battlefield settings, has been a defining feature of post-9/11 American military policy as much as the conflicts in Iraq or Afghanistan. Based on open source reporting, drones have conducted lethal strikes in six countries: Iraq, Afghanistan, Libya, Pakistan, Yemen, and Somalia. Of these countries, Iraq, Afghanistan, and Libya have been declared combat zones by the United States.

The two main actors in America's third war are Joint Special Operations Command (JSOC) and the CIA. Each organization runs their own drone program, utilizing similar technology and operational tactics but for very different purposes. The JSOC program is the military's version of the drone war. This part of the ongoing conflict is publicly acknowledged and operates in the recognized warzones of Afghanistan and Iraq, targeting U.S. enemies. It is an extension of the conventional battle waged by American forces in Afghanistan and Iraq. In these two theaters, drones have functioned in a support role to combat operations: they primarily provide surveillance, and secondly they strike targets using precision-guided munitions. In declared combat zones, JSOC operates drones overtly, under a specific chain of command, and according to rules of engagement.

The CIA conducts the second campaign of the third war. The agency targets terror suspects around the world, including countries where U.S. troops are not actively operating. This campaign has been characterized by a lack of transparency and accountability on the part of U.S. officials. As a result it has become the focal point of public discourse on drone use. The program is classified as covert- the agency declines to provide any information to the public about where it operates, how it selects targets, who is in charge, or how many people have been killed. Similarly, the deployment of drones to non-combat environments is not acknowledged by the government and therefore does not function under explicit public rules of engagement or chain of command. In Pakistan and Somalia, the CIA's lethal drone strikes are the primary tool used against suspected terrorists. In Yemen, the agency covertly operates drones in conjunction with special operations forces and the Yemeni Air Force to target suspected members of al Qaeda in the Arabian Peninsula.

It is not difficult to understand the appeal of a "push-button" approach to fighting terrorist and militant groups like al Qaeda. However, the Obama Administration has embraced the drone program while maintaining the minimal governmental oversight that was present during the Bush

Administration. As a result, the burgeoning drone debate reflects broad discontent among the population directed at the hidden bureaucracy that has directed the drone strike program. The public outcry first began following the killing of Anwar Awlaki, the first time since the Civil War that the United States government deliberately killed an American citizen as a wartime enemy and without a trial.The event caused a change in both the volume of coverage, which increased dramatically, and also the tone and depth. After the strike, journalists at *The New York Times*, *The Washington Post*, and other media outlets began to write more analytical and investigative articles about the targeted-killing program. Since then, the debate has grown; information pertaining to presidential directives, target selection, and the institutionalization of drone policies has slowly leaked to the public, spurring a public consensus for disclosure as well as reform. Due to the Obama Administration's lack of transparency regarding the drone program, critics argue that the administration's failure to provide legal justification for the assassination of individual targets that are not declared combatants or operate within defined battlefield implicates the United States in violating international legal frameworks regarding the use of force.

Justification for the Third War

The Obama Administration has drawn on international law to justify the use of drones in response to public calls for transparency regarding targeted killings. Under the terms of the Laws of Armed Conflict and International Humanitarian Law, first the Bush Administration and now Obama Administration have argued that the attacks of 9/11 and the global campaign against groups like al Qaeda should be viewed as an ongoing war. As former U.S. State Department legal advisor Harold Koh put it, "As a matter of international law, the U.S. is in an armed conflict with al Qaeda, as well as the Taliban and associated forces, in response to the horrific 9/11 attacks, and may use force consistent with its inherent right to self-defense under international law."

The Bush and Obama Administrations have also cited Article 51 of the UN Charter as further justification for drone use. The article cites that a state may use force if either a foreign nation agrees to the use of force within its territory or fails to take action against threats emanating from within its borders. In the cases of Pakistan, Somalia, and Yemen, both conditions are satisfied; all three countries have consented to the United States operating drones within their territories, and all three are safe havens for groups that have launched violent attacks against the United States and American interests. In Afghanistan, Iraq, and Libya, the United States was already engaged in combat operations. Therefore, the issue of legality regarding the use of drones does not apply.

Since 2011, the drone debate has expanded from concerns regarding legality to focusing on the moral and ethical challenges created by the Obama Administration's controversial growth of the drone program in what is shaping up to be a landmark episode in American history and both domestic and international law. Drone critics believe that strikes will soon occur in the United States, even though U.S. Attorney General Eric Holder, the primary defender of the drone program's legality, pledged in writing that this would never happen unless armed conflict breaks out on American soil. This concern highlights public fears regarding war conducted behind a classified veil, relying on missile strikes rarely acknowledged by the American government, and a president with unprecedented authority to authorize drone strikes with little congressional oversight. It goes to the heart of a deeply rooted American suspicion about the government, the military and the surveillance state; the specter of drones streaking through the skies above American cities and towns, controlled by faceless bureaucrats and equipped to spy or kill. According to Brookings scholar Ben Wittes, "Over the last year or so, this thing that was the province of a small number of technologists and national security people has exploded into the larger public consciousness."

In Defense of Drones

There are many benefits for the increased use of drones. Cruise missiles, fighter planes, and bombers work against fixed targets such as enemy forces or installations. They are not as useful, however, in today's asymmetric wars that are fought against insurgents and terrorists. Drones can loiter and maintain an "unblinking stare" over a chosen area for hours. Thanks to the drone's ability to watch and wait, its operator, often thousands of miles away, can patiently choose the best moment to fire its missiles. This increases the chances of success while minimizing collateral damage and harm to civilians. As a result, drones are relatively more ethical than other weapons systems because they can be more discriminant.

The unique capabilities of drones are evident in their operational flexibility. While there is significant public backlash against American UAV use, the alternatives of using troops or manned systems to combat the threat emanating out of terrorist havens in Pakistan or Yemen is almost unthinkable. Alternative options would cause more unintended casualties due to lack of precision. With unreliable local security forces, an American ground attack would be even more costly in human, military, and political terms than employing drones. Unmanned strikes are America's least-worst option for pursuing terrorists in terms of cost and risk to American military personal. In addition, an analysis of acquisition and operating costs reveal that drones are more cost effective to acquire and operate than conventional manned aircraft.

Drone technology has advanced to a point of sophistication that will likely give them a greatly expanded role in future wars. All currently employed drones are characterized by their staple roles in surveillance and reconnaissance operations. In addition, platforms like the Predator and Reaper have been outfitted with precision-guided munitions in order to reduce the strike time between target acquisitions and strike approval.

The evolution of drone technology has been rapid, with new developments allowing for longer flight, heavier payloads, vertical takeoff from ships, and deployment to more areas of the world. While the Predator MQ-1 and Predator B (Reaper) MQ-9 are the most used and recognizable members of the drone fleet and have carried out most surveillance missions and attacks, new platforms are being deployed, like the RQ-4 Global Hawk and the MQ-8B Fire Scout.

Ethical questions regarding current drone use are distracting us from an understanding of the significance and future implications of drones or Remotely Piloted Aircraft (RPA). In order to recognize the growing strategic framework of the technology, we need to separate the platform from impediments such as emotional and ethical concerns.

The current debate prevents a clear understanding of the technology's potential on the part of American leadership- it distracts the administration and Congress from how drones can integrate into strategic planning beyond counterterrorism operations.

While the administration is focused on institutionalizing a drone strike "playbook," drone development is far outpacing attempts at formalization. The military is already addressing the future role of UAVs, which may make any ongoing attempt to codify drone use obsolete in the near future. Thus the playbook for the tactical use of drones as well as the public debate will soon become irrelevant as drones take on their own strategic framework. In order to embrace the paradigm shift of the UAV role within military force structure, it is best to adapt policymaking and accept the technology in breaking from traditional understandings of warfare.

The Drones of the Future

In November 2012, the U.S. Navy loaded an X-47B, officially labeled an "unmanned combat air system," aboard the USS *Harry S. Truman* for the drone's first carrier-based testing. The testing represents the beginning of developing successors to contemporary drones, which will be integrated into combat platforms like aircraft carriers. This signifies a remarkable break with current practices of operating drones in a strictly tactical, non-integrated capacity. Thus the X-47B illustrates the early stages of the U.S. military's long-term vision for drone warfare through the development of an unmanned combat aerial vehicle, or UCAV. Within this program the U.S. Air Force envisions a wide array of UAVs, from insect-like robots to tanker size pilotless planes, all of which are designed to perform the functions of traditional military aircraft while replacing the human pilot.

The Air Force's plan to develop advanced drones and integrate them into an increasingly autonomous platform is laid out in their roadmap for the future titled, "Air Force Unmanned Aerial System (UAS) Flight Plan 2009-2047." The Air Force envisions small-and medium-sized drones with lethal combat capabilities that would be almost unrecognizable compared to today's drone fleet. Today's medium-sized Reapers are set to be replaced by next generation MQ-Ma drones that will be "networked, capable of partial autonomy, all-weather and modular with capabilities supporting electronic warfare, close air support, strike, and intelligence, surveillance and reconnaissance missions."

DRONE WAR JARGON

AUMF The Authorization for Use of Military Force, an act of Congresspassed days after the 9/11 attacks, giving the president authority to take "all necessary and appropriate force" against anyone involved in the attack or harboring those who were. Both Bush and Obama have claimed broad authorities to detain and kill terror suspects based on the AUMF. AQAP Al Qaeda in the Arabian Peninsula is the Yemen-based al Qaeda affiliate tied to the attempted Christmas Day airplane bombing in 2009. Over the past year, the U.S. has ramped up strikes against AQAP, targeting leaders as well as unspecified militants.

DISPOSITION MATRIX A system for tracking terror targets and assessing when – and where – they could be killed or captured. The Washington Postreported this fall that the Disposition Matrix is an attempt to codify for the long haul the administration's "kill lists."

GLOMAR A response rejecting a request for information on a classified program asserting that the information's mere existence can neither be confirmed nor denied. The name comes from 1968, when the CIA told journalists it could neither "confirm nor deny" the existence of a ship called the Glomar Explorer. The CIA has responded to information requests about its drone program with Glomar responses.

JSOC Joint Special Operations Command is a secretive, elite segment of the military. JSOC squads carried out the Bin Laden raid and run the military's drone programs in Yemen and Somalia and also conduct intelligence gathering.

PERSONALITY STRIKE A targeted attack on a particular individual identified as a terrorist leader.

SIGNATURE STRIKE A strike against someone believed to be a militant whose identity isn't necessarily known. Such strikes are reportedly based on a "pattern of life" analysis – intelligence on their behavior suggesting that an individual is a militant. The policy, reportedly begun by Bush in Pakistan in 2008, is now allowed in Yemen, under stricter criteria.

TADS Terror Attack Disruption Strikes, sometimes used to refer to some strikes when the identity of the target is not known. Administration officials have said that the criteria for TADS are different from signature strikes, but it is not clear exactly how.

How are targets chosen?

A series of articles based largely on anonymous comments from administration officials have given partial picture of how the U.S. picks targets and carries out strikes. Two recent reports – from researchers at Columbia Law School and from theCouncil on Foreign Relations– also give detailed overviews of what's known about the process.

The CIA and the military have reportedly longmaintained overlapping "kill lists." According to news reports last spring, the military's list was hashed out in Pentagon-run interagency meetings, with the White House approving proposed targets. Obama would authorize particularly sensitive missions himself.

This year, the process reportedly changed, to concentrate the review of individuals and targeting criteria in the White House. According to the Washington Post, the reviews now happen at regular interagency meetings at the National Counterterrorism Center. Recommendations are sent to a panel of National Security Council officials. Final revisions go through White House counterterror adviser John Brennan to the president. Several profiles have highlightedBrennan's powerful and controversial role in shaping the trajectory of the targeted killing program. This week, Obama nominated Brennan to head the CIA.

At least some CIA strikes don't have to get White House signoff. The director of the CIA canreportedly green-light strikes in Pakistan. In a 2011 interview, John Rizzo, previously the CIA's top lawyer, said agency attorneys did an exhaustive review of each target.

According to the Washington Post, the Obama administration's recent effort to impose more stringent requirements for kill lists and signature strikes exempts the CIA's campaign in Pakistan. The CIA will have at least a year to continue strikes in Pakistan according to its own protocols.

Doesn't the U.S. sometimes target people whose names they don't know?

Yes. While administration officials often have frequently framed drone strikes as going after "high-level al Qaeda leaders who are planning attacks" against the U.S., many strikes go after apparent militants whose identities the U.S. doesn't know. The so-called "signature strikes"began under Bush in early 2008 and were expanded by Obama. Exactly what portion of strikes are signature strikes isn't clear.

At various points the CIA's use of signature strikes in Pakistan in particular have caused tensions with the White House and State Department. One official told the New York Times about a joke that for the CIA, "three guys doing jumping jacks," was a terrorist training camp.

In Yemen and Somalia, there is debate about whether the militants targeted by the U.S. are in fact plotting against the U.S. or instead fighting against their own country. Micah Zenko, a fellow at the Council on Foreign Relations who has been critical of the drone program, toldProPublica that the U.S. is essentially running "a counterinsurgency air force" for allied countries. At times, strikes have relied on local intelligence that later proves faulty. The Los Angeles Times recently examined the case of a Yemeni man killed by a U.S. drone and the complex web of allegiances and politics surrounding his death.

How many people have been killed in strikes?

The precise number isn't known, but some estimates peg the total around 3,000.

A number of groups are tracking strikes and estimating casualties:

- The Long War Journal covers Pakistan and Yemen.
- The New America Foundation covers Pakistan.
- The London Bureau of Investigative Journalism covers Yemen, Somalia, andPakistan, as well as statistics from on drone strikes carried out in Afghanistan.

How many of those killed are have been civilians?

It's impossible to know.

There has been considerable back-and-forth about the tally of civilian casualties. For instance, the New America Foundation estimates between 261 and 305 civilians have been killed in Pakistan; The Bureau of Investigative Journalism gives a range of 475 - 891. All of the counts are much higher than the very low numbers of deaths the administration claims. (We've detailed inconsistencies even within those low estimates.) Some analyses show that civilian deaths have dropped proportionally in recent years.

The estimates are largely compiled by interpreting news reports relying on anonymous officials or accounts from local media, whose credibility may vary.

The controversy has been compounded by the fact that the U.S. reportedly counts any military-age male killed in a drone strike as a militant. An administration official told ProPublica, "If a group of fighting age males are in a home where we know they are constructing explosives or plotting an attack, it's assumed that all of them are in on that effort." It's not clear what if any investigation occurs after the fact. Columbia Law School conducted an in-depth analysis of what we know about the U.S.'s efforts to mitigate and calculate civilian casualties. It concluded that the drone war's covert nature hampered accountability measures taken in traditional military actions.Another report from Stanford and NYU documented "anxiety and psychological trauma" among Pakistani villagers. This fall, the U.N. announced an investigation into the civilian impact – in particular, allegations of "double-tap" strikes, in which a second strike targets rescuers.

Why just kill? What about capture?

Administration officials have said in speeches that militants are targeted for killing when they pose an imminent threat to the U.S. and capture isn't feasible. But killing appears to be is far more common than capture, and accounts of strikes don't generally shed light on "imminent" or "feasible." Cases involving secret, overseas captures under Obama show the political and diplomatic quandaries in deciding how and where a suspect could be picked up.

This fall, the Washington Post described something called the "disposition matrix" – a process that has contingency plans for what to do with terrorists depending where they are. The Atlantic mapped out how that decision-making might happen in the case of a U.S. citizen, based on known examples. But of course, the details of the disposition matrix, like the "kill lists" it reportedly supplants, aren't known.

What's the legal rationale for all this?

Obama administration officials have given a series of speeches broadly outlining the legal underpinning for strikes, but they never talk about specific cases. In fact, they don't officially acknowledge the drone war at all. The White House argues that Congress' 2001 Authorization for Use of Military

Force as well as international law on nations' right to self-defense provides sound legal basis for targeting individuals affiliated with Al Qaeda or "associated forces," even outside Afghanistan. That can include U.S. citizens.

"Due process," said Attorney General Eric Holder said in a speech last March, "takes into account the realities of combat." What form that "due process" takes hasn't been detailed. And, as we've reported, the government frequently clams up when it comes to specific questions – like civilian casualties, or the reasons specific individuals were killed.

NBC News obtained a Justice Department memo that was given to some members of Congress in June laying out the administration's legal case for targeted killing in more detail. The memo, which was not classified, says that a U.S. citizen who is a "senior operational leader of al-Qaida or an associated force" can be targeted even if they are not tied to an active plot against the U.S. It also offers more detail on criteria for determining that capture is not feasible.

A federal judge had ruled earlier this year that the government did not have to release a separate secret legal memo making the specific case for the killing of Anwar al-Awlaki, a U.S. citizen. The judge also ruled the government did not have to respond to other requests seeking more information about targeted killing in general. (In making the ruling, the judge acknowledged a "Catch-22," saying that the government claimed "as perfectly lawful certain actions that seem on their face incompatible with our Constitution and laws while keeping the reasons for their conclusion a secret.")

The U.S. has also sought to dismiss a lawsuit brought by family members over Awlaki's death and that of his 16-year-old son – also a U.S. citizen — who was killed in a drone strike.

When does the drone war end?

The administration has reportedly discussed scaling back the drone war, but by other accounts, it is formalizing the targeted killing program for the long haul. The U.S.estimates there Al Qaeda in the Arabian Peninsula has a "few thousand" members; but officials have also said the U.S. cannot "capture or kill every last terrorist who claims an affiliation with al Qaeda."

Jeh Johnson, who just stepped down as general counsel for the Pentagon, gave a speechlast month entitled, "The Conflict Against Al Qaeda and its Affiliates: How Will It End?" He didn't give a date.

John Brennan has reportedly said the CIA should return to its focus on intelligence-gathering. But Brennan's key role in running the drone war from the White House has led to debate about how much he would actually curtail the agency's involvement if he is confirmed as CIA chief.

What about backlash abroad?

There appears to be plenty of it. Drone strikes are deeply unpopular in the countries where they occur, sparking frequent protests. Despite that, Brennan said last August that the U.S. saw,"little evidence that these actions are generating widespread anti-American sentiment or recruits." General Stanley McChrystal, who led the military in Afghanistan, recently contradicted that, saying, "The resentment created by American use of unmanned strikes... is much greater than the average American appreciates. They are hated on a visceral level, even by people who've never seen one or seen the effects of one." The New York Times recently reported that Pakistani militants have carried out a campaign of brutal reprisals against locals, accusing them of spying for the U.S.

As for international governments: Top U.S. allies have mostly kept silent. A 2010 U.N. report raised concerns about the precedent of a covert, boundary-less war. The President of Yemen, Abdu Hadi, supports the U.S. campaign, while Pakistan maintains an uneasy combination of public protest and apparent acquiescence.

THE DRONE-INDUSTRIAL COMPLEX

These concerns are unlikely to sway political opinion in Washington—in part because drones also represent an unholy nexus of political expediency and commercial opportunity.

Politicians like drones because they don't have to worry about the potential scandal of soldiers left behind enemy lines. The arms industry likes them because high-tech R&D is a reliable cash cow. The drones may be unmanned, but it takes 168 individuals to keep one aloft for 24 hours, many of whom are employed through private contractors.

While the original Predator was attractive for its low price tag, the per-unit cost of newer drones now exceeds those of planes with a pilot in the cockpit. The Reaper is more expensive than the F-16, Cockburn notes, and twice as likely to crash. The Global Hawk is more expensive than the F-35 and has remained in production even though a 2011 Pentagon test office report declared it "not operationally effective." Yet despite their increasingly high price, the drones now have a 7,500-strong lobby on the Capitol that will continue to find uses for them.

Neither book, however, is a technophobic jeremiad. Woods makes clear that as a weapon of war, a Predator drone is no worse than an F-16; indeed, potentially a drone, armed with a Hellfire missile, with its limited blast radius, can be a more discriminating weapon. The problem is not so much with their battlefield deployment as with their use as cheap cross-border assassination tools.

But drones do take much away in the way of human judgment. Woods highlights this with a study by Lawrence Lewis of the Center for Naval Analyses who, after analysing classified data from U.S. airstrikes carried out in Afghanistan from mid-2010 to mid-2011, concluded that drone attacks were 10 times more likely to result in civilian casualties than attacks by non-remotely controlled aircraft.

Cockburn cites instances in which, during combat operations in Afghanistan, pilots flying A10s showed better judgment in the heat of battle than drone operators did from the safety of their air-conditioned trailers in the Nevada desert.

Drones also place a certain emotional distance between the target and the executioner that seems to make killing easier. The military further eases moral constraints by assigning dehumanizing labels such as MAM ("military-aged males"), which turns a whole category of humans into acceptable targets. The dangers were made dramatically clear in a *New York Times* revelation that the Obama administration had "embraced a disputed method for counting civilian casualties" that, according to several administration officials, "in effect counts all military-age males in a strike zone as combatants ... unless there is explicit intelligence posthumously proving them innocent."

Cockburn highlights this empathy deficit with the aforementioned Uruzgan incident. Thanks to a subsequent investigation, we have access to the transcripts of the chatter among the operators that preceded the killing of the family. The attitude is not just cavalier; it is callous.

Pilot: Our screeners are currently calling 21 MAMs, no females, and two possible children. How copy?

Jaguar 25: Roger, and when we say children, are we talking teenagers or toddlers?

Sensor: I would say about 12. Not toddlers; something more towards adolescents or teens.

Pilot: Yeah, adolescents.

Apparently satisfied with the assessment that the children were "not toddlers," drone operators continued with the strike. A little while later, all the "adolescents" were dead.

These deaths weren't unusual. As Woods notes, in Iraq, the U.S. had set the non-combatant casualty value (NCV) at 30—i.e., US forces could carry out an operation as long as it killed no more than 30 civilians. For an NCV higher than 30, an attack would require the personal authorisation of the secretary of defence. Cockburn notes that according to General Michael Moseley, then-vice chief of staff of the U.S. Air Force, such authority was sought on at least 50 occasions after the invasion—and not once denied. The first successful attack of the drone war killed Al Qaeda deputy Mohammed Atef along with his seven companions; it also killed 100 others.

DRONES: LESS MESSY THAN JAIL

But nowhere has the administration's policy been more cynical than in its adoption of assassinations as a less messy alternative to detention. On several occasions, according to Woods (and corroborated by journalists Mark Mazzetti and Daniel Klaidman), the administration has avoided the political complications of detaining terrorism suspects by having them killed instead.

As a former law professor, Obama is perhaps conscious that the Geneva conventions forbid torture under any circumstances but permit killing in war. Killing is his way of pre-empting fraught questions of detention, jurisdiction and torture.

But Woods reveals an even more disturbing reality: "One former officer with ISAF later recounted for the author an incident in which an Afghan suspected insurgent was being held in custody. It was decided that, while there was not enough evidence to hold the man, there were suitable grounds to assassinate him."

The CIA, Woods argues, implicated the administration in its assassination policy early, making it impossible for it to disavow it without incriminating itself. But if the CIA is cynical, the administration is hardly blameless. Bush had restored the CIA's license to kill, but Obama formalized and expanded it.

'Never seen, never known, never hated'

In their different ways, Woods and Cockburn have made important contributions to a subject that is otherwise mired in secrecy, disinformation and polemical excess. To be sure, Cockburn has sharp polemical chops, but his witticisms don't come at the expense of facts. He takes a more historically informed view and adds substantial original reporting to it.

Woods, by contrast, takes a more focused approach: His book is perhaps the most comprehensive and scrupulous treatment of the subject. (Though it also is overly cautious, sometimes to a fault. For example, on the two occasions he mentions casualties of the Iraq War, he ignores extensive peer-reviewed surveys in favour of the methodologically dubious, establishment-friendly Iraq Body Count figures).

For students of the subject, both books are indispensable; but for citizens concerned with the political and humanitarian consequences of the drone war, Woods, with his systematic approach, will prove more useful. Meanwhile, as the U.S. monopoly on drones slips, the menace is likely to grow. Benjamin Netanyahu has already embraced U.S. rationales in carrying out drone strikes in Gaza and overseas in the Sinai and the Sudan. But the tortured rationales that were offered for U.S. drone assassinations will look even less convincing once a leader like Vladimir Putin adopts them.

It is perhaps time to visit the warning (quoted by Cockburn) that Vietnam War veteran Eric Herter had issued at an anti-war soldiers' meeting in Boston long before the age of drones:

The new forms of war that are to replace the unpopular struggle of infantry and patrol against guerrilla bands ... This new war will not produce My Lais. It will be a war not of men at arms, but of computers and weapons systems against whole populations. Even the tortured bond of humanity between enemies at war will be eliminated. Under its auspices, the people of the villages have gone from being "gooks" and "dinks" to being grid-coordinates, blips on scan screens, dots of light on infrared film. They are never seen, never known, never even hated. ... It is hard to feel responsible for this type of war, even for those who were close to it. There is little personal involvement. The atrocity is the result of a chain of events in which no man plays a single decisive part."

With decision-making obscured by procedural secrecy, and with public censure pre-empted by disinformation, moral constraints on killing are lifted. The act of killing becomes casual, even banal. Responsibility is deferred. If there is any lesson to be drawn from these books, it's that transparency is the necessary first step to repairing chains of responsibility and ensuring accountability.

NATURE OF TARGETS BY DRONE

The approach that the Obama administration has taken to identify the targets of drone strikes is also new and stands in stark contrast with the American approach during previous armed conflicts. According to the law of armed conflict, the identification of a target in an armed conflict involves a positive determination of their conflict status – i.e., whether that individual serves as a direct combatant, such as a soldier, in a recognised armed conflict. This determination, supported by both state practice and customary international law, involves designating as a combatant all those involved in combatant armies, even those not directly fighting, with the exception of religious and medical personnel. In classical interstate wars, this is a relatively straightforward determination as the combatant is typically clothed as a soldier, carries some clear national identification, and is participating in conflict in a direct way. In these cases, states are not generally required to pinpoint the precise identity of an individual before targeting them, but they are required to determine if their actions are materially related to the armed conflict before attacking. They are also not required to provide combatants with access to legal process if they are in *hors d'combat*, but they must treat them as a privileged combatant and accord them prisoner of war status if captured.

For irregular wars, the designation of combatant status has always been more complex. The chief problem with these conflicts is that insurgents and other irregular fighters have often not been clothed or self-identified as combatants. For many insurgent groups, blurring their combatant status by hiding amidst the civilian population has allowed them to fight a stronger power and exploit the fact that governments are obliged to use force with the principle of distinction, avoiding civilian casualties if at all possible. Nevertheless, Article 4 of the Third Geneva Convention requires governments to accord to these irregular fighters prisoner of war status if they fulfil the following conditions: (1) that of being commanded by a person responsible for his subordinates; (2) that of having a fixed distinctive sign recognisable at a distance; (3) that of carrying arms openly; (4) that of conducting their operations in accordance with the laws and customs of war. During the Vietnam War, the US generally applied the Geneva Conventions to the Viet Cong forces and accorded captured insurgents humane treatment, though not always full prisoner of war status. During the Bush administration, the US adopted a different approach and unsuccessfully advanced the argument that al-Qaeda and Taliban members were unlawful combatants because they failed to fulfil these conditions and should not enjoy trial by jury in civilian courts. Their argument – that unlawful combatants should be tried by military tribunals at Guantanamo Bay and elsewhere – was ultimately rejected by the Supreme Court.

The Obama administration has confronted similar problems with its drones programme. Many of the targets of drones do not wear uniforms and are part-time combatants, fighting at one moment but engaging in peaceful civilian activities at the next. The fact that many insurgent and terrorist groups do not have a clear command structure or distinction between political and military leaders produces a series of important moral dilemmas. Many facilities and vehicles used by insurgents are dual use: they are used for military activity at one moment, and for combat at another. Even more so than guerrillas during the Cold War, today's insurgents are embedded in the civilian population, intermixing with them in ways that make analytically separating combatants and civilians difficult, if not impossible, in some cases. How governments can justly and carefully fight non-state actors, while maintaining the principle of distinction and not slipping into the barbarism that its abandonment would imply, is a key question that any government facing insurgent warfare in the twenty-first century must answer.

The Obama administration has acknowledged these problems but has maintained that the difficulties associated with identifying combatants in today's messy intra-state wars should not be an insurmountable barrier against using drones for targeted killings. It insists that the monitoring technology associated with its drones allows operators to abide by the principle of distinction and carefully distinguish between combatants and civilians. Koh has argued that the American drone strike programme easily meets the international humanitarian law requirements of necessity, distinction and proportionality. On the question of necessity, the US has consistently argued that it is legally permitted to attack members of al-Qaeda and the Taliban as irregular combatants because they are engaged in a protracted armed conflict with the US. For distinction and proportionality, the Obama administration has insisted that it has carefully avoided civilian casualties and abided by the principle of proportionality in its drone strikes, killing relatively few civilians compared to other available military means.President Obama has admitted that some civilian casualties are inevitable with drone strikes, but has insisted that reports of high levels of civilian casualties are overstated. From an ethical vantage point, the Obama administration argues that the drones programme is humane in that it kills relatively few civilians, all of whom would be covered under the principle of double effect given the military necessity of the strikes.

Yet the Obama administration's arguments both presume, and are dependent upon, a novel definition of the nature of the enemy not widely accepted by the international community. Recognising the problems associated with the Bush approach, the Obama administration has expanded the definition of the target in a way which avoids the difficulties associated with using the terms illegal or enemy combatants. In 2009, the Attorney General announced the Obama administration was abandoning the term 'enemy combatant' while reaffirming its broad powers to fight and detain terrorist suspects. This allowed the Obama administration to avoid many of the legal headaches that the Bush administration experienced with that definition, although in practice it meant little for those held as prisoners in Guantanamo Bay. At the same time, the Obama administration advanced, without fanfare, a more expansive definition of the potential targets of American military action than President Bush articulated. First, the Obama administration rejected the notion that it was limited to striking only al-Qaeda and the Taliban and insisted that it could also target 'associated forces'. Although the AUMF language requires some connection be drawn to the 11 September attacks or that the enemy be at the least a co-belligerent of al-Qaeda and the Taliban, the Obama administration has in practice attacked groups linked to al-Qaeda or the Taliban in a variety of indirect, often immaterial, ways. These 'associated forces' are not precisely defined by the US government and in practice have ranged from Pakistani Taliban to even Somali militants. All are now considered co-belligerents of al-Qaeda under the Obama approach. In effect, it has drawn a functional equivalence between 'associated forces' and 'co-belligerents', thus providing legal cover to strike a growing array of targets. It has used this expansive definition of the enemy to target the Islamic State in Iraq and Syria (ISIS), which was expelled from al-Qaeda in February 2014 and had no contemporary organisational link to it. In fact, its authorisation for the Iraq operation declared that ISIS was a successor to al-Qaeda, and thus it can be considered a co-belligerent, a determination now also supported by the UN. Its expansive interpretation of 'associated forces' or 'co-belligerents' is also not public, as the US refuses to make the list of what it considers an associated force of al-Qaeda or the Taliban public. While the Pentagon maintains that a target must be defined as a co-belligerent of al-Qaeda or the Taliban, it does not specify how an actor operating far outside a recognised theater of conflict (Afghanistan) can be considered a co-belligerent of an actor in that conflict. While there is a plausible case that transnational terrorist groups could be considered co-belligerents even if they are not physically co-located with a combatant, the legal standard for making that determination remains a mystery. By equating the term 'associated force' with 'co-belligerent', the Obama administration has enabled itself to attack any group operating in the same radical Islamist milieu as al-Qaeda by deeming it an 'associated force'.

Second, the Obama administration has adopted vague language about a group being 'linked' to a recognised combatant group without explaining exactly what that link is. If the linkage was material support, that connection could be considered relatively obvious as a group supplying weapons or key equipment to a fighting group could be considered a combatant under the normal interpretation of the laws of war. Equally, groups that are fighting alongside an original combatant – for example, the Haqqani network and the Islamic Movement of Uzbekistan (IMU) in Afghanistan – could plausibly be considered a combatant, and hence a target, under international law. Yet the administration has acted in ways that suggest that the linkage could consist of purely ideological or political support for al-Qaeda or the Taliban, rather than direct material support. For example, the Obama administration has reportedly used drone strikes to target elements of al-Shabaab in Somalia without specifying how it is materially linked to the original combatants in Afghanistan and Pakistan. Similarly, some Pakistani Islamist groups have been targeted on the basis of a tangential connection to al-Qaeda or the Taliban. This administration's expansive definition of linkage allows for many possible connections, even political or ideological links, to be sufficient to make a group 'linked' to al-Qaeda and hence targetable.

Third, the Obama administration has adopted a policy of engaging in periodic signature strikes, directing drone strikes against training camps and compounds which were suspected of harbouring militants. These strikes are premised on the basis that the patterns of behaviour of the potential target are sufficient to indicate that they intended to engage in combat against American or local allied forces.

Critics have argued that signature strikes carry with them a greater risk of civilian casualties than so-called personality strikes, as the risk of false positives – that is, a mistaken identification of a target – is greater in these cases. This approach may also fall below the standard for distinction that is required under international law, as it is generally accepted that the person launching the strikes must be certain, within reason, that the activity witnessed is materially aiding the enemy's military effort.

Conducted at a substantial remove from the actual target, signature drone strikes do not always achieve that standard and can fall afoul of the principle of proportionality, depending on the nature of the target and what they appear to be doing. For example, striking people simply because they were moving towards a conflict zone, or stopping at a rest area known to be used by al-Qaeda, is insufficient as grounds for a signature strike. Although he did not mention signature strikes by name, President Obama promised to employ a higher standard for drone strikes, which would eliminate many of these strikes, after his May 2013 speech. It remains unclear whether this has taken place, although drone strikes in Pakistan and Yemen declined sharply after that speech.

AFTER DRONES: THE INDELIBLE MARK OF AMERICA'S REMOTE CONTROL WARFARE

Nabila's favorite memories of her grandmother come from weddings. It didn't matter who was getting married – relative or neighbor – her grandmother, Mamana, was an active participant, owing to her matriarchal perch above their village. Mamana was as responsible as she was festive. An uneducated woman, she was the local midwife, and served as an impromptu primary care physician, even a veterinarian, when the need arose.

On a fall afternoon in 2012, Mamana called Nabila and a squad of her siblings and cousins outside to the family's okra fields, part of their sprawling garden in tribal Pakistan. It was about to be the Eid festival and the Rehman family needed to gather and prepare vegetables. Nabila, nine years old, had set to work when the drone fired its missiles.

A dark plume of dust rose from the garden and mixed with acrid smoke. It spared Nabila and the other children the sight of their grandmother's mutilated corpse.

Her older cousins, all male, ran to help the screaming children. Nabila's hand and her arm were injured with burns and shrapnel. Her three-year-old brother, Safdar, who was watching the harvest from the roof of their home, had fallen to the ground, breaking bones in his chest and shoulders. The teenagers had gotten Nabila and some of the others out of the way when the second round of missiles hit, in what the CIA refers to as a "double-tap", to make sure it kills its targets.

Because US drone strikes are cloaked in secrecy, occur in remote or dangerous locales and target people presumed to be terrorists, Americans rarely hear from survivors or their relatives. But a theme emerges in interviews the Guardian has conducted with more than half a dozen drone survivors: the pain from the strike never ends, as the apparatus of secrecy renders closure unobtainable.

According to six people in Pakistan and Yemen who have lost their brothers, sons and grandparents to drone strikes, the strike lasts a moment and the consequences last a lifetime. Most of them have never told their stories to an American reporter. Some of them have theories about whom the US was targeting, while others are left guessing. The interviews were facilitated by the human rights group Reprieve and the Foundation for Fundamental Rights and conducted in translation.

The people are left impoverished, anguished and infuriated. Justice, let alone apologies, never arrives, even as a modest amount of blood money flows from the local governments. The United States, which styles itself a force for justice in the world, is to them the remote force that introduced death into their lives and treats them like they are subhuman, fit only to be targeted. At any moment, they fear, another drone could come for them.

The White House has said it will soon release of a tally of drone deaths. Relatives of the dead and survivors of the attacks expect little of it to include the truth, and doubt it will lead to the public apologies they desire – particularly since a senior aide to Barack Obama recently told the Atlantic that the president "has not had a second thought about drones".

The CIA would not comment for this piece. An Obama administration official said: "It is certainly not the case that lives of a certain nationality are more valuable to us than those of any other. What is true, however, is that the president has said ... that the American people need information to hold their government accountable. That is in part why we have been especially transparent when it comes to the deaths of US citizens."

Nabila's father, and Mamana's son, Rafiq ur-Rehman, took a different view. "If America kills any westerner, one of their own, white people, they apologize and compensate. But if it's Pakistanis like us, they don't care. In my opinion, America treats us worse than animals."

7

The Military Intelligence Function in Future War

The *Indian Army Doctrine* accepts Intelligence as "an addition to the widely accepted principles of war because of its pre-eminence in any future conflict." This clearly brings out the great emphasis placed on this function by the military and rightly so in light of India's historical experience of both success and shortcomings. Instances of inadequacy include the 1947 tribal bid for Kashmir even as India remained sanguine with its Standstill Agreement. The surprises of 1962 and the Kargil War are examples. The materialisation of an additional armoured division in the 1965 War on the Pakistani orbat was also unexpected. This has been the case with Operations Other than War also such as the limitations in tactical intelligence in the Golden Temple and Jaffna battles.

Consensus on future wars being that they would be short and lethal, the luxury of time and resources to regain the initiative lost due to faulty intelligence would not exist. Therefore, to prevent history from repeating itself, there is a need to incorporate the additional and fresh areas of intelligence interest brought on by the asymmetric and nuclear dimensions of future conflict. This commentary dilates on the implications of these features of conflict on the intelligence function in future conflict.

The foremost lesson of recent conflicts is that irregulars would form part of the opposition armies in hostile territory. This is not a new phenomenon given Napoleon's experience in Spain and later in Russia. But the dimension has changed exponentially since the Iraqi and al Qaeda challenge to US stabilisation operations in Iraq War II. Even the Israelis faced an unconventional foe in both their recent forays into Lebanon and Gaza. The 'lessons learnt' of both armies needs critical study, not necessarily for replication since their way of war is very different, but incorporation of best practices suitably modified for Indian conditions.

Since conventional conflict may arise in fairly short order in case of a punitive Indian response to future 26/11 type situations, it behoves its military to ready itself for these. Implementation of the 'Cold Start' strategy may involve broad front offensives to limited depth. These would not only be contested by defenders but their action will be supplemented by employment of irregulars as force multipliers. In which case, the military needs to employ its intelligence resources as also task the Research and Analysis Wing to spot possible prior preparations and the latent networks that would be activated. Pakistan has not only promised an unconventional counter but is also known to have trained fighters for the purpose. Areas such as southern Punjab in Pakistan, in which may figure future military objectives, have of late inclined towards fundamentalism. Across the Line of Control, numbers of irregulars familiar with the terrain and irregular methods can be expected to be much more. Thus, cannon fodder would be readily available to complicate India's offensives and its immediate and longer term aftermath.

In addition, a sociological profile of prospective areas of offensive thrusts needs to be built up so that the occupation for howsoever brief a duration is successfully conducted. This effort would help in countering insurgency during stabilisation operations and fulfilling the duties of an occupying power. Follow on forces tasked to restore order in the communication zone need to have personnel with language skills and training in psychological war.

Next, since perception management is an intelligence function, the intelligence community would require formulating responses to likely scenarios that would develop. These include putting the lid on collateral damage that would be inevitable both in developed terrain and in the heavily populated Line of Control and explaining the benefits of cooperation. The Israeli discourse in the wake of the Goldstone Report may have pointers. It is a separate matter that the Report would be more useful reading for those conducting operations, particularly on the imperative of fighting within the laws of armed conflict; the instrumental logic being that lesser collateral damage would mean quicker stabilisation and easier the temporary occupation.

The second expanded dimension of the intelligence function is nuclear related. An interesting aspect here is that while in peacetime nuclear information security is equivalent to security of crown jewels, in war there would be a need for an element of transparency on both sides. This is because of the need to reassure the enemy against any move towards pre-emption. The requirements of nuclear signalling may also necessitate a deliberate showing of one's hand. This could be for instance done by discreetly displaying a heightened nuclear alert status.

Intelligence agencies would require awareness of the nuances of this game in order that the intelligence assets are suitably tasked to search for and pick up the required information. This means a degree of integration between military intelligence, RAW and NTRO doing this overseen by the JIC, NSCS and the HQs, Strategic Forces Command. Given that nuclear decision making would be a high tension exercise in real time, less ambiguity would make for rational decision making. This aspect needs inclusion in exercises involving multiple agencies and war gaming of the staff and decision makers.

Arriving at an understanding with and networking foreign intelligence agencies on this score would be crucial, given that the United States in particular is known to have privileged access to information. The channel can also be used for making escalation pressures recede. Such interaction would be particularly useful in case of a face off against China. While technical means are improving, their system would be considerably more impervious. Therefore, assistance from foreign intelligence agencies could help. This obviously requires to be pre-programmed.

The problem would be less with collection of information than with analysis. For instance, if preparation for missile launch has been picked up, it cannot by default be taken as nuclear related. Likewise, detecting a change in nuclear alert status should not trigger pressures for pre-emption. Alarming instances of misreading information occurred during the Cold War. Some analysts opine that this is accentuated in the South Asian setting in which technology is less capable and flight times are shorter. Coping with these problems require being sensitive to the possibility as a first step.

More importantly, given that non-state actors can have an autonomous agenda, an accurate reading of the source of a strike would be critical in determining the violence of response. The 'insider-outsider' threat to the Pakistani nuclear complex has been in evidence over the past few years. It bears recall here that India's No First Use is liable to be reconsidered in case of a 'major' attack by chemical and biological weapons also. The link to state sponsorship of terrorist action as exploding a radiological device would require to be discerned for appropriate response.

The nuclear intelligence dimension needs special effort at foregrounding in India. This owes to the possibility of being lulled into a false sense of complacency by two oft-repeated views. One is that nuclear weapons are political weapons. Second is that the Pakistani threshold is likely to be a high enough for India to prosecute conventional military operations, albeit informed by the Limited War concept. That the nuclear initiative would be with Pakistan, which may think differently, is a sobering thought. The scenario of the Cold Start offensives overstepping predetermined lines in the fog of war is a case in point. Therefore, alert intelligence and competent analysis is vital in order that Indian forces do not inadvertently nudge the nuclear threshold. Picking up signals of nuclear preparation can help in timely reversing of provocative military action and in establishing communication and contact with the opposite side to defuse in-conflict nuclear crisis. For the greater good, incidental exposure of the source of the information should not come in way of preventive action.

Intelligence from own potential nuclear targets needs to be accurate. For instance, in case an air field is hit, there is bound to be collateral damage to the urban centre in the vicinity. How this is viewed – as a counter value or counter military strike – could influence if not determine the nature of the counter. Even as India's deterrence doctrine promises 'unacceptable damage' in retaliation, conflict strategy could instead be a measured one, since escalation is undesirable. Reporting the nature of nuclear damage suffered under emotive conditions needs specially emplaced and practiced measures. The existing system of military and civil reporting channels can be supplemented by the network of the National Disaster Management Authority.

It is possible that the intelligence leg of officer courses and pedagogy in the intelligence school is already cognisant of this expansion in the intelligence function. Nevertheless, the reemphasis done is useful given the military's propensity to focus on the conventional level in any discussion of war. The subconventional and nuclear levels being equally salient in future conflict, a conscious effort is required to expand the focus to include these levels. In any case, the nuclear dimension of intelligence warrants a deeper look.

IMPOSITION OF AN ASYMMETRIC WAR

We are aware that the concept of 'asymmetry' is as old as warfare itself. Military commanders down the ages have invested in manipulating the rules of armed engagement in a manner as to generate tactical advantages of their strengths while exploiting the adversary's limitations. Obviously, it is usual to impose *asymmetry* upon the opponent by fielding greater numbers of troops and weaponry.

However, history teaches us that there are other ingenuous ways – some tangible (quantitative, technological, logistic) and others intangible (qualitative, tactical, psychological) - to achieve that end . The PLA too, faced with prospects of conflict with the all-powerful US military forces on the Taiwan issue, has been propagating her version of asymmetric warfare - she illustrates the idea by a dramatic description : *"Assasin's Mace".*

In view of the PLA's overwhelming military superiority, the recourse adopted by the Indian armed forces must aim at finding strategic and tactical ingenuity to negate the advantages of such superiority. The point to ponder here is that can such a recourse be in the realm of possibility? The answer is offered by what one of our finest generals had to state. Writing for the 'Seminar' in early 1962, General Thimmayya stated :

"I cannot ... envisage India taking on China in an open conflict on its own. China's present strength ... exceeds our resources a hundred fold, ...we could not hope to match China in the foreseeable future... .

The country is a mass of mountains right up to the highest ridges of the Himalayas. The passes are practically impossible for over six months except for the men and animals, and that too with difficulty. China is, therefore, deprived of the use of its overwhelming superiority ... . This is where we should make full use of our manpower and light equipment ... .

If the Chinese attack us with the intention of recovering territory which they believe to be theirs, we must meet them in those regions with commandos and highly equipped and fast moving infantry. If the Chinese penetrate the Himalayas ... , we must be in a position to take advantage of our superior fire power and manoeuvrability to defeat them and at the same time continue to harass their lines of communications by the use of commandos and guerrillas ...".

Of course, the General was thinking of fighting a war that played mismatch to PLA's tactical strengths while permitting exposure of its vulnerabilities .

Let us then examine certain core aspects of strategic asymmetry in the Sino-Indian context. We may begin with the fundamental factor of war: terrain.

Leveraging the Terrain

We are aware of the much lamented 'tactical advantages' enjoyed by the PLA on the open Tibetan Plateau. But we are also conscious of the fact that every item of PLA's war wherewithal on the Indo-Tibet frontline must be carted over 1500 kilometers from their logistic hubs at Lhasa and Kashgarh, which in turn must be stocked from central China, a further 2000 kilometers away. The entire logistic connectivity by road, rail, pipeline and air depends upon tenuous lines of communication and static staging yards, all situated over a terrain that is completely open, devoid of local resources and subject to such extreme conditions as it must obtain at 4300 meters of average altitude and sub-zero cold almost throughout the year. Even if China has engineered her transportation capacity to 24000 tons a day and therefore stated to be able to build up 30 divisions, including formations already in place, in 30 days, and sustain this force in war indefinitely, such theoretical calculations may be valid under 'test conditions', in practice this will invariably not be so. No doubt, the whole system of induction and sustenance for PLA's field forces in war would be ripe for interdiction by air power and special operations.

On the Indian side, the terrain south of the 4300 to 5400 meter high Himalayan passes, constricted and snow-bound most of the year, is characterised by razor-sharp ridgelines, steep slopes and narrow, gorge-like valleys generally running North to South. The Indian logistic installations are between 350 to 400 kilometers in depth, and therefore, in terms of turn around time, comparable to that of the PLA in Tibet. Road axes connecting Indian foothills to the Indo-Tibet Border, being aligned more or less along the narrow valley floors, are extremely difficult to interdict by air or ground fire; these are targetable only in some stretches and even then require super-skills, high-technology and load of chance to score effective hits. Notably, scope exists to make such hits even more ineffective by means of modern methods of camouflage, deception and repair.

To undertake offensive operations in such terrain, PLA formations have to confine to constricted valleys that are hemmed-in by successive ridge lines, thus limiting the scope for tactical level lateral manoeuvre. At the operational level, axes of offensive have to remain isolated from each other, while envelopment and turning movement, besides inviting risks of entrapment, would entail such heavy logistic back up as to be prohibitive in terms of resources and time. Further, some distance down the Southern slopes into Indian territory, the terrain closes down to subsume the advantages that heavy weaponry and high-technology might bring to PLA's offensive. Indeed, the ground is heavily biased towards defensive operations - if conducted with aggressive intent.

We have reasons to believe that mother earth has not been overly supportive of aggression from Tibetan Plateau across the Himalayan Passes into India. Indeed, any PLA offensive across the Indo-Tibet Border has to contend with an adverse terrain anomaly: its build-up and spring-board areas straddle a ground that exposes its war machine to disruption by inhospitable elements as well as air and ground attack, while its offensive across the watershed passes would be beleaguered by a ground that favours classically conducted defensive operations. Indeed, PLA's offensive across the passes would have to fight *'friction of terrain'* and *'tension of logistics'* before engaging Indian forces - with *"General Snow"* ever ready to cut off its lifeline. Therefore, even if the PLA commits overwhelming number of formations to its offensives, as to how many of these could actually be employable - along limited, narrow axes, and against successive lines of defences, remains a moot point to consider. China's declaration of unilateral ceasefire in 1962 may be seen in this light.

Only if Indian leadership had not lost its nerve and continued the state of war, matters would have been different.

PLA's Susceptibilities

With superior weaponry, missile arsenal, airborne forces, reconnaissance, communication, navigational and logistic capabilities, all of which are under continuous modernisation, we are well aware of PLA's overwhelming superiority over the Indian Armed Forces. Yet, the current state of Sino-India peace will be better fostered by factoring China's innate vulnerabilities in order to devise an affordable military deterrence.

Firstly, the 'hawks' in the Chinese establishment do not seem to be able to hide their hegemonic instincts till completion of the last phase of her 'four modernisations', as Deng Xioaping had advised. They have already started repudiating international norms on diplomatic, territorial, proliferation, economic and human rights issues. Reinforced with her past record of inciting trouble in the neighbourhood, this development has caused China to be seen as a predatory threat by most of her neighbours. In fact, the undercurrent of wariness of China's military build up is already evident by signs of emergence of common-cause groupings among the Austro-Asian nations - with US participation. Possibly therefore, India's joint military exercises could gradually be elevated to the status of 'military co-operation' and bonded by a corresponding diplomatic understanding. The wise Chinaman certainly realises that in the contemporary international dispensation, such grouping among her target countries cannot be to her advantage. May be that consideration would curb her militaristic urge.

Secondly, build up and war logistics of the PLA could be vulnerable to severe disruptions in Tibet. If they can be rebellious even when under the grip of a ruthless state, the discontented Uyghurs in the North-West and Tibetans in the South-East could also play a highly debilitating role on PLA's war-effort. Indian Army could leverage this vulnerability of the PLA by means of direct as well as indirect attacks on its rear echelons and thereby choking sustainability of its offensive across the watershed.

Thirdly, even as the modernisation programme imparts quantum empowerment to the PLA, there are intrinsic vulnerabilities too. Having propagated the doctrines of *"Informationalisation"* and *"War Zone Campaign"*, it has embarked upon adaptation of unfamiliar and complex concepts and practices of warfare. Therefore, its transition from a manpower intensive, low technology 'people's army' to a modern army of high-technology, heavy weaponry and logistic-intensive formations cannot be free of complex glitches. The fact that its military leadership is relatively inexperienced and yet untested against spirited opposition, adds to the PLA's burden. These vulnerabilities could afford opportunities to topple PLA's apple cart in the fog of war.

Fourthly, China is at a stage of 'wannabe superpower', when she is precariously open to losing her way by even stray developments, internal or external. Therefore, a conflict that fails to conclude with clear victory within a specified time frame will entail a serious setback to China's standing. Then there is the tactical vulnerability of the Chumbi Valley as well as across the passes in North Sikkim, Kailash Range and Aksai Chin, which present opportunities of potent riposte. Even if limited, such reverses can besmirch PLA's success elsewhere. Therefore, in a period when people's perceptions count, China may be wary of adopting military recourse against a resilient adversary. The complex concoction of time, terrain, counter-tactics and perceptions would not be easy for the PLA to tame in her adventure across the Indo-Tibet Border.

It may be noteworthy that the nuclear angle does not figure in the preceding discussion. This is deliberate. Firstly, because the nuclear doctrine espoused by both China and India - that of 'No First Use' - precludes any nuclear exchange. Secondly, should China circumvent her stated position, there is little India can do about it besides retaliation in kind to the extent of her arsenal; and then the script would be different. Lastly, beyond committing soldiers to conduct nuclear drills, Indian policy-makers have not mandated the military institution to nuclear warfare. Therefore, the Indian military hierarchy may not concern itself with what has been deliberately kept out of its orbit as a matter of higher policy of the government. The preceding discussion leads to the observation that if not diverted from the verve of military preparations, it should be possible for India to build up credible deterrence against military attack by China to settle the contentious border issue. The question, however, is that how may that goal be secured?

FUTURE OF THE ARMY AVIATION CORPS

The army is currently evaluating helicopters from Kamov, Eurocopter and AgustaWestland for the 197 light helicopter contract for lifting supplies for the troops stationed at high altitudes. The $750 million deal for the 197 helicopters for the defence forces aims to replace the aging 1970s-vintage Chetak and Cheetah helicopters and will be for high altitude, surveillance and logistics. The successful bidder will provide 60 helicopters in a flyaway condition, while the remaining 137 aircraft will be licence-produced by Hindustan Aeronautics Limited (HAL). Under the offsets clause, the winning bidder must also invest at least 30% of the contracted cost in India. In December 2014, Kamov Ka-226T was selected for the role of Light Utility Helicopter and as an initial replacement for Obsolete Chetak and Cheetah, while the LUH is under development. Kamov would set up a production plant in India and around 197 would be procured under the "Make in India" program.

The army is also planning to acquire HAL Light Combat Helicopter, which is under development by the Hindustan Aeronautics Limited to meet its requirements for an attack helicopter which can operate at high altitude (16,300 feet) to fit into an anti-armour and anti-infantry role. The army is also planning to acquire a 3-tonne single-engine HAL Light Utility Helicopter which is also under development for recce and observation role. As of 2007 the Army Aviation Corps modernisation plans were:

Other future acquisition plans are:

- Reconnaissance and surveillance helicopters – HAL Dhruv will replace the existing fleet of Cheetah and Chetak helicopters. While some helicopters will be procured as 'Buy' category, others will be 'Designed and Developed' by HAL as 'Make' category. RFP for the former has been issued and the procurement was likely to commence soon.
- Tactical Battle Support Helicopter - This is being developed as a tri-services project by HAL. The helicopter will be called Indian Multi Role Helicopter. By 2007 the procurement process had already been "set into motion" for battle support helicopters. These machines should be capable of carrying 10–12 men into the battlefield.
- Special operations squadron - A special operations squadron is being raised to provide dedicated integral aviation support to the Para Commandos (India).
- Heli-borne early-warning – Raising of a heli-borne early warning flight has been planned for employing electronic warfare.
- The government of India, on 2 July 2014, approved purchase of 39 Apache helicopters.
- Light fixed-wing aircraft – The army is also planning to induct light fixed-wing aircraft in future for surveillance and communication tasks.
- DRDO Imperial Eagle

THE STRUCTURAL CHALLENGES OF THE INDIAN DEFENCE SECTOR

Through this seminal account, Dr. Harsh Pant brings in a diverse set of scholars who take the understanding of India's defense policy beyond the conventional understanding which hitherto restricted its focus to the armed forces and took India's independence as a starting point for evolution of military policies. The scholarship Dr. Pant engages with, presents a multidimensional analysis consisting of the social, historical, structural and doctrinal issues which have guided the evolution and development of India's defense policy.

Soldier, State and Society in India

The chapter gives an elaborate account of the fundamental structure of Indian Army, which had its origins in the colonial era. Specifically, the book explains the recruitment policies of the British, based on the myth of 'martial races' (according to which only certain classes were fit to fight).

In the post-independence period, the civil- military relations were heavily skewed in favor of the former as Prime Minister Nehru was skeptical of military domination owing to his leanings towards liberal democratic institutions where a civilian supremacy was the norm. The hierarchical arrangement of civilian authority over the armed forces has its own complexities which have led to simmering tensions between them. Conflicting objectives between these domains have presented themselves in a wide variety of contexts ranging from wars, secessionist movements, developing nuclear doctrines, organizing a strategic culture and instituting defense reforms. Each of the above mentioned points is intricately as well as critically discussed to give an insight regarding the challenges which the armed forces have faced in their transition from a colonial to a post-colonial era.

The Services—Indian Army

The army is faced with a twin challenge of maintaining the internal as well as external security. Additionally, the emergence of a nuclear Pakistan has undermined the conventional superiority of the army which was evident with the Pakistan's Kargil venture in 1999.

The domestic arena has kept the Indian army more occupied where it has faced insurgencies ever since the days of independence, first in the north-east, then in Punjab and finally in Kashmir. In the present times, the army is occupied in its counter insurgency operations in the Kashmir region, which took a violent turn in early 1990s and continues to challenge the state till date. Here, the book sheds light on problems such as an over-emphasis on internal security which is seen as something regressive for the army, but it should be realized that at this moment, there is no alternative to the army as the police and the paramilitary forces still operate sub optimally, which the book explains later.

Indian Navy

The Indian Navy's role came to be recognized in the 1971 Indo-Pak war when its operations in the twin fronts of West and East Pakistan led to a decisive Indian victory. With the realization of its crucial role, the year's post 1971 witnessed a massive modernization and expansion of the naval infrastructure.

The end of Cold war reoriented the naval vision and the quest to emerge as a regional maritime powers expanded its operations across the full spectrum of Indian Ocean region (IOR), from the Horn of Africa to the Straits of Malacca.

Despite its visible presence in the region, maritime security was severely undermined during the 2008 Mumbai attacks where the attackers entered India through the Arabian Sea. Another challenge was in the years 2013-14 when a series of blasts in the ageing fleet of naval ships and submarines resulted in resignation of the then navy chief. Heavy reliance on imports is yet another issue which has to be addressed. India's growing influence as a regional power in the IOR states that it is high time that the navy is used as an effective instrument of state policy.

Indian Air Force

The Air Force is the most innovative and adaptive entity among the three services, which has been active since Kashmir dispute began in 1947 where it performed to task of transporting troops to defend Kashmir against Pakistani invasion. Though it was not used during the 1962, Sino-Indian war, its role was very effective in 1971 war. Besides this, it has been engaged in numerous missions of domestic as well as international nature including UN operations.

Despite the impressive feats achieved by each of these organizations in their individual capacity, a unified command is yet to be established, only after which an optimal and coordinated decision making will utilize the full potential of the armed forces, which still lack unity.

Doctrines

The successive wars fought by the Indian army helped shape its doctrinal evolution. Long delayed, Indian army's doctrine got released in 2004(on conventional warfare) and 2006(on sub-conventional warfare). Events like the end of Cold War, nuclearization of the Indian subcontinent, Operation Parakram and the Cold Start doctrine have heavily influenced Indian army's doctrine making and its offensive posture. However, if analyzed along with the nuclear doctrine, a disconnect appears as the nuclear policy is a political domain kept out of military influence, an anomaly which must be worked upon.

Known as the 'Iron fist in a velvet glove', the doctrine on sub-conventional warfare is principled on a humane, people centric approach but the presence extrajudicial powers with the army in conflict zones makes the role of the armed forces controversial . Further, an aggressive approach to deal with insurgency in the following doctrine of 2010 makes the people centric principles of this approach questionable. The loss of civilian lives in conflict zones cannot be ignored in this regard the accountability for such loss is yet to be established.

Regarding the navy, a key highlight about the Indian navy stated in the book is that it has seen some strategic maneuvering after the end of Cold War and has expanded its outreach considerably, especially in the crucial maritime zones of Asia and Africa. Its presence among the near as well as far flung island states indicates in form of cordial maritime relations indicates its emergence as a net security provider in the IOR. The navy is also an important element of the nuclear strategy; hence the focus on induction of Nuclear powered submarine and Submarine Launched Ballistic Missiles.

For Indian Air Force, the credit for giving it a doctrinal structure goes to Air Commodore Jasjit Singh whose works equipped the aviation strategists with the understanding of modern western air power theory and operations at a time when India opened its doors to western hardware. The air power came to be seen not as an adjunct of the land power, but a distinct entity capable of decisive action. Today, full spectrum capability (ability to carry out conventional as well as a limited air warfare) have become an integral part of Indian Air Power. However, achieving an inter dependency and a complete understanding of air power by other two forces would result in complete doctrinal evolution of the forces.

Defense and Development

India's defense budget has come a long way since the days of independence, from a meagre INR 92 crores in 1947 to a staggering INR 2.29 lakh crores in 2014. Initially not considered important, the Indian leadership was compelled to focus on defense spending after it faced the humiliating defeat in the 1962 war and a twin threat from China and Pakistan. At present, despite the high absolute numbers, the defense spending is only 1.78% of the nation's GDP for the year 2014-15, falling from 3.25% in 1988.

Noticeably, allocation to R&D has been on the rise with an emphasis on creation of a robust indigenous base. However, time and cost overruns in many projects have raised widespread criticism regarding the utilization and efficacy of the R&D sector in India. Another issue confronting the army is gross under-utilization of capital acquisition budget.

Moving on to the defense procurements, the book locates the challenges confronting this sector in the undeveloped strategic vision of India's post-colonial leadership which was opposed to India attaining a military posture. Even despite facing several wars and conflicts throughout, it took the Kargil War in 1999 to give a wakeup call to the Indian establishment to set up an organizational structure for this sector, which finally came up in 1999. Private players were invited to invest and the Defense Procurement Procedure was promulgated for capital acquisitions. The book explains structure of procurement procedures along with the shortcomings which have impeded some big ticket reforms to streamline the procurement procedure.

Security

The book takes a pan-Indian analysis of the major issues challenging India's internal security, namely the Islamic terrorism, the Naxalite movement and the insurgency in India's north-eastern states.

Islamic extremism

The Islamic extremism began in India in early 1990s when a nationwide communal polarization led to the demolition of Babri Mosque in 1992. The disenchantment among the Muslim population, along with their marginalization from mainstream representation was a ready fertile ground for Pakistan's proxy agencies to recruit youth which solved the twin objectives of carrying out destabilizing activities as well an indigenization of militancy. Groups like the Indian Mujahedeen were a creation of this network and reached its operational apogee in 2008, when several major cities across India were targeted with serial blasts.

At present, what is alarming is the reports on a possible alliance of these groups with Al-Qaeda, after its leader Ayman Al Zawahiri announced the creation of Al-Qaeda in Indian Subcontinent (AQIS) in 2014. In this regard, the book could have recommended steps for inclusion of the marginalized minorities and to dissuade them from being radicalized, as these aspects are crucially linked to national security too.

Naxal/Maoist Movement

Beginning out of a communist revolt in the state of West Bengal 1967, the Naxalite movement has made deep inroads in India's hinterland region. Its influence spans from Andhra Pradesh in South to the Indo-Nepal border in the north.

Functioning under different leaderships, the movement organized itself into a unified structure as the Communist Party of India (Maoist) in 2004. Recognizing the superiority of state's forces, the Maoist movement relies on popular mobilization strategies and guerrilla warfare which has been so powerful that fatalities due to their violent actions prompted the 'Operation Green Hunt' in 2009 to tackle this challenge.

Absence of a strategy is evident due to ad-hoc shifts in state's approach to this challenge. Added to this, a low police to people ratio, ill-equipped police and a thin presence of state's administrative apparatus complicate the situation. Here, the book rightly argues that it is also the miscarriage of justice which has fostered a popular resentment among the people, something that is a bitter reality to be accepted by the Indian establishment.

North-east India

The insurgency in India's north-east is as old as India's independence when several groups emerged demanding secession. The protracted nature of conflict in this region is due to recurring emergence of factions and new entrants, known as the 'vacuum fillers'. The states of Assam, Manipur, Nagaland and Tripura have recorded a spike in insurgent violence. However, counter insurgency efforts have been successful in Tripura due to a people centric approach and have also helped in effective intelligence gathering. This needs to be applied to other affected regions.

A significant challenge is the cross-border nature of these insurgencies where rebels have successfully used the porous borders to establish training bases in Bangladesh, Myanmar and even Bhutan. Support from Bhutanese and Bangladeshi authorities has been overwhelming and has given a blow to insurgent activities. With challenges abound, the book argues that the complacency on part of government while dealing with insurgency is detrimental to the north-east's stability.

The suggestions provided in the book to deal with these issues are very important, yet limit themselves to providing structuring solutions to these problems, which are socioeconomic in nature, and hence demand a bottom-up approach, where the civilian(and not military) establishment must play a preponderant, especially in reaching out to those placed in the lowest rungs of the society.

Institutional Infrastructure

This unit highlights the structural deficiencies which affect India's national security apparatus which primarily include an absence of a military Chief of Defense Staff (CDS) and a paucity of long term defense planning. In fact, the position of a CDS is pending since the days of its recommendation by Lord Mountbatten to the then Nehru government. Besides this, the military chiefs are hierarchically placed below the Ministry of Defense whose highest decision making committees are staffed by generalist officers from the civil services. Time and again, these deficiencies have surfaced during the war times. Moreover, the exigencies of delivering on social and economic issues in a coalition government era resulted in the Cabinet Committee on Security (the highest level decision making body on defense issues) relegating defense related decisions.

A positive development took place in the aftermath of Kargil war, following which an Integrated Defense Staff was established within the Ministry of Defense but it too became a victim of bureaucratic staffing, thereby affecting its efficiency.

The book, then explains the functioning of India's intelligence institutions since independence in light of the constant threats faced on internal as well as the external front. For instance, the R&AW's biggest achievement was its twin successes in liberating Bangladesh and raiding the Northeastern rebel hideouts operating from Chittagong Hill Tracts.

Contrary to the popular perception that intelligence failures have led India into crises, the book mentions that failure of quick response in the Kargil crisis and later the 2008 Mumbai attacks were more to do with structural failures to respond to the intelligence inputs, which were times provided by the agencies. In today's world with changing nature of threats, it is important that these agencies adopt future oriented reforms soon, but this crucial aspect doesn't receive consideration beyond mere mention. In an increasingly globalized world with rapid technological advancements, the book falls short of explaining the course of action taken by Intelligence agencies in light of the latest and most dangerous threats, which come from transnational terrorist groups (especially the ISIS) or from cyber warfare. This has blurred the internal and external dimensions of threats. How the Intel agencies plan to cooperate in addressing these threats is not mentioned. Also, in this regard, the preparedness of India's intelligence agencies to deal with the growing menace of cyber warfare is missing. This is important to highlight as along with a conventional threat of a direct confrontation, the cyber-attacks from China and Pakistan are a regular and rising phenomenon.

Indian Police

The Police in India is still dawns a colonial character, drawing from the Indian Police Act of 1861. It still functions as it did earlier to meet colonial requirements, that is, maintaining order by force. Reform committees too have fallen short of meeting these key issues. Connecting with the community, gender sensitivity, scientific investigations and formulating a concrete approach to fight insurgencies are key reforms which are required as soon as possible.

Similarly, the paramilitary forces require some crucial reforms, most importantly, achieving interoperability between various paramilitary forces for a coordinated response to future crises.

Nuclear Weapons and Space

The book takes up the crucial issue of the need for an interface between conventional and the nuclear command. Here, the domains of cooperation identified are techno-industrial, infrastructural, personnel and Command & Control, focusing on which a conventional-nuclear interface can make the defense institutions effective. Besides this, such interface also requires an oversight coordinating mechanism which can come only if a CDS is established. Another anomaly highlighted by the book is the non- involvement of military in decision making related to nuclear issue(which is under civilian control) which contributes to the already existing schism between conventional and nuclear forces.

Lastly, the book touches upon India's policy on space security and its missile defense program which are being pursued with greater concern after the realization that the space too is a strategic domain with changing technical nature of warfare.

Conclusion

Overall, the achievements as well as the challenges facing the defense policymaking are put in an elaborate framework, with a thrust on the latter. However, an overemphasis is placed on undermining Nehru's decision to make the post-independence armed forces under the civilian establishment. This decision by the Nehru led government is considered as a key factor for the continuing civil-military schisms.

What should have been realized is the immediate spatio-temporal context in which the Nehruvian regime was operating, which made the civilian authority over the army quintessential, notwithstanding its colonial origins and continuing traditions.

Besides this, in an ambitious attempt to cover each and every aspect of the defense and security domain, some of the key issues fall short of analyzing key issues with rigor, as more focus has been given on explaining their historical origins.

Because of this, analysis of future challenges has not been adequately discussed. Also, despite the book being themed upon overhauling India's defense infrastructure to meet future challenges, a quintessential challenge in the cybersecurity realm doesn't find any mention.

However on the positive side, Dr. Pant deliberately chose to focus on the challenges so that the security problems arising from the present policies can be analyzed comprehensively and a future course of action should be charted out only after having grasped these issues. The book comes at a time when the India got a full majority leadership led by Prime Minister Narendra Modi and hopes are high that the new dynamic leadership under him will implement these long delayed course corrections, which will lay a clear path for India's emergence as a formidable global power.

MODERN WARFARE: WHY THE U.S. ARMY MUST REFORM

Structural reform in the military is long overdue. Thirty years ago, when the last major overhaul of the military's structure was implemented due to the passage of the Goldwater Nichols Act, desktop computers and cell phones were largely viewed as novelty items, the Berlin Wall still stood firm, and terrorists were seen as more of a nuisance than an existential national security threat. The world has changed a lot in the past thirty years, and so has the nature of the threats faced by our military. So far, proposals to reform the military's structure to better address contemporary challenges have been focused on the service Chiefs of Staff and above. That should change, starting with a closer examination of the military's largest service, the US Army.

Structural reform, hardly the stuff of cocktail hour repartee, is finally on the agendas of our most senior civilian officials. Just last month, for example, Secretary of Defense Ashton Carter unveiled a plan to reform aspects of the military's command and control structure, and the issue is currently under discussion as Congress debates the form of the FY2017National Defense Authorization Act. One of the themes underlying these conversations is a sense that the service chiefs have been frozen out of major decisions such as acquisition and operational planning—to the detriment of the military as a whole. Another theme is that the military has become too "top-heavy"—i.e., that the sheer number of top brass is depleting valuable resources and detracting from the agility of the force.

The tone in any organization is set at the top, so it's no surprise that similar problems with inefficient decision-making, top-heavy commands, and outmoded organizational structures permeate into each of the services. The size of the Army alone provides reason to examine its structure more closely for inefficiencies. But, for a service that may be 'outmanned and outgunned' in its next war; that is shrinkingwhile the threats that it may need to address in the future continually expand, structural reform provides a way to improve the efficacy of the Army, regardless of the resource constraints that it currently faces or may face in the future.

The changing threat environment since 1986 has also drawn the role of ground forces into question more than naval, amphibious, or air-based instruments of military power. Russia's *revanche* and the ongoing conflict against ISIS notwithstanding, large land wars, a la Desert Storm or Iraqi Freedom, have become increasingly unpalatable to the civilian political class. The need for a large standing Army has thus been drawn into question, not least of all by the current administration. The Army has and is taking several steps to adapt to changing budgetary and threat environments, including undertaking projects that rethink the role of ground forces both in and out of kinetic conflict. But, so far, many of the structural problems facing the Army have received less attention.

Take the Army's decision-making process, or rather, preoccupation with process. A Center for Army Lessons Learned-issued summary of the various decision-making processes available to Army officers opens with General Patton's rejection of over-analysis: that "a good plan violently executed now is better than a perfect plan executed next week." Yet the section for "analysis" alone prescribes no fewer than fourteen labor-intensive, time-consuming steps, and not explicitly following the outlined processes is blamed as a cause of bad decision-making throughout the document. Processes are important; they are what make bureaucracies tick. But a preoccupation with process can lead to an overreliance on it, which in turn can lead to a failure to adapt.

An overemphasis on process has both strategic and tactical consequences. At the strategic level, one of the primary reasons that "grey zone" issues have proven so challenging to the US Army is that they confound traditional planning models and the doctrinaire responses tied to such frameworks. At the tactical level, the implementation of the similarly rigid "tactical decision-making process" often leads to a "single tracking" of plans, which narrows the commander's field of vision and undermines a commander's ability to respond flexibly to changing circumstances.

A top-heavy command structure exacerbates this problem. The House Armed Services Committee's draft of the 2017 NDAA recognizes the military-wide nature of this problem, but it's worth examining the Army-specific trend more closely: even though the size of the total force decreased by 39 percent between 1986 and 2016, the ratio of general and flag officers to enlisted personnel increased by 26 percent during the same period. Not only does a glut of general and flag officers furthercomplicate the decision-making process, it also reduces morale and pulls resources away from other priorities, from readiness to end strength. This problem is particularly critical as the Army continues to face cuts to its base budget and more spending is shifted to the government's new preferred flexible spending account, overseas contingency operations—very little which has gone to personnel funding in recent years.

Inefficiency is not just a function of process or of leadership. It is also a function of inputs—and the Army, like other services, has struggled to achieve an appropriate balance between different types of forces. Take, for example, the overuse of special operations forces and the comparative operational din of their conventional counterparts. The Army has done a better job of integrating best practices from special operations forces into the doctrine of the conventional force, but the roles of each could still be better delineated to reduce redundancies of effort.

The Army's underutilized reserve component provides another example of misused inputs. Though some argue that maintaining a large, educated officer corps better prepares the force to meet evolving, technology-driven threat environments, the harsh reality is that much of the expertise necessary to counter such threats is best represented in the private sector. For an all-volunteer military, the reserve component can serve a critical role in injecting new ways of thinking into a comparatively ossified bureaucracy and in providing a bridge between public and private sectors—but only if it is effectively leveraged.

Overemphasis on process, leadership bloat, and structural disjointedness each contribute to organizational inertia and detract from the ability to adapt. One thing that's needed is what is referred to in management literature as organizational "ambidexterity," in which a balance is achieved between effective organizational alignment and the ability to adapt. Because it faces many challenges at the same time, the Army must also focus on agility to improve its ability shift among threat environments with greater ease and speed.

There are several concrete steps that the Army could take to improve both ambidexterity and agility. First, it could take more seriously efforts to decentralize decision-making. Special operations units, in which many Army officers spend time at some point in their careers, generally operate with more autonomy than their conventional counterparts; there is no reason to believe that this isn't part of the recipe for their successes. The chain-of-command is sacrosanct in the Army, for good reason, but that doesn't mean that every decision needs to be made by the officer in charge, something that even the Center for Army Lessons Learned recognizes in its decision-making process guide.

Second, the Army should continue efforts to reduce the number of general and flag officers in its ranks, but it should also trim the number of layers within the chain-of-command in order to speed up and improve the decision-making process. This would improve the ability of Army leadership to make the decisions that cannot be delegated downward and free up resources for other pressing needs. And the savings wouldn't just be short-term: Because of the generous sums that retired general and flag officers collect in retirement, the benefits of reducing so-called "star creep" compound over time.

Third, the Army should foster flexibility and innovation throughout every level of its hierarchy. It should take a closer look at the concept of "modularity;" the shift from divisions to brigade combat teams should be viewed as the beginning, not the end of the conversation about how the Army's basic deployable units could become more flexible. As I've arguedelsewhere, it should take a hard look at the way special operations forces operate for lessons on how to quickly adapt to changing circumstances. It should rethink the way that it incentivizes service in the Army reserves, especially for professionals from technical, managerial, or communications backgrounds, as the sharpest skill sets in these and many other fields lie outside of the permanent bureaucracy. It should also re-think how it uses its reserve officers once they have matriculated.

The Army is not the only part of the Defense Department that is in need of internal reform to better address contemporary threats. The officer-to-enlisted ratio of the Air Force, for example, is far worse than that of the Army, and the currently proposed Defense-wide acquisition reformsarguably do not go far enough. But given the fact that the Army is currently facing, as one author bluntly put, an identity crisis, it has the opportunity to lead the way on meaningful structural reform. Pursuing greater agility, adaptability, and ambidexterity will increase the ability of the Army to face both current and future threats, regardless of what future budgets might bring.

8

A Nuclear Environment in Future Battlefields

Today, the world is in a historical period of drastic changes, the pattern of multipolar forces is taking shape, the international situation is moving toward relaxation, and peace and development have become the theme of the present world.

Therefore, we can anticipate that a new world war will not break out and nuclear warfare is avoidable. However, the world today is not trouble free, hegemony and power politics still have not withdrawn from the historical arena, the international situation is still very complicated, and the flames of war arising from local conflicts have never died out. Owing to multifarious factors, the nuclear shadow still cannot be cast away from future battlefields.

Warfare is violent action. More than 100 years ago, the capitalist strategist Clausewitz pointed out, "The use of violence knows no bounds. Therefore, a belligerent will oblige its opponent to use force as it will itself, thus producing a kind of interaction. As viewed from this conception, such interaction will inevitably lead to extreme." Warfare is the continuation of politics, and a kind of bloody politics at that. Nuclear warfare and high-tech warfare are both instruments subordinate to the purposes and requirements of wars. When countries possessing nuclear weapons and high-tech conventional weapons are involved in a war in which the conflict is intensifying, the possible use of nuclear weapons cannot be ruled out. Nuclear weapons, therefore, are still a trump card in the hands of nuclear nations.

Thomas F. Ramos, science adviser to the senior officer responsible for nuclear weapons in the U.S. Department of Defense said: "No reasonable evidence indicates that conventional weapons will be reliable shelters to cope with enemies possessing and intending to use nuclear weapons." His remarks express the consensus of some military strategists studying the Gulf War.

As estimated by some Western specialits/analysts, there are at least 12 countries which claim to have ballistic missiles and at least 25 countries that have probably developed or are developing nuclear, biological, and chemical weapons. Using this estimation, some Western publications maintain that "the world has ushered in an age of nuclear proliferation." In 1974, India carried out its first nuclear blast, which kicked off the nuclear emulation in South Asia. In 1988, India successfully developed the PRITHVI medium-range ground-to-ground missile with a range of 2,000 meters, and the capability of carrying nuclear warheads. On March 24, 1993, South African President De Klerk addressed a special session of the National Assembly, saying that South Africa worked out a limited nuclear deterrent program in 1974 and had produced six atomic bombs by the end of 1989, and that all the said nuclear weapons had been dismantled and destroyed in early 1990. It was also revealed by the South African media that if the expansion of nuclear powers shown an intimidating color, South Africa will install warheads into its missiles and will probably develop and deploy neutron weapons. Israel is one of the countries that had nuclear weapons in its possession relatively earlier. Moreover, it was prepared to use them during the fourth Middle-East war.

Other data also stated that countries like Argentina and Brazil will also be able to manufacture nuclear weapons. With the rapid development of science and technology, the technology of making nuclear weapons has almost become an open secret. The disintegration of the former Soviet Union not only resulted in a brain drain of a vast number of scientists engaged in nuclear weapon development, but also threw the supervision of nuclear materials into chaos, considerably enlarging the scope of nuclear proliferation. A terrorist organization or a maniac could, some day, claim possession of an atomic bomb and use it as a tool of intimidation and blackmail, and no one would think that this was a tale from the Arabian Nights.

What merits our attention is that in a high-tech conventional war, a nuclear environment may still emerge even if nuclear weapons are not used. The more society advances, the greater the demands for energy will be. In order to satisfy the demands for energy, nuclear power stations were built. According to the data released by the International Atomic Energy Agency in March 1994, at the end of 1993 there were 430 nuclear power plants with a total installed capacity of approximately 345 million kw operating in various places throughout the world; these accounted for more than 17 percent of the world's gross power generation. It is predicted that by 2001, there will be 558 nuclear power generating units with a total installed capacity of approximately 460 million kw all worldwide, which will account for 24 percent of the world's gross power generation. The peaceful utilization of nuclear energy is a piece of joyous news to mankind.

Meanwhile, the extensive use of nuclear energy also constitutes a latent threat to peace and the existence of human beings. The accident at the Chernobyl Nuclear Power Plant that occurred in April 1986 inflicted air pollution on 16 Russian oblasts and victimized 250,000 people. In Ukraine, 370,000 people suffered injuries in varying degrees as land covering 40,000 square meters was polluted, and more than 2,000 residential areas were evacuated. In future high-tech warfare, if an enemy intentionally or unintentionally attacks nuclear power plants or other facilities using nuclear energy with high-tech conventional weapons, the secondary nuclear radiation produced and the nuclear environment brought about would likewise do harm.

In June 1981, Israel dispatched four aircraft to launch a sudden attack on an Iraqi nuclear reactor southeast of the capital Baghdad, dropping 16 tons of bombs in two minutes and hitting all the targets. Fortunately, the reactor was not yet operational; otherwise the attack would have resulted in very serious consequences.

NUCLEAR DETERRENCE WILL BE USED IN LOCAL WARS

The local wars that broke out after World War II were mostly carried out under the conditions of nuclear deterrence if the Western powers were involved in them. During the Korean War, U.S. Commander-in-Chief MacArthur once threatened a sudden attack of atomic bombs on China's northeast and coastal strategic targets. After Eisenhower came to power, he again ordered the Pentagon to formulate a nuclear program aimed at China. During its war of aggression in Vietnam, the United States also made nuclear threats and was prepared to resolve the issue with nuclear weapons.

After the armed conflicts on Zhenbao Island between China and the Soviet Union in 1969, Brezhnev considered initiating a nuclear attack on China in an attempt to ruin China's nuclear facilities. In the Malvinas Islands War, Britain carried tactical nuclear weapons on its huge fleet and was prepared to use them if its conventional operations failed. In particular, the multinational coalition troops headed by the United States used extremely advanced high-tech weapons in the Gulf War, and although they held the trump card, they still deployed 800 to 850 tactical nuclear weapons on three sides of Iraq.

What is more, U.S. troops considered using radio flash bombs but, because of political considerations, they were not approved by U.S. President Bush. In response to Saddam's repeated threats to use chemical weapons, the British

Government warned again and again that its troops would retaliate by using tactical nuclear weapons should Iraq resort to using chemical weapons. Bush also hinted that he would give field commanders freedom when necessary. These countries threatened to use nuclear weapons in conventional wars because they believed that with nuclear weapons in hand, psychologically they would be able to hold a dominant position, which would enhance troop morale and frighten the enemy on the one hand, and restrict the enemy's use of some conventional means on the other, thus changing the direction of the war. These past events should not be forgotten.

At present, nuclear deterrence is still a strategic pillar of military power. U.S. President Clinton thinks that the United States must build up military muscle that suits the new age, and this military muscle must have the capacity of nuclear deterrence. Nuclear deterrent force is an effective form of security. The 1993 defense report submitted by the U.S. Defense Department to Congress proposed that an all directional global defense system of strategic nuclear deterrence to prevent limited nuclear attacks should be set up, under which the former nuclear deterrent strategy chiefly aimed at the Soviet Union should be readjusted to an all-direction and multilevel nuclear deterrent strategy aimed at both the former Soviet Union and other regions.

On September 25, 1995, President Clinton ordered the Energy Department to maintain the three major nuclear weapon laboratories to ensure that U.S. nuclear deterrent capacity remains effective. Russia set up a defense ministry in March 1992, then founded its nuclear strategic forces and made the development of strategic nuclear weapons a top priority in the future development of eight technical weapons.

President Yeltsin said that a strategic nuclear force was the foundation of Russia's military strength. In November 1993, giving sanction to the new Russian military theory, he officially abandoned the Kremlin's 11-year-old commitment that in a conflict it would not be the first to use nuclear weapons. In its 1992 defense report, France claimed that it merely wanted to have the "most rudimentary" nuclear deterrent for as a way to cope with various kinds of unexpected events and check possible encroachments on its interests by potential enemies.

In the meantime, France announced that it is continuing to focus on the development of a submarine-launched strategic nuclear missile system to ensure the reliability of its nuclear deterrent strategy. At his first news conference after assuming office as president on June 13, 1995, Chirac declared that France would resume its nuclear tests in the South Pacific. The French Defense Minister maintained that President Chirac had made a "very serious decision."

British Prime Minister Major said, "As far as Britain is concerned, laying down the nuclear shield in whatever manner is an indiscreet move. Britain holds on to its views that as long as the CIS countries are still in possession of nuclear weapons, Britain should retain its own. The number of British nuclear weapons will not be determined by that of other countries, but by whether or not they are sufficient to make potential enemies feel incapable of sustaining their losses."

Deterrence and actual combat are complementary and closely interrelated. Generally speaking, the military strategy of all countries has a dual character of deterrence and actual combat. Before a war breaks out, a country will, by way of military deterrence, try to make the opposite side refrain from launching an attack rashly, so as to provide a powerful backing for its own political, economic, and diplomatic activities. Once military deterrence does not work, it will strive to win a victory through actual combat, so as to remove obstacles to its political, economic, and diplomatic activities.

Militarily, the immense effect of nuclear weaponry is that it can serve as a deterrent force and, at the same time, as a means of actual combat. Some countries, even those of the Third World, also consider possession of limited nuclear strength to be a significant way to contend against the deterrence of big powers or to deter one another in order to make up for the deficiency of their conventional forces. Military history after World War II has principally centered on the two superpowers that applied nuclear deterrence to each other and contended with each other for nuclear hegemony. After one of the superpowers disintegrated, a "crowd of heroes" rose up. As a result, conflicts that were in the past covered up by the Cold War surfaced with each passing day, and the collision and coalition of various political forces intensified simultaneously. Some regional powers were not weakened by the superpowers' relaxed control over them. On the contrary, they will, perhaps, go their own way even more willfully on the issues of possessing and using nuclear weapons. Both the United States and Russia believe that future nuclear threats will primarily stem from small nuclear nations in certain regions. Hence, the world situation of nuclear deterrence will be transformed from the previous global nuclear deterrence and confrontation between the United States and the Soviet Union to multiple and regional nuclear deterrence and confrontation. In future high-tech local wars, the struggle between nuclear deterrence and counter nuclear deterrence will be even more complex.

We are materialists, so when we study an issue, we must proceed from the objective reality rather than from a subjective wish and, through investigation and study of objective reality, we derive our principles, policies, and measures. The study of issues concerning warfare can be conducted in the same way. Comrade Mao Zedong said a long time ago: Investigation and study are very important. When we see someone hold something in his hand, we should look into the matter. What is he holding in his hand? It is a knife. What is the use of a knife? It can kill a person. Whom will he kill with the knife? He will kill the people. After probing into these matters, we should further the investigation: The Chinese people also have hands, and they can hold knives too. They can forge one if they have none. . . .

We love peace. China's development and possession of a small number of nuclear weapons is entirely for self-defense. Since the very first day when China had nuclear weapons in 1964, it solemnly proclaimed that it would never be the first to use nuclear weapons at any time and under any circumstances. China also made the commitment that it would never use or threaten to use nuclear weapons toward nuclear-free countries or regions. At the same time, we clearly understand that only by relying on the arduous work of the people all over the world can the objective of genuinely eliminating nuclear wars and genuinely obtaining world peace be realized: "It is a universal truth since ancient times that proficiency in warfare is not tantamount to bellicosity." The stronger our national defense muscle and the more sufficient our preparations for high-tech warfare under the condition of nuclear deterrence, the smaller the possibility of the outbreak of nuclear war.

We wish that the day will come when the nuclear shadow will disappear from the blue sky and the people the world over will live under the sunshine of genuine peace. To hail the early arrival of this day, we should work with greater stamina and diligence.

ALTERATIONS OF THE GLOBAL ENVIRONMENT

A nuclear war would involve such prodigious and concentrated short term release of high temperature energy that it is necessary to consider a variety of potential environmental effects. It is true that the energy of nuclear weapons is dwarfed by many natural phenomena. A large hurricane may have the power of a million hydrogen bombs. But the energy release of even the most severe weather is diffuse; it occurs over wide areas, and the difference in temperature between the storm system and the surrounding atmosphere is relatively small. Nuclear detonations are just the opposite—highly concentrated with reaction temperatures up to tens of millions of degrees Fahrenheit. Because they are so different from natural processes, it is necessary to examine their potential for altering the environment in several contexts.

High Altitude Dust

It has been estimated that a 10,000-megaton war with half the weapons exploding at ground level would tear up some 25 billion cubic meters of rock and soil, injecting a substantial amount of fine dust and particles into the stratosphere. This is roughly twice the volume of material blasted loose by the Indonesian volcano, Krakatoa, whose explosion in 1883 was the most powerful terrestrial event ever recorded. Sunsets around the world were noticeably reddened for several years after the Krakatoa eruption, indicating that large amounts of volcanic dust had entered the stratosphere.

Subsequent studies of large volcanic explosions, such as Mt. Agung on Bali in 1963, have raised the possibility that large-scale injection of dust into the stratosphere would reduce sunlight intensities and temperatures at the surface, while increasing the absorption of heat in the upper atmosphere.

The resultant minor changes in temperature and sunlight could affect crop production. However, no catastrophic worldwide changes have resulted from volcanic explosions, so it is doubtful that the gross injection of particulates into the stratosphere by a 10,000-megaton conflict would, by itself, lead to major global climate changes.

Ozone

More worrisome is the possible effect of nuclear explosions on ozone in the stratosphere. Not until the 20th century was the unique and paradoxical role of ozone fully recognized. On the other hand, in concentrations greater than I part per million in the air we breathe, ozone is toxic; one major American city, Los Angeles, has established a procedure for ozone alerts and warnings. On the other hand, ozone is a critically important feature of the stratosphere from the standpoint of maintaining life on the earth.

The reason is that while oxygen and nitrogen in the upper reaches of the atmosphere can block out solar ultraviolet photons with wavelengths shorter than 2,420 angstroms (Å), ozone is the only effective shield in the atmosphere against solar ultraviolet radiation between 2,500 and 3,000 Å in wavelength. Although ozone is extremely efficient at filtering out solar ultraviolet in 2,500-3,OOO Å region of the spectrum, some does get through at the higher end of the spectrum. Ultraviolet rays in the range of 2,800 to 3,200 Å which cause sunburn, prematurely age human skin and produce skin cancers. As early as 1840, arctic snow blindness was attributed to solar ultraviolet; and we have since found that intense ultraviolet radiation can inhibit photosynthesis in plants, stunt plant growth, damage bacteria, fungi, higher plants, insects and annuals, and produce genetic alterations.

Despite the important role ozone plays in assuring a livable environment at the earth's surface, the total quantity of ozone in the atmosphere is quite small, only about 3 parts per million. Furthermore, ozone is not a durable or static constituent of the atmosphere. It is constantly created, destroyed, and recreated by natural processes, so that the amount of ozone present at any given time is a function of the equilibrium reached between the creative and destructive chemical reactions and the solar radiation reaching the upper stratosphere.

The mechanism for the production of ozone is the absorption by oxygen molecules (O_2) of relatively short-wavelength ultraviolet light. The oxygen molecule separates into two atoms of free oxygen, which immediately unite with other oxygen molecules on the surfaces of particles in the upper atmosphere. It is this union which forms ozone, or O_3. The heat released by the ozone-forming process is the reason for the curious increase with altitude of the temperature of the stratosphere (the base of which is about 36,000 feet above the earth's surface).

While the natural chemical reaction produces about 4,500 tons of ozone per second in the stratosphere, this is offset by other natural chemical reactions which break down the ozone. By far the most significant involves nitric oxide (NO) which breaks ozone (O_3) into molecules. This effect was discovered only in the last few years in studies of the environmental problems which might be encountered if large fleets of supersonic transport aircraft operate routinely in the lower stratosphere. According to a report by Dr. Harold S. Johnston, University of California at Berkeley— prepared for the Department of Transportation's Climatic Impact Assessment Program—it now appears that the NO reaction is normally responsible for 50 to 70 percent of the destruction of ozone.

In the natural environment, there is a variety of means for the production of NO and its transport into the stratosphere. Soil bacteria produce nitrous oxide (N_2O) which enters the lower atmosphere and slowly diffuses into the stratosphere, where it reacts with free oxygen (O) to form two NO molecules. Another mechanism for NO production in the lower atmosphere may be lightning discharges, and while NO is quickly washed out of the lower atmosphere by rain, some of it may reach the stratosphere. Additional amounts of NO are produced directly in the stratosphere by cosmic rays from the sun and interstellar sources.

It is because of this catalytic role which nitric oxide plays in the destruction of ozone that it is important to consider the effects of high-yield nuclear explosions on the ozone layer. The nuclear fireball and the air entrained within it are subjected to great heat, followed by relatively rapid cooling. These conditions are ideal for the production of tremendous amounts of NO from the air. It has been estimated that as much as 5,000 tons of nitric oxide is produced for each megaton of nuclear explosive power.

What would be the effects of nitric oxides driven into the stratosphere by an all-out nuclear war, involving the detonation of 10,000 megatons of explosive force in the northern hemisphere? According to the recent National Academy of Sciences study, the nitric oxide produced by the weapons could reduce the ozone levels in the northern hemisphere by as much as 30 to 70 percent.

To begin with, a depleted ozone layer would reflect back to the earth's surface less heat than would normally be the case, thus causing a drop in temperature—perhaps enough to produce serious effects on agriculture. Other changes, such as increased amounts of dust or different vegetation, might subsequently reverse this drop in temperature—but on the other hand, it might increase it.

Probably more important, life on earth has largely evolved within the protective ozone shield and is presently adapted rather precisely to the amount of solar ultraviolet which does get through. To defend themselves against this low level of ultraviolet, evolved external shielding (feathers, fur, cuticular waxes on fruit), internal shielding (melanin pigment in human skin, flavenoids in plant tissue), avoidance strategies (plankton migration to greater depths in the daytime, shade-seeking by desert iguanas) and, in almost all organisms but placental mammals, elaborate mechanisms to repair photochemical damage.

It is possible, however, that a major increase in solar ultraviolet might overwhelm the defenses of some and perhaps many terrestrial life forms. Both direct and indirect damage would then occur among the bacteria, insects, plants, and other links in the ecosystems on which human well-being depends. This disruption, particularly if it occurred in the aftermath of a major war involving many other dislocations, could pose a serious additional threat to the recovery of postwar society. The National Academy of Sciences report concludes that in 20 years the ecological systems would have essentially recovered from the increase in ultraviolet radiation—though not necessarily from radioactivity or other damage in areas close to the war zone. However, a delayed effect of the increase in ultraviolet radiation would be an estimated 3 to 30 percent increase in skin cancer for 40 years in the Northern Hemisphere's mid-latitudes.

Some Conclusions

We have considered the problems of large-scale nuclear war from the standpoint of the countries not under direct attack, and the difficulties they might encounter in postwar recovery. It is true that most of the horror and tragedy of nuclear war would be visited on the populations subject to direct attack, who would doubtless have to cope with extreme and perhaps insuperable obstacles in seeking to reestablish their own societies. It is no less apparent, however, that other nations, including those remote from the combat, could suffer heavily because of damage to the global environment. Finally, at least brief mention should be made of the global effects resulting from disruption of economic activities and communications. Since 1970, an increasing fraction of the human race has been losing the battle for self-sufficiency in food, and must rely on heavy imports. A major disruption of agriculture and transportation in the grain-exporting and manufacturing countries could thus prove disastrous to countries importing food, farm machinery, and fertilizers—especially those which are already struggling with the threat of widespread starvation. Moreover, virtually every economic area, from food and medicines to fuel and growth engendering industries, the less-developed countries would find they could not rely on the "undamaged" remainder of the developed world for trade essentials: in the wake of a nuclear war the industrial powers directly involved would themselves have to compete for resources with those countries that today are described as "less-developed."

Similarly, the disruption of international communications—satellites, cables, and even high frequency radio links—could be a major obstacle to international recovery efforts. In attempting to project the after-effects of a major nuclear war, we have considered separately the various kinds of damage that could occur. It is also quite possible, however, that interactions might take place among these effects, so that one type of damage would couple with another to produce new and unexpected hazards.

For example, we can assess individually the consequences of heavy worldwide radiation fallout and increased solar ultraviolet, but we do not know whether the two acting together might significantly increase human, animal, or plant susceptibility to disease. We can conclude that massive dust injection into the stratosphere, even greater in scale than Krakatoa, is unlikely by itself to produce significant climatic and environmental change, but we cannot rule out interactions with other phenomena, such as ozone depletion, which might produce utterly unexpected results.

We have come to realize that nuclear weapons can be as unpredictable as they are deadly in their effects. Despite some 30 years of development and study, there is still much that we do not know. This is particularly true when we consider the global effects of a large-scale nuclear war.

Nuclear Weapons Yield

The most widely used standard for measuring the power of nuclear weapons is "yield," expressed as the quantity of chemical explosive (TNT) that would produce the same energy release. The first atomic weapon which leveled Hiroshima in 1945, had a yield of 13 kilotons; that is, the explosive power of 13,000 tons of TNT. (The largest conventional bomb dropped in World War II contained about 10 tons of TNT.)

Since Hiroshima, the yields or explosive power of nuclear weapons have vastly increased. The world's largest nuclear detonation, set off in 1962 by the Soviet Union, had a yield of 58 megatons—equivalent to 58 million tons of TNT. A modern ballistic missile may carry warhead yields up to 20 or more megatons.

Even the most violent wars of recent history have been relatively limited in terms of the total destructive power of the non-nuclear weapons used. A single aircraft or ballistic missile today can carry a nuclear explosive force surpassing that of all the non-nuclear bombs used in recent wars. The number of nuclear bombs and missiles the superpowers now possess runs into the thousands.

NUCLEAR WEAPONS DESIGN

Nuclear weapons depend on two fundamentally different types of nuclear reactions, each of which releases energy: Fission, which involves the splitting of heavy elements (e.g. uranium); and fusion, which involves the combining of light elements (e.g. hydrogen). Fission requires that a minimum amount of material or "critical mass" be brought together in contact for the nuclear explosion to take place. The more efficient fission weapons tend to fall in the yield range of tens of kilotons. Higher explosive yields become increasingly complex and impractical.

Nuclear fusion permits the design of weapons of virtually limitless power. In fusion, according to nuclear theory, when the nuclei of light atoms like hydrogen are joined, the mass of the fused nucleus is lighter than the two original nuclei; the loss is expressed as energy. By the 1930's, physicists had concluded that this was the process which powered the sun and stars; but the nuclear fusion process remained only of theoretical interest until it was discovered that an atomic fission bomb might be used as a "trigger" to produce, within one- or two-millionths of a second, the intense pressure and temperature necessary to set off the fusion reaction. Fusion permits the design of weapons of almost limitless power, using materials that are far less costly.

Radioactivity

Most familiar natural elements like hydrogen, oxygen, gold, and lead are stable, and enduring unless acted upon by outside forces. But almost all elements can exist in unstable forms. The nuclei of these unstable "isotopes," as they are called, are "uncomfortable" with the particular mixture of nuclear particles comprising them, and they decrease this internal stress through the process of radioactive decay. The three basic modes of radioactive decay are the emission of alpha, beta and gamma radiation:

- Alpha—Unstable nuclei frequently emit alpha particles, actually helium nuclei consisting of two protons and two neutrons. By far the most massive of the decay particles, it is also the slowest, rarely exceeding one-tenth the velocity of light. As a result, its penetrating power is weak, and it can usually be stopped by a piece of paper. But if alpha emitters like plutonium are incorporated in the body, they pose a serious cancer threat.
- Beta—Another form of radioactive decay is the emission of a beta particle, or electron. The beta particle has only about one seven-thousandth the mass of the alpha particle, but its velocity is very much greater, as much as eight-tenths the velocity of light. As a result, beta particles can penetrate far more deeply into bodily tissue and external doses of beta radiation represent a significantly greater threat than the slower, heavier alpha particles. Beta-emitting isotopes are as harmful as alpha emitters if taken up by the body.
- Gamma—In some decay processes, the emission is a photon having no mass at all and traveling at the speed of light. Radio waves, visible light, radiant heat, and X-rays are all photons, differing only in the energy level each carries. The gamma ray is similar to the X-ray photon, but far more penetrating (it can traverse several inches of concrete). It is capable of doing great damage in the body.

Common to all three types of nuclear decay radiation is their ability to ionize (i.e., unbalance electrically) the neutral atoms through which they pass, that is, give them a net electrical charge. The alpha particle, carrying a positive electrical charge, pulls electrons from the atoms through which it passes, while negatively charged beta particles can push electrons out of neutral atoms. If energetic betas pass sufficiently close to atomic nuclei, they can produce X-rays which themselves can ionize additional neutral atoms. Massless but energetic gamma rays can knock electrons out of neutral atoms in the same fashion as X-rays, leaving them ionized. A single particle of radiation can ionize hundreds of neutral atoms in the tissue in multiple collisions before all its energy is absorbed. This disrupts the chemical bonds for critically important cell structures like the cytoplasm, which carries the cell's genetic blueprints, and also produces chemical constituents which can cause as much damage as the original ionizing radiation.

For convenience, a unit of radiation dose called the "rad" has been adopted. It measures the amount of ionization produced per unit volume by the particles from radioactive decay.

Nuclear Half-Life

The concept of "half-life" is basic to an understanding of radioactive decay of unstable nuclei. Unlike physical "systems" — bacteria, animals, men and stars — unstable isotopes do not individually have a predictable life span. There is no way of forecasting when a single unstable nucleus will decay. Nevertheless, it is possible to get around the random behavior of an individual nucleus by dealing statistically with large numbers of nuclei of a particular radioactive isotope. In the case of thorium-232, for example, radioactive decay proceeds so slowly that 14 billion years must elapse before one-half of an initial quantity decayed to a more stable configuration. Thus the half-life of this isotope is 14 billion years. After the elapse of second half-life (another 14 billion years), only one-fourth of the original quantity of thorium-232 would remain, one eighth after the third half-life, and so on.

Most manmade radioactive isotopes have much shorter half-lives, ranging from seconds or days up to thousands of years. Plutonium-239 (a manmade isotope) has a half-life of 24,000 years. For the most common uranium isotope, U-238, the half-life is 4.5 billion years, about the age of the solar system. The much scarcer, fissionable isotope of uranium, U-235, has a half-life of 700 million years, indicating that its present abundance is only about 1 percent of the amount present when the solar system was born.

NUCLEAR WEAPONS

The history of nuclear weapons chronicles the development of nuclear weapons. Nuclear weapons are devices that possess enormous destructive potential derived from nuclear fission or nuclear fusion reactions. Starting with the scientific breakthroughs of the 1930s which made their development possible, and continuing through the nuclear arms race and nuclear testing of the Cold War, the issues of proliferation and possible use for terrorism still remain in the early 21st century. The first fission weapons, also known as "atomic bombs," were developed jointly by the United States, Britain and Canada during World War II in what was called the Manhattan Project to counter the assumed Nazi German atomic bomb project. In August 1945 two were dropped on Japan ending the Pacific War. An international team was dispatched to help work on the project. The Soviet Union started development shortly thereafter with their own atomic bomb project, and not long after that both countries developed even more powerful fusion weapons called "hydrogen bombs."

During the Cold War, the Soviet Union and United States each acquired nuclear weapons arsenals numbering in the thousands, placing many of them onto rockets which could hit targets anywhere in the world. Currently there are at least nine countries with functional nuclear weapons. A considerable amount of international negotiating has focused on the threat of nuclear warfare and the proliferation of nuclear weapons to new nations or groups. There have been (at least) four major false alarms, the most recent in 1995, that resulted in the activation of either the US's or Russia's nuclear attack early warning protocols.

Physics and Politics in the 1930s

In the first decades of the twentieth century, physics was revolutionized with developments in the understanding of the nature of atoms. In 1898, French physicist Pierre Curie and his Polish wife Maria Sklodowska-Curie had discovered that present in pitchblende, an ore of uranium, was a substance which emitted large amounts of radioactivity, which they named radium. This raised the hopes of both scientists and lay people that the elements around us could contain tremendous amounts of unseen energy, waiting to be tapped. Experiments by Ernest Rutherford in 1911 indicated that the vast majority of an atom's mass was contained in a very small nucleus at its core, made up of protons, surrounded by a web of whirring electrons. In 1932, James Chadwick discovered that the nucleus contained another fundamental particle, the neutron, and in the same year John Cockcroft and Ernest Walton "split the atom" for the first time, the first occasion on which an atomic nucleus of one element had been successfully changed to a different nucleus by artificial means.

In 1934 the idea of chain reaction via neutron was proposed by Leó Szilárd, who patented the idea of the atomic bomb. The patent was transferred in secret to Britain's Royal Navy in 1936. In a very real sense, Szilárd was the father of the atomic bomb academically. In 1934, French physicists Irène and Frédéric Joliot-Curie discovered that artificial radioactivity could be induced in stable elements by bombarding them with alpha particles, and in the same year Italian physicist Enrico Fermi reported similar results when bombarding uranium with neutrons. In December 1938, the German chemists Otto Hahn and Fritz Strassmann sent a manuscript to *Naturwissenschaften* reporting they had detected the element barium after bombarding uranium with neutrons; simultaneously, they communicated these results to Lise Meitner. Meitner, and her nephew Otto Robert Frisch, correctly interpreted these results as being nuclear fission. Frisch confirmed this experimentally on 13 January 1939. Even before it was published, Meitner's and Frisch's interpretation of the work of Hahn and Strassmann crossed the Atlantic Ocean with Niels Bohr, who was to lecture at Princeton University. Isidor Isaac Rabi and Willis Lamb, two Columbia University physicists working at Princeton, heard the news and carried it back to Columbia. Rabi said he told Fermi; Fermi gave credit to Lamb. Bohr soon thereafter went from Princeton to Columbia to see Fermi. Not finding Fermi in his office, Bohr went down to the cyclotron area and found Herbert Anderson. Bohr grabbed him by the shoulder and said: "Young man, let me explain to you about something new and exciting in physics."

It was clear to a number of scientists at Columbia that they should try to detect the energy released in the nuclear fission of uranium from neutron bombardment. On 25 January 1939, an experimental team at Columbia University conducted the first nuclear fission experiment in the United States, which was done in the basement of Pupin Hall; the members of the team were Herbert L. Anderson, Eugene T. Booth, John R. Dunning, Enrico Fermi, G. Norris Glasoe, and Francis G. Slack. As the Nazi army marched into first Czechoslovakia in 1938, and then Poland in 1939, beginning World War II, many of Europe's top physicists had already begun to flee from the imminent conflict. Scientists on both sides of the conflict were well aware of the possibility of utilizing nuclear fission as a weapon, but at the time no one was quite sure how it could be done. In the early years of the Second World War, physicists abruptly stopped publishing on the topic of fission, an act of self-censorship to keep the opposing side from gaining any advantages.

From Los Alamos to Hiroshima

By the beginning of World War II, there was concern among scientists in the Allied nations that Nazi Germany might have its own project to develop fission-based weapons. Organized research first began in Britain as part of the "Tube Alloys" project, and in the United States a small amount of funding was given for research into uranium weapons starting in 1939 with the Uranium Committee under Lyman James Briggs. At the urging of British scientists, though, who had made crucial calculations indicating that a fission weapon could be completed within only a few years, by 1941 the project had been wrested into better bureaucratic hands, and in 1942 came under the auspices of a Military Policy Committee led by General Leslie Groves as the Manhattan Project.

Scientifically led by the American physicist Robert Oppenheimer, the project brought together the top scientific minds of the day (many exiles from Europe) with the production power of American industry for the goal of producing fission-based explosive devices before Germany could. Britain and the U.S. agreed to pool their resources and information for the project, but the other Allied power—the Soviet Union under Joseph Stalin—was not informed. A massive industrial and scientific undertaking, the Manhattan Project involved many of the world's great physicists in the scientific and development aspects. The United States made an unprecedented investment into wartime research for the project, which was spread across more than 30 sites in the U.S. and Canada. Scientific knowledge was centralized at a secret laboratory known as Los Alamos, previously a small ranch school near Santa Fe, New Mexico.

Uranium appears in nature primarily in two isotopes: uranium-238 and uranium-235. When the nucleus of uranium-235 absorbs a neutron, it undergoes nuclear fission, splitting into two "fission products" and releasing energy and 2.5 neutrons on average. Uranium-238, on the other hand, absorbs neutrons but does not split, effectively putting a stop to any ongoing fission reaction. It was discovered that an atomic bomb based on uranium would need to be made of almost completely pure uranium-235 (at least 80% pure), or else the presence of uranium-238 would quickly curtail the nuclear chain reaction. The team of scientists working on the Manhattan Project immediately realized that one of the largest problems they would have to solve was how to remove uranium-235 from natural uranium, which was composed of 99.3% uranium-238. Two methods were developed during the wartime project, both of which took advantage of the fact that uranium-238 has a slightly greater atomic mass than uranium-235: electromagnetic separation and gaseous diffusion—methods which separated isotopes based on their differing weights. Another secret site was erected at rural Oak Ridge, Tennessee, for the large-scale production and purification of the rare isotope. It was a massive investment: at the time, one of the Oak Ridge facilities (K-25) was the largest factory under one roof. The Oak Ridge site employed tens of thousands of employees at its peak, most of whom had no idea what they were working on.

Though uranium-238 cannot be used for the initial stage of an atomic bomb, when U-238 absorbs a neutron, it transforms first into an unstable element, uranium-239, and then decays into neptunium-239, and finally the relatively stable plutonium-239, an element which does not exist in nature. Plutonium is also fissile and can be used to create a fission reaction, and after Enrico Fermi achieved the world's first sustained and controlled nuclear chain reaction in the creation of the first "atomic pile"—a primitive nuclear reactor—in a basement at the University of Chicago, massive reactors were secretly created at what is now known as Hanford Site in the state of Washington, using the Columbia River as cooling water, to transform uranium-238 into plutonium for a bomb.

For a fission weapon to operate, there must be a critical mass—the amount needed for a self-sustaining nuclear chain reaction—of fissile material bombarded with neutrons at any one time. The simplest form of nuclear weapon is a gun-type fission weapon, where a sub-critical mass of fissile material (such as uranium-235) would be shot at another sub-critical mass of fissile material. The result would be a super-critical mass which, when bombarded with neutrons, would undergo fission at a rapid rate and create the desired explosion. The weapons envisaged in 1942 were the two gun-type weapons, Little Boy (uranium) and Thin Man (plutonium), and the Fat Man plutonium implosion bomb. In early 1943 Oppenheimer determined that two projects should proceed forwards: the "Thin Man" project (plutonium gun) and the "Fat Man" project (plutonium implosion). The plutonium gun was to receive the bulk of the research effort, as it was the project with the most uncertainty involved. It was assumed that the uranium gun-type bomb could then be adapted from it.

But in April 1944 it was found by Emilio Segrè that plutonium produced by the Hanford reactors had too high a level of background neutron radiation, and underwent spontaneous fission to a very small extent, due to the presence of impurities of the Pu-240 isotope. If such plutonium were used in a "gun assembly," the chain reaction would start in the split seconds before the critical mass was assembled, blowing the weapon apart before it would have any great effect (this is known as a fizzle). So development of Fat Man, the implosion bomb, was given high priority. Chemical explosives were used to implode a sub-critical sphere of plutonium, thus increasing its density and making it into a critical mass. The difficulties with implosion were in the problem of making the chemical explosives deliver a perfectly uniform shock wave upon the plutonium sphere— if it were even slightly asymmetric, the weapon would fizzle (which would be expensive, messy, and not a very effective military device). This problem was circumvented by the use of hydrodynamic "lenses"—explosive materials of differing densities—which would focus the blast waves inside the imploding sphere, akin to the way in which an optical lens focuses light rays.

After D-Day, General Groves had ordered a team of scientists—Project Alsos—to follow eastward-moving victorious Allied troops into Europe in order to assess the status of the German nuclear program (and to prevent the westward-moving Russians from gaining any materials or scientific manpower). It was concluded that while Nazi Germany had also had an atomic bomb program, headed by Werner Heisenberg, the government had not made a significant investment in the project, and had been nowhere near success. Historians claim to have found a rough schematic showing a Nazi nuclear bomb. Research was conducted in the German nuclear energy project. In March 1945, a Nazi scientific team was directed by the physicist Kurt Diebner to develop a primitive nuclear device in Ohrdruf, Thuringia.

By the unconditional surrender of Germany on May 8, 1945, the Manhattan Project was still months away from a working weapon. That April, after the death of American President Franklin D. Roosevelt, former Vice-President Harry S. Truman was told about the secret wartime project for the first time. Because of the difficulties in making a working plutonium bomb, it was decided that there should be a test of the weapon, and Truman wanted to know for sure if it would work before his meeting with Joseph Stalin at an upcoming conference on the future of postwar Europe.

On July 16, 1945, in the desert north of Alamogordo, New Mexico, the first nuclear test took place, code-named "Trinity," using a device nicknamed "the Gadget." The test, a plutonium implosion type device, released the equivalent of 19 kilotons of TNT, far mightier than any weapon ever used before. The news of the test's success was rushed to Truman, who used it as leverage at the upcoming Potsdam Conference, held near Berlin.

After hearing arguments from scientists and military officers over the possible uses of the weapons against Japan (though some recommended using them as "demonstrations" in unpopulated areas, most recommended using them against "built up" targets, a euphemistic term for populated cities), Truman ordered the use of the weapons on Japanese cities, hoping it would send a strong message which would end in the capitulation of the Japanese leadership and avoid a lengthy invasion of the island.

There were suggestions to drop the atomic bomb on Tokyo, the capital of Japan, but concerns about Tokyo's cultural heritage changed the plan. On May 10–11, 1945 The Target Committee at Los Alamos, led by J. Robert Oppenheimer, recommended Kyoto, Hiroshima, Yokohama, and the arsenal at Kokura as possible targets.

On August 6, 1945, a uranium-based weapon, "Little Boy", was let loose on the Japanese city of Hiroshima. Three days later, a plutonium-based weapon, "Fat Man", was dropped onto the city of Nagasaki. The atomic bombs killed at least one hundred thousand Japanese outright, most of them civilians, with the heat, radiation, and blast effects. Many tens of thousands would die later of radiation sickness and related cancers. Truman promised a "rain of ruin" if Japan did not surrender immediately, threatening to eliminate Japanese cities, one by one; Japan surrendered on August 15. Truman's threat was in fact a bluff, since the US had but one remaining uranium-gun type bomb completed.

Soviet Atomic Bomb Project

The Soviet Union was not invited to share in the new weapons developed by the United States and the other Allies. During the war, information had been pouring in from a number of volunteer spies involved with the Manhattan Project (known in Soviet cables under the code-name of *Enormoz*), and the Soviet nuclear physicist Igor Kurchatov was carefully watching the Allied weapons development. It came as no surprise to Stalin when Truman had informed him at the Potsdam conference that he had a "powerful new weapon." Truman was shocked at Stalin's lack of interest. The Soviet spies in the U.S. project were all volunteers and none were Russians. One of the most valuable, Klaus Fuchs, was a German émigré theoretical physicist who had been a part in the early British nuclear efforts and had been part of the UK mission to Los Alamos during the war. Fuchs had been intimately involved in the development of the implosion weapon, and passed on detailed cross-sections of the "Trinity" device to his Soviet contacts. Other Los Alamos spies—none of whom knew each other—included Theodore Hall and David Greenglass. The information was kept but not acted upon, as Russia was still too busy fighting the war in Europe to devote resources to this new project.

In the years immediately after World War II, the issue of who should control atomic weapons became a major international point of contention. Many of the Los Alamos scientists who had built the bomb began to call for "international control of atomic energy," often calling for either control by transnational organizations or the purposeful distribution of weapons information to all superpowers, but due to a deep distrust of the intentions of the Soviet Union, both in postwar Europe and in general, the policy-makers of the United States worked to attempt to secure an American nuclear monopoly. A half-hearted plan for international control was proposed at the newly formed United Nations by Bernard Baruch ("The Baruch Plan"), but it was clear both to American commentators—and to the Soviets—that it was an attempt primarily to stymie Russian nuclear efforts. The Soviets vetoed the plan, effectively ending any immediate postwar negotiations on atomic energy, and made overtures towards banning the use of atomic weapons in general.

All the while, the Soviets had put their full industrial and manpower might into the development of their own atomic weapons. The initial problem for the Soviets was primarily one of resources—they had not scouted out uranium resources in the Soviet Union and the U.S. had made deals to monopolise the largest known (and high purity) reserves in the Belgian Congo. The USSR used penal labour to mine the old deposits in Czechoslovakia—now an area under their control—and searched for other domestic deposits (which were eventually found). Two days after the bombing of Nagasaki, the

U.S. government released an official technical history of the Manhattan Project, authored by Princeton physicist Henry DeWolf Smyth, known colloquially as the Smyth Report. The sanitized summary of the wartime effort focused primarily on the production facilities and scale of investment, written in part to justify the wartime expenditure to the American public.

The Soviet program, under the suspicious watch of former NKVD chief Lavrenty Beria (a participant and victor in Stalin's Great Purge of the 1930s), would use the Report as a blueprint, seeking to duplicate as much as possible the American effort. The "secret cities" used for the Soviet equivalents of Hanford and Oak Ridge literally vanished from the maps for decades to come. At the Soviet equivalent of Los Alamos, Arzamas-16, physicist Yuli Khariton led the scientific effort to develop the weapon. Beria distrusted his scientists, however, and he distrusted the carefully collected espionage information. As such, Beria assigned multiple teams of scientists to the same task without informing each team of the other's existence. If they arrived at different conclusions, Beria would bring them together for the first time and have them debate with their newfound counterparts. Beria used the espionage information as a way to double-check the progress of his scientists, and in his effort for duplication of the American project even rejected more efficient bomb designs in favour of ones which more closely mimicked the tried-and-true "Fat Man" bomb used by the U.S. against Nagasaki.

Working under a stubborn and scientifically ignorant administrator, the Soviet scientists struggled on. On August 29, 1949, the effort brought its results, when the USSR tested its first fission bomb, dubbed "Joe-1" by the U.S., years ahead of American predictions. The news of the first Soviet bomb was announced to the world first by the United States, which had detected the nuclear fallout it generated from its test site in Kazakhstan. The loss of the American monopoly on nuclear weapons marked the first tit-for-tat of the nuclear arms race. The response in the U.S. was one of apprehension, fear, and scapegoating, which would lead eventually into the Red-baiting tactics of McCarthyism. Yet recent information from unclassified Venona intercepts and the opening of the KGB archives after the fall of the Soviet Union show that the USSR had useful spies that helped their program, although none were identified by the McCarthy. Before this, though, President Truman would announce his decision to begin a crash program to develop a far more powerful weapon than those which were used against Japan: the hydrogen bomb.

The First Thermonuclear Weapons

The notion of using a fission weapon to ignite a process of nuclear fusion can be dated back to 1942. At the first major theoretical conference on the development of an atomic bomb hosted by J. Robert Oppenheimer at the University of California, Berkeley, participant Edward Teller directed the majority of the discussion towards Enrico Fermi's idea of a "Super" bomb which would utilize the same reactions which powered the Sun itself. It was thought at the time that a fission weapon would be quite simple to develop and that perhaps work on a hydrogen bomb would be possible to complete before the end of the Second World War. However, in reality the problem of a "regular" atomic bomb was large enough to preoccupy the scientists for the next few years, much less the more speculative "Super." Only Teller continued working on the project—against the will of project leaders Oppenheimer and Hans Bethe.

After the atomic bombings of Japan, many scientists at Los Alamos rebelled against the notion of creating a weapon thousands of times more powerful than the first atomic bombs. For the scientists the question was in part technical—the weapon design was still quite uncertain and unworkable—and in part moral: such a weapon, they argued, could only be used against large civilian populations, and could thus only be used as a weapon of genocide. Many scientists, such as Bethe, urged that the United States should not develop such weapons and set an example towards the Soviet Union. Promoters of the weapon, including Teller, Ernest Lawrence, and Luis Alvarez, argued that such a development was inevitable, and to deny such protection to the people of the United States—especially when the Soviet Union was likely to create such a weapon themselves—was itself an immoral and unwise act.

Oppenheimer, who was now head of the General Advisory Committee of the successor to the Manhattan Project, the Atomic Energy Commission, presided over a recommendation against the development of the weapon. The reasons were in part because the success of the technology seemed limited at the time (and not worth the investment of resources to confirm whether this was so), and because Oppenheimer believed that the atomic forces of the United States would be more effective if they consisted of many large fission weapons (of which multiple bombs could be dropped on the same targets) rather than the large and unwieldy predictions of massive super bombs, for which there were a relatively limited amounts of targets of the size to warrant such a development.

Furthermore, were such weapons developed by both the U.S. and the USSR, they would be more effectively used against the U.S. than by it, as the U.S. had far more regions of dense industrial and civilian activity which would serve as ideal targets for the large weapons than the Soviet Union did.

In the end, President Truman made the final decision, looking for a proper response to the first Soviet atomic bomb test in 1949. On January 31, 1950, Truman announced a crash program to develop the hydrogen (fusion) bomb. At this point, however, the exact mechanism was still not known: the "classical" hydrogen bomb, whereby the *heat* of the fission bomb would be used to ignite the fusion material, seemed highly unworkable. However, an insight by Los Alamos mathematician Stanislaw Ulam showed that the fission bomb and the fusion fuel could be in separate parts of the bomb, and that *radiation* of the fission bomb could first work in a way to *compress* the fusion material before igniting it.

Teller pushed the notion further, and used the results of the boosted-fission "George" test (a boosted-fission device using a small amount of fusion fuel to boost the yield of a fission bomb) to confirm the fusion of heavy hydrogen elements before preparing for their first true multi-stage, Teller-Ulam hydrogen bomb test. Many scientists initially against the weapon, such as Oppenheimer and Bethe, changed their previous opinions, seeing the development as being unstoppable. The first fusion bomb was tested by the United States in *Operation Ivy* on November 1, 1952, on Elugelab Island in the Enewetak (or Eniwetok) Atoll of the Marshall Islands, code-named "Mike". "Mike" used liquid deuterium as its fusion fuel and a large fission weapon as its trigger. The device was a prototype design and not a deliverable weapon: standing over 20 ft (6 m) high and weighing at least 140,000 lb (64 t) (its refrigeration equipment added an additional 24,000 lb as well), it could not have been dropped from even the largest planes.

Its explosion yielded 10.4 megatons of energy—over 450 times the power of the bomb dropped onto Nagasaki— and obliterated Elugelab, leaving an underwater crater 6240 ft (1.9 km) wide and 164 ft (50 m) deep where the island had once been. Truman had initially tried to create a media blackout about the test—hoping it would not become an issue in the upcoming presidential election—but on January 7, 1953, Truman announced the development of the hydrogen bomb to the world as hints and speculations of it were already beginning to emerge in the press. Not to be outdone, the Soviet Union exploded its first thermonuclear device, designed by the physicist Andrei Sakharov, on August 12, 1953, labeled "Joe-4" by the West. This created concern within the U.S. government and military, because, unlike "Mike," the Soviet device was a deliverable weapon, which the U.S. did not yet have. This first device though was arguably not a "true" hydrogen bomb, and could only reach explosive yields in the hundreds of kilotons (never reaching the megaton range of a "staged" weapon). Still, it was a powerful propaganda tool for the Soviet Union, and the technical differences were fairly oblique to the American public and politicians.

Following the "Mike" blast by less than a year, "Joe-4" seemed to validate claims that the bombs were inevitable and vindicate those who had supported the development of the fusion program. Coming during the height of McCarthyism, the effect was most pronounced by the security hearings in early 1954 which revoked former Los Alamos director Robert Oppenheimer of his security clearance, on the grounds that he was unreliable, had not supported the American hydrogen bomb program, and had made long-standing, left-wing ties in the 1930s. Edward Teller participated in the hearing as the only major scientist to testify against Oppenheimer, a role which resulted in his virtual expulsion from the physics community. On February 28, 1954, the U.S. detonated its first deliverable thermonuclear weapon (which used isotopes of lithium as its fusion fuel), known as the "Shrimp" device of the "Castle Bravo" test, at Bikini Atoll, Marshall Islands. The device yielded 15 megatons of energy, over twice its expected yield, and became the worst radiological disaster in U.S. history. The combination of the unexpectedly large blast and poor weather conditions caused a cloud of radioactive nuclear fallout to contaminate over 7,000 square miles, including Marshall Island natives and the crew of a Japanese fishing boat, as a snow-like mist. The contaminated islands were evacuated (and are still uninhabitable), but the natives received enough of a radioactive dose that they suffered far elevated levels of cancer and birth defects in the years to come.

The crew of the Japanese fishing boat, *Lucky Dragon 5*, returned to port suffering from radiation sickness and skin burns. Their cargo, many tons of contaminated fish, managed to enter into the market before the cause of their illness was determined. When a crew member died from the sickness and the full results of the contamination were made public by the U.S., Japanese concerns were reignited about the hazards of radiation and resulted in a boycott on eating fish (a main staple of the island country) for some weeks. The hydrogen bomb age had a profound effect on the thoughts of nuclear war in the popular and military mind. With only fission bombs, nuclear war could be considered something which could easily be "limited." Dropped by planes and only able to destroy the most built up areas of major cities, it was possible to consider fission bombs simply a technological extension of previous wartime bombing (such as the extensive firebombing which took place against Japan and Germany during World War II), and claims that such weapons could lead to worldwide death or harm were easily brushed aside as grave exaggeration.

Even the decades before the development of fission weapons there had been speculation about the possibility for human beings to end all life on the planet by either accident or purposeful maliciousness, but technology had never allowed for such a capacity. The far greater power of hydrogen bombs made this seem ever closer. The "Castle Bravo" incident itself raised a number of questions about the survivability of a nuclear war. Government scientists in both the U.S. and the USSR had insisted that fusion weapons, unlike fission weapons, were "cleaner" as fusion reactions did not result in the dangerously radioactive by-products as did fission reactions. While technically true, this hid a more gruesome point: the last stage of a multi-staged hydrogen bomb often used the neutrons produced by the fusion reactions to induce fissioning in a jacket of natural uranium, and provided around half of the yield of the device itself.

This fission stage made fusion weapons considerably more "dirty" than they were made out to be, a fact made evident by the towering cloud of deadly fallout which followed the "Bravo" test. When the Soviet Union tested its first megaton device in 1955, the possibility of a limited nuclear war seemed even more remote in the public and political mind: even if a city or country was not the direct target of a nuclear attack, the clouds of fallout and harmful fission products would disperse along with normal weather patterns and embed themselves in the soil and water of non-targeted areas of the planet as well. Speculation began to look towards what would happen as the fallout and dust created by a full-scale nuclear exchange would affect the world as a whole, rather than just the cities and countries which had been directly involved. In this way, the fate of the world was now tied to the fate of the bomb-wielding superpowers.

Deterrence and Brinkmanship

Throughout the 1950s and the early 1960s a number of trends were enacted between the U.S. and the USSR as they both endeavored in a tit-for-tat approach to disallow the other power from acquiring nuclear supremacy. This took form in a number of ways, both technologically and politically, and had massive political and cultural effects during the Cold War. The first atomic bombs dropped on Hiroshima and Nagasaki were large, custom-made devices, requiring highly trained personnel for their arming and deployment. They could be dropped only from the largest bomber planes—at the time the B-29 Superfortress—and each plane could only hold a single bomb in its hold.

The first hydrogen bombs were similarly massive and complicated. This ratio of one plane to one bomb was still fairly impressive in comparison with conventional, non-nuclear weapons, but against other nuclear-armed countries it was considered to be a grave danger. In the immediate postwar years, the U.S. expended much effort on making the bombs "G.I.-proof"—capable of being used and deployed by members of the U.S. Army, rather than Nobel Prize–winning scientists, and in the 1950s a program of nuclear testing was undertaken in order to improve the nuclear arsenal. Starting in 1951, the Nevada Test Site (in the Nevada desert) became the primary location for all U.S. nuclear testing (in the USSR, Semipalatinsk Test Site in Kazakhstan served a similar role). Tests were divided into two primary categories: "weapons related" (verifying that a new weapon worked or looking at exactly how it worked) and "weapons effects" (looking at how weapons behaved under various conditions or how structures behaved when subjected to weapons).

In the beginning, almost all nuclear tests were either "atmospheric" (conducted above ground, in the atmosphere) or "underwater" (such as some of the tests done in the Marshall Islands). Testing was used as a sign of both national and technological strength, but also raised questions about the safety of the tests, which released nuclear fallout into the atmosphere (most dramatically with the Castle Bravo test in 1954, but in more limited amounts with almost all atmospheric nuclear testing). Because testing was seen as a sign of technological development (the ability to design usable weapons without some form of testing was considered dubious), halts on testing were often called for as stand-ins for halts in the nuclear arms race itself, and many prominent scientists and statesmen lobbied for a ban on nuclear testing. In 1958, the U.S., USSR, and the United Kingdom (a new nuclear power) declared a temporary testing moratorium for both political and health reasons, but by 1961 the Soviet Union had broken the moratorium and both the USSR and the U.S. began testing with great frequency.

As a show of political strength, the Soviet Union tested the largest-ever nuclear weapon in October 1961, the massive Tsar Bomba, which was tested in a reduced state with a yield of around 50 megatons—in its full state it was estimated to have been around 100 Mt. The weapon was largely impractical for actual military use, but was hot enough to induce third-degree burns at a distance of 62 mi (100 km) away. In its full, "dirty" design, it would have increased the amount of worldwide fallout since 1945 by 25%. In 1963, all nuclear and many non-nuclear states signed the Limited Test Ban Treaty, pledging to refrain from testing nuclear weapons in the atmosphere, underwater, or in outer space. The treaty permitted underground tests.

Most tests were considerably more modest, and worked for direct technical purposes as well as their potential political overtones. Weapons improvements took on two primary forms. One was an increase in efficiency and power, and within only a few years fission bombs were being developed which were many times more powerful than the ones created during World War II. The other was a program of miniaturization, reducing the size of the nuclear weapons themselves. Smaller bombs meant that bombers could carry more of them, and thus become even more of a threat against even the most rigorous air defenses, and they could also be used in conjunction with the development in rocketry during the 1950s and 1960s. U.S. rocket efforts had received a large boost in the postwar years, largely from the acquiring of engineers who had worked on the Nazi rocketry program during the war, such as Wernher von Braun, who had been involved in the design and manufacture of the V-2 rockets which were launched across the English Channel. An American program, Project Paperclip, had endeavored to move scientists of this sort into American hands (and kept out of Soviet hands) and put them to work on projects for the U.S.

Weapons Improvement

The first nuclear-tipped rockets, such as the MGR-1 Honest John, first deployed by the U.S. in 1953, were surface-to-surface missiles with relatively short ranges (around 15 mi/25 km maximum) with yields around twice the size of the first fission weapons. The limited range of these weapons meant that they could only be used in certain types of potential military situations—the U.S. rocket weapons could not, for example, threaten the city of Moscow with the threat of an immediate strike, and could only be used as "tactical" weapons (that is, for small-scale military situations). For "strategic" weapons—weapons which would serve to threaten an entire country—for the time being, only long-range bombers capable of penetrating deep into enemy territory would work. In the U.S. this resulted in the creation of the Strategic Air Command in 1946, a system of bombers headed by General Curtis LeMay (who had previously presided over the firebombing of Japan during WWII), which kept a number of nuclear-armed planes in the sky at all times, ready to receive orders to attack Moscow whenever commanded.

These technological possibilities enabled nuclear strategy to develop a logic considerably different than previous military thinking had allowed. Because the threat of nuclear warfare was so awful, it was first thought that it might make any war of the future impossible. President Dwight D. Eisenhower's doctrine of "massive retaliation" in the early years of the Cold War was a message to the USSR, saying that if the Red Army attempted to invade the parts of Europe not given to the Eastern bloc during the Potsdam Conference (such as West Germany), nuclear weapons would be used against the Soviet troops and potentially the Soviet leaders. With the development of more rapid-response technologies (such as rockets and long-range bombers), this policy began to shift. If the Soviet Union also had nuclear weapons and a policy of "massive retaliation" was carried out, it was reasoned, then any Soviet forces not killed in the initial attack, or launched while the attack was ongoing, would be able to serve their own form of nuclear "retaliation" against the U.S. Recognizing this to be an undesirable outcome, military officers and game theorists at the RAND think tank developed a nuclear warfare strategy that would eventually become known as Mutually Assured Destruction (MAD).

MAD divided potential nuclear war into two stages: first strike and second strike. A first strike would be the first use of nuclear weapons by one nuclear-equipped nation against another nuclear-equipped nation. If the attacking nation did not prevent the attacked nation from a nuclear response, then a second strike could be deployed against the attacking nation. In this situation, whether the U.S. first attacked the USSR or the USSR first attacked the U.S., the end result would be that both nations would be damaged perhaps to the point of utter social collapse. According to game theory, because starting a nuclear war would be suicidal, no logical country would willfully enter into a nuclear war. However, if a country were capable of launching a first strike which would utterly destroy the ability of the attacked country to respond in kind, then the balance of power would be disturbed and nuclear war could then be safely undertaken.

MAD played on two seemingly opposed modes of thought: cold logic and emotional fear. The phrase by which MAD was often known, "nuclear deterrence", was translated as "dissuasion" by the French and "terrorization" by the Russians. This apparent paradox of nuclear war was summed up by British Prime Minister Winston Churchill as "the worse things get, the better they are"—the greater the threat of mutual destruction, the safer the world would be. This philosophy made a number of technological and political demands on participating nations. For one thing, it said that it should always be assumed that an enemy nation may be trying to acquire "first strike capability," something which must always be avoided. In American politics this translated into demands to avoid "missile gaps" and "bomber gaps" where the Soviet Union could potentially "out shoot" American efforts (most of these supposed "gaps" proved to be political figments, but this hardly mattered at the time). It also encouraged the production of thousands of nuclear weapons by both the U.S. and the USSR, far more than would be needed to simply destroy the major civilian and military infrastructures of the opposing country.

These policies and strategies were satirized in the 1964 Stanley Kubrick film Dr. Strangelove, in which the Soviets, unable to keep up with the US's first strike capability, instead plan for MAD by building a Doomsday Machine, and thus, after a (literally) mad US General orders a nuclear attack on the USSR, the end of the world is brought about. The policy also encouraged the development of the first early warning systems. Conventional war, even at its fastest, was fought over time scales of days and weeks. With long-range bombers, the time from the start of an attack to its conclusion was reduced to mere hours. With rockets, it could be reduced to minutes. It was reasoned that conventional command and control systems could not be expected to adequately respond to a nuclear attack, and so great lengths were taken to develop the first computers which could look for enemy attacks and direct rapid responses. In the U.S., massive funding was poured into the development of SAGE, a system which would track and intercept enemy bomber aircraft using information from remote radar stations, and was the first computer system to feature real-time processing, multiplexing, and display devices—the first "general" computing machine, and a direct predecessor of modern computers.

Anti-nuclear

Bombers and short-range rockets were not reliable: planes could be shot down, and earlier nuclear missiles could cover only a limited range— for example, the first Soviet rockets' range limited them 'to targets in Europe. However, by the 1960s, both the United States and the Soviet Union had developed intercontinental ballistic missiles, which could be launched from extremely remote areas far away from their target; and submarine-launched ballistic missiles, which had less range but could be launched from submarines very close to the target without any radar warning. This made any national protection from nuclear missiles increasingly impractical. The military realities made for a precarious diplomatic situation. The international politics of brinkmanship led leaders to exclaim their willingness to participate in a nuclear war rather than concede any advantage to their opponents, feeding public fears that their generation may be the last. Civil defence programs undertaken by both superpowers, exemplified by the construction of fallout shelters and urging civilians about the "survivability" of nuclear war, did little to ease public concerns.

The climax of brinksmanship came in early 1962, when an American U-2 spy plane photographed a series of launch sites for medium-range ballistic missiles being constructed on the island of Cuba, just off the coast of the southern United States, beginning what became known as the Cuban Missile Crisis. The U.S. administration of John F. Kennedy concluded that the Soviet Union, then led by Nikita Khrushchev, was planning to station Russian nuclear missiles on the island, which was under the control of Communist Fidel Castro. On October 22, Kennedy announced the discoveries in a televised address, and declared that a naval quarantine would be put around Cuba to turn back any Soviet nuclear shipments, and warned that the military was prepared "for any eventualities." The missiles would have a range of 2,400 miles (4,000 km), and allow the Soviet Union to easily destroy many major American cities on the Eastern Seaboard if a nuclear war were started. The leaders of the two superpowers stood nose to nose, seemingly poised over the beginnings of a third world war. Khrushchev's ambitions for putting the weapons on the island were motivated in part by the fact that the U.S. had stationed similar weapons in Britain, Italy, and nearby Turkey, and had previously attempted to sponsor an invasion of Cuba the year before in the failed Bay of Pigs Invasion. On October 26, an offer was sent from Khrushchev to Kennedy offering to withdraw all missiles if Kennedy would commit to a policy of no future invasions of Cuba. Khrushchev worded the threat of assured destruction eloquently: "You and I should not now pull on the ends of the rope in which you have tied a knot of war, because the harder you and I pull, the tighter the knot will become. And a time may come when this knot is tied so tight that the person who tied it is no longer capable of untying it, and then the knot will have to be cut. What that would mean I need not explain to you, because you yourself understand perfectly what dreaded forces our two countries possess."

A day later, however, the Russians put forward another offer, this time demanding that the U.S. remove its missiles from Turkey before any missiles would be withdrawn from Cuba. On the same day, a U-2 plane was shot down over Cuba and another was almost intercepted over Russia, and Soviet merchant ships were nearing the quarantine zone. Kennedy responded by accepting the first deal publicly, and sending his brother Robert to the Soviet embassy to accept the second deal in private. On October 28, the Soviet ships stopped at the quarantine line and, after some hesitation, turned back towards the Soviet Union. Khrushchev announced that he had ordered the removal of all missiles in Cuba, and U.S. Secretary of State Dean Rusk was moved to comment, "We went eyeball to eyeball, and the other fellow just blinked."

The Crisis was later seen as the closest the U.S. and the USSR ever came to nuclear war and had been narrowly averted by last-minute compromise by both superpowers. Fears of communication difficulties led to the installment of the first hotline, a direct link between the superpowers which would allow them to more easily discuss future military activities and political maneuverings. It had been made clear that with their missiles, bombers, submarines, and computerized firing systems, the escalation of any situation to Armageddon could be done far more easily than anybody desired. After stepping so close to the brink, both the U.S. and the USSR worked to reduce their nuclear tensions in the years immediately following. The most immediate culmination of this work was the signing of the Partial Test Ban Treaty in 1963, in which the U.S. and USSR agreed to no longer test nuclear weapons in the atmosphere, underwater, or in outer space. Testing underground continued, allowing for further weapons development, but the worldwide fallout risks were purposefully reduced, and the era of using massive nuclear tests as a form of saber-rattling ended.

In December 1979, NATO decided to deploy cruise and Pershing II missiles in Western Europe in response to Soviet deployment of intermediate range mobile missiles, and in the early 1980s, a "dangerous Soviet-US nuclear confrontation" arose. In New York on June 12, 1982, one million people gathered to protest nuclear weapons, and to support the second UN Special Session on Disarmament. As the nuclear abolitionist movement grew, there were many protests at the Nevada Test Site. For example, on February 6, 1987, nearly 2,000 demonstrators, including six members of Congress, protested against nuclear weapons testing and more than 400 people were arrested. Four of the significant groups organizing this renewal of anti-nuclear activism were Greenpeace, The American Peace Test, The Western Shoshone, and Nevada Desert Experience.

Initial Proliferation

The United Kingdom had been an integral part of the Manhattan Project following the Quebec Agreement in 1943. The passing of the McMahon Act by the United States in 1946 unilaterally broke this partnership and prevented the passage of any further information to the United Kingdom. The British Government under Clement Attlee determined that it would be essential for there to be a British Bomb. Because of the involvement in the Manhattan Project Britain had extensive knowledge in some areas, but not in others.

An improved version of 'Fat Man' was developed, and on 26 February 1952, Prime Minister Winston Churchill announced that the United Kingdom also had an atomic bomb and a successful test took place on the 3rd October 1952. At first these were free-fall bombs and then there was a missile, Blue Steel, and a later-canceled MRBM, Blue Streak. Anglo-American cooperation on Nuclear weapons was restored by the 1958 US-UK Mutual Defence Agreement. As a result of this and the Polaris Sales Agreement, the United Kingdom has bought United States designs for submarine missiles and fitted its own warheads. It retains full independent control over the use of the missiles. It no longer possesses any free-fall bombs. France had been heavily involved in nuclear research before World War II through the work of the Joliot-Curies. This was discontinued after the war because of the instability of the Fourth Republic and the lack of finance available. However, in the 1950s a civil nuclear research program was started, a byproduct of which would be plutonium.

In 1956 a secret Committee for the Military Applications of Atomic Energy was formed and a development program for delivery vehicles started. With the return of Charles de Gaulle to the presidency of France in 1958 the final decisions to build a bomb were taken, and a successful test took place in 1960. Since then France has developed and maintained its own nuclear deterrent. In 1951 China and the Soviet Union signed an agreement whereby China would supply uranium ore in exchange for technical assistance in producing nuclear weapons. In 1953 China had established a research program under the guise of civilian nuclear energy. Throughout the 1950s the Soviet Union provided large amounts of equipment, but as the relations between the two countries worsened, the amount of assistance was reduced, and in 1959 the donation of a bomb for copying purposes was refused. Despite this, rapid progress was made with the test of an atomic bomb on the 16th October 1964 at Lop Nur, a nuclear missile on 25 October 1966, and of a hydrogen bomb on the 14th June 1967.

Nuclear warheads were produced from 1968 and thermonuclear warheads from 1974. It is also thought that Chinese warheads have been successfully miniaturised from 2200 kg to 700 kg through the use of designs obtained by espionage from the United States. The current number of weapons is unknown owing to strict secrecy, but it is thought that up to 2000 warheads may have been produced, though far fewer may be available for use. China is the only nuclear weapons state to have guaranteed the non-first use of nuclear weapons.

Cold War

After World War II, the balance of power between the Eastern and Western blocs, resulting in the fear of global destruction, prevented the further military use of atomic bombs. This fear was even a central part of Cold War strategy, referred to as the doctrine of Mutually Assured Destruction ("MAD" for short). So important was this balance to international political stability that a treaty, the Anti-Ballistic Missile Treaty (or ABM treaty), was signed by the U.S. and the USSR in 1972 to curtail the development of defenses against nuclear weapons and the ballistic missiles which carry them. This doctrine resulted in a large increase in the number of nuclear weapons, as each side sought to ensure it possessed the firepower to destroy the opposition in all possible scenarios and against all perceived threats. Early delivery systems for nuclear devices were primarily bombers like the United States B-29 Superfortress and Convair B-36, and later the B-52 Stratofortress. Ballistic missile systems, based on Wernher von Braun's World War II designs (specifically the V2 rocket), were developed by both United States and Soviet Union teams (in the case of the U.S., effort was directed by the German scientists and engineers although the Soviet Union also made extensive use of captured German scientists, engineers, and technical data).

These systems, after testing, were used to launch satellites, such as Sputnik, and to propel the Space Race, but they were primarily developed to create the capability of Intercontinental Ballistic Missiles (ICBMs) with which nuclear powers could deliver that destructive force anywhere on the globe. These systems continued to be developed throughout the Cold War, although plans and treaties, beginning with the Strategic Arms Limitation Treaty (SALT I), restricted deployment of these systems until, after the fall of the Soviet Union, system development essentially halted, and many weapons were disabled and destroyed. There have been a number of potential nuclear disasters. Following air accidents U.S. nuclear weapons have been lost near Atlantic City, New Jersey (1957); Savannah, Georgia (1958); Goldsboro, North Carolina (1961); off the coast of Okinawa (1965); in the sea near Palomares, Spain (1966); and near Thule, Greenland (1968). Most of the lost weapons were recovered, the Spanish device after three months' effort by the DSV Alvin and DSV Aluminaut.

The Soviet Union was less forthcoming about such incidents, but the environmental group Greenpeace believes that there are around forty non-U.S. nuclear devices that have been lost and not recovered, compared to eleven lost by America, mostly in submarine disasters. The U.S. has tried to recover Soviet devices, notably in the 1974 Operation Jennifer using the specialist salvage vessel *Hughes Glomar Explorer*. On January 27, 1967, more than 60 nations signed the Outer Space Treaty, banning nuclear weapons in space.

The end of the Cold War failed to end the threat of nuclear weapon use, although global fears of nuclear war reduced substantially. In a major move of symbolic de-escalation, Boris Yeltsin, on January 26, 1992, announced that Russia planned to stop targeting United States cities with nuclear weapons.

Second Nuclear Age

Although it had started before the end of the Cold War, the *second nuclear age*-proliferation of nuclear weapons among lesser powers and for reasons other than the American-Soviet rivalry-really began with the end of the Cold War. India's first atomic-test explosion was in 1974 with Smiling Buddha, which it described as a "peaceful nuclear explosion". India tested fission and perhaps fusion devices in 1998, and Pakistan successfully tested fission devices that same year, raising concerns that they would use nuclear weapons on each other. All of the former Soviet bloc countries with nuclear weapons returned their warheads to Russia by 1996.

In January 2004, Pakistani metallurgist and weapons scientist Abdul Qadeer Khan confessed to having been a part of an international proliferation network of materials, knowledge, and machines from Pakistan to Libya, Iran, and North Korea. South Africa also had an active program to develop uranium-based nuclear weapons, but dismantled its nuclear weapon program in the 1990s. It is not believed that it actually tested such a weapon though it later claimed to have constructed several crude devices which it eventually dismantled. In the late 1970s American spy satellites detected a "brief, intense, double flash of light near the southern tip of Africa." Known as the Vela Incident, it was speculated to have been a South African or possibly Israeli nuclear weapons test,. though some feel that it may have been caused by natural events.

Israel is widely believed to possess an arsenal of potentially up to several hundred nuclear warheads, but this has never been officially confirmed or denied (though the existence of their Dimona nuclear facility were confirmed by Mordechai Vanunu in 1986). North Korea announced in 2003 that it also had several nuclear explosives though it has not been confirmed and the validity of this has been a subject of scrutiny amongst weapons experts. The first detonation of a nuclear weapon by the Democratic People's Republic of Korea was the 2006 North Korean nuclear test, conducted on October 9, 2006. On the 25th of May 2009 North Korea continued nuclear testing, violating United Nations Security Council Resolution 1718. In Iran, Ayatollah Ali Khamenei issued a fatwa forbidding the production, stockpiling and use of nuclear weapons on August 9, 2005. The full text of the fatwa was released in an official statement at the meeting of the International Atomic Energy Agency (IAEA) in Vienna. Despite this, however, there is mounting concern in many nations about Iran's refusal to halt its nuclear power program, which many (including some members of the US Government) fear is a cover for weapons development.

NUCLEAR MISSILES: A SOURCE OF POWER

In 1991, General Sundarji, the Indian Army Chief of Staff, said that the "Gulf War emphasized once again that nuclear weapons are the ultimate coin of power. In the final analysis the US could go in because it had nuclear weapons and Iraq did not." India clearly sees nuclear weapons as a source of power and has made a decision to maintain nuclear weapons and to develop ballistic missiles of various ranges to deliver them.

Indian Satellite & Nuclear Technology

India now is producing and selling satellite imagery on the world market. In 1992, Professor U. R. Rao, Chairman of ISRO said that enormous opportunities were opening for Indian industry to sell satellites, rocket engines and even space launch vehicles for export. Mr. Rao noted that Indian's version of France's Viking rocket engine compares with the best but costs much less. India could, therefore, become a major source of ballistic missile technology and components for countries trying to develop a long range missile capability.

India whose current generation of imaging satellites can take pictures of the earth with 5.8 metre resolution has recently obtained government's approval to build and launch a satellite (Cartosat) capable of taking images with 1 metre resolution. It is expected to cost about 2.3 billion rupees ($49.7 million). It will be launched by ISRO's Polar Satellite Launch Vehicle in 2003 or 2004. The spacecraft is expected to cost less than its predecessor, Cartosat 1 that costs around 2.5 billion rupees.

Expected to launch next year, Cartosat-1 will have two panchromatic cameras for taking pictures with 2.5 metre spatial resolution. The cameras will provide stereo imaging useful for creating terrain elevation maps. Cartosat-1 also will carry a solid-state recorder for storing payload data.

The camera optics for both satellites is being developed at ISRO's Laboratory for Electro Optic Systems in Bangalore. Some Cartosat 2 camera technologies will be tested on India's Technology Experimental Satellite set to launch in 2001.

It would undoubtedly put India in a position where it would stand not too far behind the US and Russia in satellite based reconnaissance and intelligence gathering activities. Seeing these advancements along with India's recent deals with France and Russia for joint production of nuclear submarines, submarine launched missiles and cruise missiles leaves no doubt as to how India plans to enhance its capabilities in space based warning, identification and tracking in the achievement of its nuclear designs. India has expressed particular interest in the Israeli Arrow-2 of the Russian S 300. Recently, unconfirmed reports have suggested that India may have entered into a covert arrangement with Israel to obtain technology related to the Arrow-2.

Conclusion

India's designs to be the dominating power in the region resulted in the development and testing of its nuclear device in 1974. The country has been pursuing a plan to develop an indigenous capability to produce nuclear weapon systems complete with delivery systems based on ballistic missiles deployed from land, air, and sea.

India's missile development programme is well supported and augmented by its space programme, which has already demonstrated its satellite launch capabilities into polar orbits (PSLV), and for geo-synchronous orbit (GSLV).

These launch vehicles could be easily converted to deliver nuclear warheads to about 14,000 km. India has also demonstrated its indigenous capability for communication and environment monitoring, reconnaissance (pre-launch monitoring, as well as for early warning (launch alert) satellites. Such systems are not only highly sophisticated and expensive, and play a very important role in the command and control of nuclear ballistic missile systems.

With INSAT series of communication satellites, and high-resolution remote sensing systems, India is in a position to have a comprehensive system to provide almost instantaneous warning of launch indications. The fact that South Asian subcontinent is geographically compact has significantly enhanced the scope for distributed deployment of ballistic missiles from nuclear submarines.

The above situation has put Pakistan in a very difficult situation with regard to its security and is being forced to divert its resources to negate India's offensive missile program. Fresh acquisitions of the nuclear submarines and missiles has made the matter only worst.

NUCLEAR RISK REDUCTION REDUX IN SOUTH ASIA

Although New Delhi and Islamabad are resuming official talks after the nineteen-month hiatus resulting from the Mumbai attacks, the impulse to promote bilateral nuclear risk-reduction measures (NRRMs) has largely dissipated. India wants to focus on terrorism, while Pakistan wants to focus on water and Kashmir. Other subjects once covered under the previously agreed "composite dialogue" format, including the agenda item on peace and security in which NRRMs were discussed, now appear to be of secondary interest.

Delhi's and Islamabad's mutual disinterest in intensive diplomatic engagement is both understandable and unfortunate. Previous spurts of hopeful engagement have been ruptured by acts of mass casualty terrorism directed by Pakistani nationals against symbolic venues in India. The perpetrators have usually had ties to extremist groups that have not been greatly disturbed by Pakistan's security apparatus. Delhi now expects little to come from resuscitating dialogue, and Islamabad refuses to want diplomatic success stories more than India. All parties, including Washington, the subcontinent's presumed crisis manager, await the next big explosion on Indian soil. In the meantime and in the absence of high-level interventions, cautious Indian and Pakistani civil servants who have been entrusted with the stately process of re-engagement will continue to meet and issue polite press statements.

In December 2001, promising India-Pakistan ties were severed after an attack by Pakistani nationals against the Indian Parliament building, which led to the mobilization of both armies. A subsequent mass casualty attack directed against the dependents of Indian soldiers in May 2002 raised fears of another conventional war on the subcontinent, but the Indian Prime Minister, A.B. Vajpayee, saw a war as doing more harm than good.

At this point, the Carnegie Corporation and the Nuclear Threat Initiative enabled the Stimson Centre to convene Track II workshops to lend impetus to NRRMs on the subcontinent. Stimson convened workshops in 2002 and 2003 with well-connected Indians and Pakistanis, most of whom had previously served with distinction in government positions and military assignments. Among the participants were future national security advisers M.K. Narayanan and Mahmud Durrani, as well as Salman Haidar, V.P. Malik, S.K. Mehra, V.R. Raghavan, Rahul Roy-Chaudhury, Raja Menon, Jehangir Karamat, Najmuddin Shaikh, Shaharyar Khan, and Feroz Khan. A few U.S. nongovernment and academic experts - Peter Lavoy and Scott Sagan, among them - served as facilitators. We met at quiet spots in the United Kingdom because it was easier than hassling with visas for cross-border venues and more conducive to pursuing problem-solving approaches.

At our 2002 workshop, held in the shadow of the "Twin Peaks" crisis, participants discussed two worrisome scenarios - unconventional attacks leading to an escalatory spiral, and a conventional war leading to a nuclear exchange. Back then, such discussions were unusual, even in Track II. But because we focused on the scenario of extremist groups acting beyond governmental control - and perhaps because both governments could no longer be dismissive about this scenario - New Delhi and Islamabad "green lighted" our unofficial discussions.

At the conclusion of this workshop, participants endorsed an ambitious work agenda for their governments, including the following items:

1) Improving bilateral relations
   - o Initiating bilateral dialogue
   - o Establishing a solid bilateral relationship before a crisis occurs
   - o Sharing knowledge of decision-making processes
   - o Increasing transparency in nuclear doctrine and capabilities
   - o Developing a common vocabulary regarding doctrines and red lines
   - o Avoiding conventional war
   - o Establishing a quiet LoC

- Increasing public awareness of nuclear dangers 2) Nuclear risk reduction and strategic restraint

- o Negotiating verifiable agreements on nuclear restraint
- o Negotiating an agreement not to launch missiles during periods of crisis
- o Ceasing bellicose nuclear rhetoric
- o Agreeing not to develop or deploy tactical nuclear weapons
- o Negotiating intrusive treaties relating to nuclear capabilities
- o Avoiding new, destabilizing, nuclear developments

- Giving consideration to provisions found in the Prevention of Dangerous Military Activities Agreement between the United States and the Soviet Union
  - o Establishing nuclear risk reduction centers
  - o Establishing symmetry in nuclear doctrines
  - o Mutually declaring, akin to the Reagan-Gorbachev statement, that a nuclear war could not be won and must never be fought
  - o Avoiding sensitive targets in the event of a conventional war-especially airfields
  - o Refraining from giving pre-delegation of authority to use nuclear weapons
- Conducting similar, scenario-based discussions on the possible use of chemical or biological weapons 3) Safety and security measures
  - o Establishing improved and comprehensive safety and security norms in both countries
  - o Strengthening personnel reliability programs and systems
  - o Conducting nuclear safety and security audits by units that might "check the checkers"
  - o Enlisting third-party facilitation on nuclear security
  - o Stronger understanding by national leaders of their own nuclear capabilities and procedures
- Greater public awareness of nuclear dangers 4) Improving intelligence
  - o Acquiring technology to help provide prompt and accurate information concerning missile launches and nuclear detonations
  - o Refining forensic and diagnostic tools for determining the source and circumstances surrounding nuclear accidents
- Greater utilization of commercial satellite imagery to prevent surprises 5) Communication
  - o Hardening communication channels
  - o Establishing nuclear risk reduction centers in both countries

- Establishing a multi-nodal and multi-level structure of bilateral communication, including a hotline between the employment control committee in Pakistan and its functional equivalent in India
    - o Upgrading the existing DGMO hotline
    - o Establishing a dedicated hotline between the air force chiefs
- Keeping lines of communication active. When they become inactive, it is harder to make proper use of them in a crisis. Hotlines have sometimes been used multiple times daily in previous crises
- Hotlines could have greater utility if they had conference calling capabilities

The 2003 workshop entered deeper uncharted waters by using the scenarios of a terrorist attack using a "dirty" bomb and an improvised nuclear device that produced a mushroom cloud. The discussions that followed prompted a commonly agreed work agenda to reduce nuclear dangers. Our participants agreed to focus on "practicable as well as desirable measures that could be implemented as soon as possible." These included: Establishment of National Risk Reduction Centers in order to: (a) serve as a focal point for the administration of CBMs that require notifications; (b) help revive existing CBMs; (c) provide a mechanism for notifications for new CBMs; and (d) provide a channel of communication that would be utilized regardless of the state of bilateral relations.

Missile-related Measures, including: (a) formalizing and properly implementing the agreement concerning prior notification of missile launches, and formalizing the time line for such notifications; (b) agreeing not to flight test missiles in the direction of the other country; (c) agreeing to flight test missiles only from designated test ranges; and (d) providing advance notification of the movement of missiles for training purposes.

Clarifying Terminology: Government and military officials could meet to discuss terms and definitions with a view toward the joint or separate publication of a glossary. Leadership Declarations Affirming Responsible Nuclear Stewardship: Participants agreed that joint statements at the highest level could help defuse nuclear dangers and facilitate an improvement in bilateral relations. Such declarations might focus on the obligation of national leaders to: (a) decrease or to end bellicose nuclear rhetoric; (b) negotiate and properly implement measures to reduce nuclear dangers, whether bilateral or unilateral; (c) implement improved safety and security measures; and (d) refrain from deploying "tactical" nuclear weapons.

Increasing Awareness of Nuclear Dangers: Participants agreed that greater awareness of nuclear dangers, particularly with regard to the possible acquisition of nuclear materials by terrorist groups, would be advisable.

The 2003 workshop also proposed a work agenda for subsequent Track II meetings. These topics included the impact of new military technologies (including ballistic missile defense) on strategic stability in southern Asia; intelligence, misperception and escalation control; tactical nuclear weapons; and measures to improve command, control, and communication.

Bilateral relations between India and Pakistan subsequently improved. The LoC in divided Kashmir quieted down considerably. Both governments began to take NRRMs more seriously. In 2005, they finalized an agreement on advance notifications of ballistic missile flight tests, and in 2007, they reached an agreement on protocols for nuclear accidents. Helpful ideas were injected into discussions of a Kashmir settlement. Foundation grant makers turned to more pressing problems. And then came Mumbai. This excursion down memory lane was triggered by a press release dated June 24, 2010, announcing that a University of Ottawa-led Track II program with former officials, retired military officers, and academics from India and Pakistan produced an action plan to help stabilize their nuclear relationship. Their "to do" list is indistinguishable from the ones Stimson compiled eight years ago.

Unless India, Pakistan and the United States can summon greater urgency to take preventative measures, eight years hence, after more mass casualty acts of terrorism and more crises, another NGO may see fit to convene another Track II event that produces similar recommendations. For now, Delhi seems convinced that NRRMs aren't worth significant effort, as they do not fundamentally alter the behaviour of Pakistan's security apparatus and the outfits that provokes crises. Pakistan's military leadership sees little sense of urgency to pursue this agenda, focusing instead on more concrete manifestations of security, such as modernizing its nuclear deterrent and preparing to counter India's Cold Start military doctrine. Nor is the pursuit of NRRMs high on Washington's list of talking points, which are dominated by Afghanistan, al-Qaeda, and Pakistan's selective military campaigns against extremist groups.

These well rehearsed arguments leave little room for traction on the diplomatic front. One central irony here is that, if these rationales for complacency are correct, they nonetheless point toward the greater relevance of NRRMs. Moreover, little creativity or heavy lifting is required to add to their number, since preparatory work has already been done.

NUCLEAR SHADOW OVER THE MIDDLE EAST

In the summer of 1984, *Newsweek* published the results of a Gallup poll of hundreds of top-ranking American military officers. Among the questions was this: where did they see the greatest threat of a conflict situation which might escalate to nuclear war? The majority responded clearly: the Middle East.

They might have had in mind those times that leaders of the two superpowers have threatened to use nuclear weapons in a Middle East showdown. According to former Senator Henry Jackson, Harry Truman invoked their presence in the US arsenal when he demanded that the Soviet Union withdraw from Iran after World War II. Nikita Khrushchev brandished nuclear-tipped missiles when Britain, France and Israel teamed up to invade Egypt in 1956. Lyndon Johnson and Alexei Kosygin felt compelled to use the Washington/Moscow hotline for the first time in June 1967, as Israel launched a preemptive attack that devastated Egypt, Syria and Jordan. In late October 1973, as Israel and Egypt slugged it out again in the Sinai and Richard Nixon fought off the Watergate prosecutor, Secretary of State Henry Kissinger decided that the best way to convince Moscow that American war-making capacity remained unimpaired was to call a quick DefCon 3 alert — sort of a nuclear fire drill. Then there was the scene in the middle of August 1980. In response to "clear but ambiguous" indications of a Soviet military buildup along the border north of Iran, American war planners debated the first use of tactical nuclear weapons; the Joint Chiefs told Defense Secretary Harold Brown that the US had "no other" military option to prevent the Soviets from moving south.

In 1984, when Gallup posed his questions, Congress was debating a Pentagon budget that would increase spending for Third World intervention ("power projection" is the budget rubric) by 34 percent, against 13 percent for the military as a whole. The officers quizzed by Gallup knew that some of the "power projection" weapons systems were "dual capable" — able to fire nuclear as well as conventional warheads. The big guns on the USS New Jersey that shelled Lebanon a few months earlier, for instance. The difference between "conventional" weapons and tactical nukes — the "nuclear firebreak" — was fast eroding. The newest conventional shells combined firepower and accuracy to a degree that made them as devastating as nuclear shells, while from the other end of the "conflict spectrum" nuclear warheads had been miniaturized for battlefield use.

Responding to developments such as these, the US Army had formulated a new battle doctrine — the first since World War II. Once the president approves the use of nuclear weapons, operational questions — when and how?are delegated to field commanders. AirLand Battle Operations Manual FM100-5 foresees that: "A relatively small rapidly deployable force with nuclear weapons may be assigned a contingency mission. This force might succeed as a deterrent while a larger, conventional force might deploy too late."

Oil War?

Too late for what? We've all seen the *Time* magazine cover showing an enormous bear, hammer-and-sickle medallion on his chest, reaching down across the Caucasus to menace a dozen miniature oil derricks in the Persian Gulf. Phrases like "oil jugular" trip off the tongues of news anchormen. Buried in the op-ed rejects is the fact that the Soviet Union has for a long while been the world's largest oil producer. Ten years ago, Washington "leaked" a report that showed the USSR becoming a net oil importer by the mid-1980s, with an insatiable lust for "our" oil. The figures, it turned out, had been cooked in the kitchen where William Casey is now head chef.

Suppose the CIA had been right. The Soviet Union needs to import lots of wheat, year after year. Yet the Russians have not taken over Argentina or Canada, never mind Kansas. There are branches of Bank Novostni throughout the Arab world. Moscow has plenty of experience buying or bartering for what it needs on the world market.

The Soviet Union knows very well, because the United States has made it very clear, that any effort to seize the oil of Arabia and the Gulf would lead to war. The Kremlin has demonstrated a very cautious attitude toward any steps that might lead to war with the US — much more cautious than their counterparts on the Potomac. The only situation in which the Soviet Union might move militarily against the Persian Gulf would be if a general war had already started or was truly imminent, to interdict supplies vital to the US war machine.

The national security advisors with their illuminated maps in the White House basement know this better than the rest of us. If we read their "guidance documents" closely, we see that what they fear most are political changes in the Middle East that might affect Western access to the region's resources and markets. Decisions about how much oil to produce, and the price at which it will be available, might be made in Tehran, in Baghdad and in Jeddah rather than in New York or London.

To some extent, the locus of such decision-making has shifted over the last two decades. True, the giant oil companies are still major players (six of these companies are still in the top 10 of Fortune's famous 500, and their profits account for a steady one-seventh of total profits of the 500). The world market has resiliently protected industrial societies against the aberrant behavior of people of color. This is largely because those exercising power in the oil-exporting states are people who see their future linked to the interests of the capitalist West. Shaikh Zaki Yamani, until recently oil minister of Saudi Arabia, is a case in point. The exceptions — Qaddafi in Libya, Khomeini in

Iran — highlight the rule. The enemy in the Gulf, in Alexander Haig's 1981 phrase, is "a change in the status quo." It would be met, he informed a Senate committee and the world, "with the full range of [US] power assets." This was a bit like saying the US would use its "full range of power assets" to stop the tides. Throughout the region, most regimes are tied politically to Washington. But they are not firmly grounded in their own societies.

Here is a world that has undergone radical and wrenching social and economic changes in the last decades, resulting in new social forces, new internal class alliances and new links with the global market. These enormous changes in the structures of society have not received political expression. Arrangements from earlier eras have been petrified in place. It is as if the oil revenues which fueled these social changes at the same time embalmed the presiding regimes. We now have the political equivalent of geological pressures that build up beneath the surface and erupt as earthquakes. We have seen one in Iran, another in Lebanon. Tremors have struck in Egypt, Tunisia, Sudan and Morocco.

Nuclear Options

Washington's cold war perspective invests any change anywhere in the world with tremendous significance for the global contest with the Soviet Union, no matter what its local origins. The Middle East would be exceedingly important to Washington by virtue of its proximity to the Soviet Union, along its southern border, even if there were not a single drop of oil there. This global aspect of US policy engages the nuclear factor in its most dangerous dimension. For nuclear war planning is geared precisely to maintaining and extending influence in a world that can only be partially controlled, a world where Washington's weight has diminished.

Though the Soviets have not correspondingly gained, the erosion of control compels American strategists to pin responsibility for unwanted change on the USSR, and emphasize US nuclear leverage. Henry Kissinger complained after the Black September 1970 crisis in Jordan that if he could not threaten to use nuclear weapons in such cases, "We weren't getting our money's worth out of them." Kissinger, whose first book was *Nuclear Weapons and Foreign Policy*, ordered a new study of nuclear "options" in 1972 "to be sure that America's strategic forces really did cast a shadow on peripheral situations."

Today the enormous US military buildup in Saudi Arabia and the Gulf, largely accomplished under the cover of the Iran-Iraq war, has made Southwest Asia a key strategic theater equipped with numbers and quality of aircraft, radar and nuclear blast-hardened command posts more advanced than those of NATO. And Kissinger, in more recent pronouncements, would have the rulers of the Gulf "understand that we are prepared to protect both their domestic structure and their frontiers, and they need to be given confidence in the means which we will use." In other words, Washington must wire nuclear weapons to the tottering thrones of the Gulf.

Washington's Mutt, Israel's Jeff

US policy in the Middle East, on first glance, presents a paradox. Western material interests are centered in the Persian Gulf/Arabian Peninsula. So why has Israel, the adversary state, counted for the greatest share of US military and economic aid in the region?

Through 1967, Washington did not display this favoritism. The key "intervention assets" in the region were neither Arab nor Israeli but the so-called "northern tier": Turkey, Iran, Pakistan. Arab states like Jordan played specific gendarme roles vis-à-vis the Palestinians, but Israel was kept at arms length.

The June War of 1967 marks a watershed in the balance of military and political forces in the region. Israel's smashing victory led to a new strategic calculation in Washington, expressed by the 1968 sale of state-of-the-art F-4 Phantom fighter-bombers. Set against the US predicament in Vietnam. Israel's impressive performance gave great weight to those in the White House and the Pentagon who argued that a generous military supply relationship with Israel (and Iran) represented the most cost-effective approach to advancing US interests in the region.

Nixon and Kissinger continued to describe US policy as "even-handed," but "protection racket" would be the more appropriate phrase. Yitzhak Rabin, then Israel's ambassador in Washington, boasts in his published diary of his direct access to Kissinger. "Some sources inform me," he wrote coyly on one occasion, "that our military operations are the most encouraging breath of fresh air the American administration has enjoyed recently.... There is a growing likelihood that the US would be interested in an escalation of our military activity with the aim of undermining Nasser's standing.... Thus the willingness to supply us with additional arms depends more on stepping up our military activity against Egypt than on reducing it." Nixon's esteem for Israel was not based on sentiment or electoral considerations, but on its policy of provocation and brutal reprisal against Palestinians and other Arabs. Israel was doing in the Middle East what Nixon wished he could do more freely in Indochina. "Every time I hear of you penetrating into their territory and hitting them hard, I get a feeling of satisfaction," Nixon told Rabin.

The virtues of this approach seemed to be confirmed by Israel's high-profile preparation to intervene in the September 1970 war between the

Jordanian army and the Palestinian resistance. The PLO and Syria, in Washington's eyes, were significant only because they received political and material support from the Soviet Union. The new US-Israeli relationship, in the words of National Security Council staffer William Quandt, was now "seen as key to combatting Soviet influence in the Arab world and attaining stability."

This new vision quickly became operational reality. Key policy decisions in 1971 significantly restructured the military ties between the US and Israel. First, the dollar value of US weapons shipped to Israel jumped nearly ten times: from $140 million in 1968-70 to $1.2 billion in 1971-73. Second, the sophistication of weapons followed the Phantom precedent. Third, weapons sales to Israel had previously been on a cash basis; now Washington extended generous credits and grants. Finally, a little-noted agreement of November 1971 provided American technical support and licenses for Israeli manufacture of sophisticated weapons systems, laying the groundwork for Israel's own military-industrial complex and making it possible for Israel to join the ranks of the world's leading arms exporters.

It is essentially the globalist perspective of the cold war which lends Israel its significance in the formulation of US policy. Regional developments and local conflicts are important only for the impact they are assumed to have on the balance of power between the US and the USSR. This coincides with a greater centralization of policy-making within the national security apparatus. Regional experts ("Arabists") who do not ratify the prevailing geostrategic priorities and prefer to emphasize local dynamics are banished from the corridors of power.

This cold war perspective also lends a certain relativity to terms like "peace." Even people who would not accept for a minute the proposition that peace is the highest priority of the Reagan administration in Central America or Southern Africa do not blink when Reagan talks about "the peace process" in the Arab-Israeli conflict. People assume that the failure to achieve a political settlement owes to incompetence or irresolution, or to the pernicious influence of the Zionist lobby.

But the "peace process" is no more about peace than the "peacekeeping force" sent to Beirut or the "peacekeeper" label that Reagan put on the MX missile. The pattern, rather, has been to reward and encourage the most belligerent political forces in Israel. Washington lavishly endows that country's military establishment and avidly tolerates its most aggressive behavior. Then Washington can turn around and extract concessions and cooperation from the Arab states as the price for restraints on Israel. This "good cop/bad cop" routine has in fact been rather productive, if we recognize that Washington's priority has been to "expel" the Soviet Union rather than bring about a political settlement. Israel is valued precisely for its antagonistic relations with key states in a region of strategic proximity to the Soviet Union.

Armageddon's Shortest Fuse

The wars and feuds that tear the Middle East apart, with terrible consequences for tens of millions of people, chiefly grow out of local and regional struggles and dynamics. Rather than try to resolve the most outstanding political contradictions in the region, Washington has exploited them to build up its military forces in the region, directly and through arms deliveries to key allies and clients. The result is devastation for many and a pervasive insecurity for the rest, as the conflicts continue and the weapons to fight them grow in number and destructive power.

The Middle East is both a potential trigger and target for a war between the US and USSR. The US president and many of his fervent evangelical supporters have varnished the prospect of nuclear conflict in the Middle East with the biblical sanction of Armageddon. Here is where American troops and warplanes have gone into battle under Reagan, against Libya and against Lebanon. This administration tacitly supported Israel's assaults against Lebanon, Iraq and Tunisia, and tried to instigate Egypt to invade Libya. Washington's chief client in the region, Israel, evidently has developed the world's sixth largest nuclear arsenal. Another key US client, Pakistan, is on the verge of joining the nuclear club. Both politically and technologically, the Middle East has breached the "nuclear firebreak."

So far, the unfolding scandal in Washington over arms sales to Iran has been limited to the contradictions this poses for official policy in the Gulf War and the ritual rants against terrorism. The extensive media attention reflects serious conflicts within the administration and the larger establishment to the scheme itself and to the White House attempt to implement it unilaterally. The important roles of Israel and Saudi Arabia in supporting Reagan's contra war against Nicaragua over many years risk becoming footnotes to this Washington power struggle. In all of this, the real scandal has been ignored and overlooked again. This is the phony "peace process," the set of policies that has backed Israeli military solutions towards the Palestinians and towards Lebanon and prompted the hostage situation in the first place. It is the intersection of this policy with the course of superpower relations which today darkens the nuclear shadow over the Middle East.

9

Traditional versus Mechanical Warfare

At the beginning of 1918 a struggle took place for control over the conduct of the war on the Western Front between Haig and his supporters on the one hand, and the British prime minister, Lloyd George and his supporters, on the other hand. One way for Lloyd George and the War Cabinet to exert control over the Western Front was to regulate the flow of manpower, and this was attempted. Another method was to change key personnel at GHQ in France, as well as the CIGS, and this was done. Finally, there was an attempt on the part of certain individuals, particularly Winston Churchill as Minister of Munitions, to change the way the war was actually fought on the Western Front. This took the form of a concerted effort to replace the traditional infantry-artillery form of warfare with a manpower-saving mechanical form of warfare, employing such weapons as tanks, aeroplanes, machine guns, mobile mortars and gas. This potential shift in the conduct of the war generated a stiff debate through the first half of 1918 and beyond, between the mechanical and traditional warfare supporters, particularly over the role of the tank.

Neither Robertson nor Douglas Haig recognized in late 1917 and early 1918 that the Cambrai tank-artillery operation and the German counterattack meant that warfare was changing. In fact, Haig's comment to his wife on the German counter-offensive of 30 November was that it would be good for the BEF officers who were 'getting careless by reason of our uninterrupted successes all this year'. Nor was Haig willing to accept that Russia's leaving the war had altered the balance on the Western Front, so that as late as mid-December 1917, Haig did not expect a German offensive in spring 1918 because of their losses in 1917 of 'nearly a million men against the British alone'. Instead Haig aimed to continue his wearing-down offensive policies of 1917 on the Western Front, although Robertson was less confident about sticking to such a policy. But Haig's point of view really provoked a crisis of inflexibility, in which the past- oriented Commander-in-Chief clearly did not mean to change his structured concept of the wearing-out battle, leading to the decisive offensive at the decisive point on the Western Front.

Haig's inflexibility ran into contrary ideas expressed by Lloyd George and the majority of the War Cabinet, who had enough of BEF casualty figures at Passchendaele and Cambrai (a total of 346,712 according to Edmonds, the official historian), and who decided to gain control of operations on the Western Front. This was all the more necessary because of Haig's deliberate refusal to face the facts—perhaps a psychological defence mechanism; for example, on 2 August 1917, Haig calculated BEF casualties on the first day of the Passchendaele offensive and remarked that they compared 'most favourably' with the attacks at Vimy and Arras. Although Haig himself wrote down the figures of casualties per division employed, he simply ignored the results, which were that the Passchendaele offensive of 31 July 1917 had cost 1,258 casualties per division, as compared to 1,003 for Vimy and 1,170 at Arras. It was not surprising, therefore, that Lloyd George and the War Cabinet decided that one way of gaining control, or at least improving efficiency at GHQ, was to change the staff, and a host of new appointments were made in late 1917 and early 1918—Lawrence as the new chief of staff; Dawnay as Major General Organization; Maxse as Inspector General Training; Cox as chief of Intelligence, replacing Charteris; Hartley to take charge of gas warfare; Wace to organize the disregarded area of Labour; Crookshank to control Transport; Heath as new chief engineer; Dill, Fuller and Nethersole to do liaison and make the staff at GHQ more efficient, and so on. As one member of the GHQ staff later acknowledged with a note of resentment: 'Over a curiously wide range of subjects swept a wave of reform and retrenchment.'

Lloyd George and the War Cabinet also decided to firmly control manpower; to go on the defensive and wait for the arrival of the Americans; to send troops to Italy; to order Haig to take over more of the French line; to form a general reserve; and to unify the Allied command either under a Supreme War Council or under one supreme commander. Haig reluctantly accepted the staff changes at GHQ, but fought against all the other decisions (apart from the arrival of the Americans), regardless of their value and regardless of whether they would enhance the war effort of the Allies, for two reasons only. These were that he wished to retain his overall command of the BEF without outside interference, and he wanted to maintain his idea of an offensive in 1918, preferably in Flanders. Haig's reaction to just one of these War Cabinet policies is worth pursuing.

On the question of taking over more line from the French, Haig mounted a two-pronged defence. On the one hand, he argued that the decision to extend the British line beyond Barisis was really a question of whether he or the Inter-Allied War Council at Versailles was responsible to the government for 'his army'—in other words, whether Haig enjoyed full powers of command or not. On the other hand, Haig argued forcefully with the French that he could not agree to the defensive exercise of extending the BEF's line, when instead he should be going on the offensive. It was better to go on the offensive, and therefore attract double the number of German divisions, than to extend the line and stand on the defensive, which would hold only the same number of German divisions as before. In fact, it was essential to go on the offensive in 1918 on the Flanders front in order to clear the coast as the great strategical objective. Thus Haig's primary objection to the BEF taking over more of the front was because of his projected offensive.

Haig's attitude toward the offensive and his position as Commander-in-Chief also applied to other areas. This was particularly true over the question of his authority. For example, the real reason that Haig did not want a general reserve formed was apparently because this would place a greater authority than his own over his actions, so that Lloyd George could force his views onto Haig. He (Haig) also told Lloyd George that no one could give him orders except for the Army Council and a field marshal senior to him. Thus, as he wrote to his wife in November 1917, Lloyd George would not be able to modify the way 'I carry out my duties here', despite the attempts of the Prime Minister to 'set aside me and my views on military plans'. Similarly, Haig would not hear of the possibility of an Allied Commander-in-Chief, who would of course diminish Haig's authority.

The conflict between Haig and Lloyd George escalated with Lloyd George's speech on 12 November to the Inter-Allied War Council in Paris; with the German counter-attack at Cambrai on 30 November; plus the decision to send divisions to Italy; the creation of the Supreme War Council at Versailles; and the organization of a cabinet committee to take control of manpower in December 1917. So much so, that Haig began to have apocalyptic visions of what was happening. According to Haig's letters to Lady Haig, in late 1917 and early 1918, Lloyd George was afraid of Haig because he had the army at his back, while Lloyd George wanted to discredit him and then break up the army into factions. Haig believed, correctly, that Lloyd George also wanted to get rid of Haig, but was afraid to do so. A little later, Haig thought that Lloyd George wanted to turn Britain into a republic, but to do this he had to get rid of the army first. The only way to do this, considered Haig, was for Lloyd George to discredit the army leaders and put in civilians instead (which he believed had been tried at the earlier Calais conference). Then in early March 1918, Haig told his wife that if he could have a go at reorganizing the House of Commons with the army at his back, with his own audience, and with the press well in hand, he would be popular!

All of this reflected Haig's shaky position at the end of 1917 and the beginning of 1918, and his curious lack of introspection or self-reflection — he simply could not imagine that any criticism directed against his army leadership and ideas might have any merit. (The closest Haig came to admitting responsibility for reverses was to threaten to resign, but perhaps he never actually intended to do so.) Although Haig may have been only half serious in his political suggestions to Lady Haig, his political solutions probably did reflect his real wishes. Strangely enough, Lloyd George may have had the same illusions about the army leadership as Haig had about Lloyd George. According to Lord Beaverbrook, (owner of the Daily Express and Minister of Information), at the end of 1917 'Lloyd George, convinced that Robertson and his military colleagues now aimed at over-throwing the Government and setting up a new administration under Army control, determined that he must get rid of both Robertson…and Haig'. Lloyd George succeeded only in regard to Robertson, who was forced to resign over the creation of a competing military executive in Versailles. Then Lloyd George sent out General Smuts to the Western Front in January 1918 ostensibly because 'he [Lloyd George] did not know many of the various generals at the front', but really with the intention of finding a better commanderin- chief than Haig.

The names of Jacob, Plumer and Rawlinson were suggested as possible replacements for Haig, but the plan came to nothing. This was partly because no one could be found who was significantly better than Haig, partly because enough of the army still had faith in Haig, partly because of the uproar that would be created by Haig's resignation, and partly because Haig was already being neutralized via Military Representatives in Versailles and the forthcoming appointment of Wilson as CIGS, who would act as the 'real' Commanderin-Chief.

So with Haig temporarily secure in early 1918, but with Lloyd George and the War Cabinet exercising greater control over GHQ, especially regarding the question of manpower, what were the alternative strategies for Haig and the War Cabinet on the Western Front? It is roughly at this point in time that an important division of opinion in the army and in London occurs regarding the direction of the war. Although there was general agreement to go on the defensive on the Western Front, and wait for the Americans to arrive, there was also the question of how the rest of the war was to be fought, and how the manpower shortage was to be dealt with. It appears that two basic alternatives emerged, which might be termed the mechanical means of warfare, versus the traditional means of warfare. On the one hand the mechanical supporters advocated the use of 'new' technology (particularly tanks and aeroplanes, but also innovations such as mobile trench mortars, gas and smoke) which would be more efficient and would replace manpower, while the other school of thought stressed the use of manpower (infantry) in the traditional manner, and advocated using more of the 'traditional' technology, such as rifles, machine guns and artillery, but did see the 'new' technology as a useful auxiliary tool.

The underlying causes of this debate were the decisions of the Cabinet and Supreme War Council committees in late 1917 and in January and February 1918 to deny manpower to the Western Front, and the ordering of priorities so that shipbuilding, aeroplanes, tanks and food production came ahead of men for France. Originally, on 24 November 1917, GHQ had estimated that infantry manpower would be 250,000 below establishment on 31 March 1918. One suggestion to deal with this difficulty was simply to maintain 31 divisions at full strength and break up the remaining divisions to supply the original 31 with men. The Army Council rejected this plan, and instead decided on 10 January 1918 to reduce battalions in the BEF from 12 to 9 in each division. GHQ responded by requesting 615,000 men for the Western Front in early 1918, but they received only 100,000 'A' men. Nevertheless, according to one source, a comparison of manpower on 1 January 1917 and 1 January 1918 showed that there were actually only 70,000 fewer fighting men on the Western Front in 1918 than in 1917. This may have been reasonably accurate, since postwar figures prepared by Lieutenant General Sir Herbert Lawrence, chief of staff at GHQ in 1918, revealed that the total of all BEF personnel in France, both combatant and non-combatant, was 1,365,394 on 1 January 1917 and 1,949,100 on 1 January 1918. However, much of the 1918 advantage was due to a large increase in labour from 87,832 in 1917 to 354,577 in 1918. (This, in passing, tends to refute GHQ's claim that it was short of labour before the German offensive of March 1918.) However, looking only at fighting troops of all kinds, Lawrence's figures show 1,077,343 on 1 January 1917 and 983,399 on 1 January 1918, for a decrease of 93,944 between January 1917 and January 1918. Since Lawrence's figures did not include the Royal Engineers for 1917, and since technical troops tended to increase markedly through the war, the original number of 70,000 fewer combatant men at the beginning of 1918 than in 1917 probably was reasonably accurate. In an army of around a million men, however, this represented only a relatively small difference of some 7 per cent. And it was certainly possible to achieve the same efficiency as before by maintaining the same number of divisions with fewer men, but with greater firepower, as in the German army, and as suggested by Foch. This option was rejected by Haig and by others at GHQ. But the key point is that the past-oriented emphasis at GHQ and elsewhere on manpower and wearing down produced the strong impression that the BEF was short of men, and this set the stage for the discussion between the two schools of thought represented by the manpower and mechanical warfare advocates.

The 'new' technology advocates were led by Winston Churchill, who set out his proposals in a paper on munitions prospects, dated 21 October 1917. Churchill concluded that the way to inflict a decisive defeat on the enemy on the Western Front was by mechanical means and not by manpower: 'If, therefore, we could by organized mechanical processes and equipment impart this faculty to our armies in 1918 or 1919 [of advancing continuously], it would be an effective substitute for a great numerical preponderance.' The means by which this would be done involved a further emphasis on artillery, but particularly a development of the air weapon, trench mortars, tanks, gas and railway or mechanical mobility. Churchill also advised applying these mechanical means to what he called the battle of Surprise rather than the 1916 and 1917 battles of Exhaustion.

On 23 November 1917, on behalf of the 'traditional' school, Haig replied to Churchill's document with caution, but argued that the true use of guns, mortars, gas, aeroplanes and tanks, 'is as an aid to infantry. Without sufficient and efficient infantry machinery can neither win victory in offence, nor save us from defeat in defence.' Curiously enough, given that the successful tank offensive at Cambrai had occurred only three days earlier, Haig went on to state that 'Tanks under conditions suitable to their use are of great value and to some extent, for certain purposes, are capable of replacing numbers of guns and economizing infantry. But suitable conditions for their employment cannot always or even often be found.' Haig's conclusion was that 'an insufficiency of infantry cannot be compensated for by a development of machinery beyond a certain point'.

Churchill's paper and Haig's reply were sufficiently significant for a conference to be held on the subject, on 5 December 1917. However, the report of the conference shows that Haig and his supporters in GHQ, as advocates of the 'traditional' school, emerged victorious from this debate. For example, the conference downplayed the importance of tanks and argued that for a large tank attack to succeed, 'Favourable weather, that is misty conditions, seem necessary'. The report conceded that tanks had certain advantages, for example, surprise, but that 'to exploit the Tank to the prejudice of rifle and manpower would be bad policy, and would end in exalting the servant above the arm it exists to assist and serve'. The recommendation was that in future the Tank Corps should be limited to 27 battalions of 60 tanks (1,620 tanks) and an establishment of 22,500 men (as opposed to the then establishment of 18 battalions). The conference concluded by stating that the infantry establishment should first be placed on a footing satisfactory to Sir Douglas [Haig], and that only then should manpower be applied, in sequence, to aircraft, artillery, transport, locomotives, tanks and rope railways.

The argument between the two schools of thought was complicated by a number of factors. Focusing only on tanks as the central feature of mechanical warfare, it was the case that there were several tank designs, with the Mark V, first used at Hamel on 4 July 1918, being considerably advanced over the Mark IV, which was used at Cambrai. The Mark V was particularly improved in the area of steering, so that now one man could control the tank rather than the four men required for the Mark IV.

Therefore, attitudes toward tanks tended to change over time, as the tanks became more reliable. Nevertheless, Haig and the senior staff at GHQ clearly saw the role of tanks as simply existing to assist the infantry, but for two reasons. First, tanks were obviously machines, and being inanimate objects, therefore by definition could not gain or hold ground. And second, stemming from earlier experiences in 1916 and early 1917, tanks were not seen as mechanically reliable and therefore could not be given a major role. These two sentiments were expressed in Haig's November 1917 reply to Churchill, quoted above, and in the GHQ tank policy statement of August 1918, which argued that tanks could only assist the infantry, because infantry 'is the only arm which can seize and hold a position, and upon its skill and endurance depends the security of the defence'.

The memo agreed that tanks could materially assist the advance of the infantry, but 'it is unwise to place too much reliance upon mechanical contrivances'. This document really reflected the way in which the tank, as a piece of technology, tended to retain its original characteristics of adjunct to infantry, and as mechanically unreliable, thereby delaying more favourable views of its potential, just as the evolution of the machine gun was delayed because of its own original mechanical flaws. The GHQ document therefore imagined a past-oriented and manpower-centred battlefield in stressing the need for tanks to cooperate with other arms in assisting the infantry, but contained a hint of uneasiness in admitting that 'As the speed of tanks is developed and their machinery perfected, it is possible that their tactical employment may develop and that their role may become more independent'. But this goal was evidently thought by GHQ to be some way in the future, for in July 1918 the VI Corps commander, Haldane, went to a tank demonstration and remarked that the GHQ staff were anti-tanks and were preventing Haig from seeing them. This may have been partly because there was a push on by the Tank Corps to break up cavalry units and put them in tanks, since there was little manpower available for the tanks.

GHQ's negative but apprehensive view of the growing power of the tanks was further reflected in its ambiguous approach to the Tank Corps. After initially conceiving of the Tank Corps as similar in structure to the Royal Flying Corps, an analogy which Elles approved of (although the War Office did not), GHQ settled down to a contradictory policy of either depreciating the value of the Tank Corps, and thus not issuing a policy on tanks at all until August 1918, or of attempting to take over the tank weapon.

There were many complaints in early 1918 of the attitude of GHQ (and the War Office) toward tanks. J.F.C.Fuller told Churchill in March 1918 that 'GHQ is inert and will lay down no policy', and in June 1918 he reported that GHQ acted as a post office concerning tanks, because it did not know them and therefore could not formulate policy.

Fuller believed that both the War Office and GHQ were devoid of the means of acquiring and sorting tank knowledge and experience. Soon after, Elles declared that the General Staff at GHQ simply 'won't function on Tanks and this has its effect throughout the Army' because 'Armies get no guidance from above except by suggestion'. As late as July 1918, the Deputy CIGS remarked that the tanks 'have never had a policy' from the General Staff. GHQ finally issued a tank policy in August 1918, but it was apparent to both Elles and Major General Sir J.E.Capper (Director General Tank Corps) that the real problem lay in not having a senior tank adviser at GHQ, like the artillery, and in not having tank advisers in each army, again like the artillery. A Supreme War Council document in May 1918 declared that 'the Tank Corps should be represented on the General Staff [GHQ] in the same way as is the Artillery, otherwise there must be misuse of tanks through a lack of understanding of their powers and limitations'. Similarly, a War Office conference in late June 1918 advised the appointment of a Tank General Staff officer at GHQ, and the acceptance of GOC Tanks as tank adviser to GHQ.

Eventually, the War Office itself was reorganized with a tank staff, but at GHQ there was no change. Essentially the Tank Corps was commencing the same long-drawn-out process as occurred earlier with the artillery in fighting for, and eventually being granted, staff advisers at the highest levels. But Haig and GHQ were simply unwilling to grant higher status to a new arm which did not accord with their vision of the battlefield.

UNILATERAL AND BILATERAL ANTI-ESCALATION STEPS FOR PAKISTAN AND INDIA

Unlike Pakistan, India is in a different position when it comes to reducing military tension between itself and Pakistan specifically and in South Asia generally. Its geographical size, central location, and military strength give India a hegemonic influence that it uncomfortably and inconsistently wields. In South Asia's turbulent history, India passed through its most dangerous decades relatively better than others, its smaller neighbors lacking adequate structure and strength to stem crises and wars. Regional security issues compounded also due to India's steadfast reluctance to accommodate its neighbors and to focus on a grand strategy of regional hegemony.

India is still searching for the right strategy to deal with its neighbors, arguably impeding its own rise. Two opposing schools of thought have emerged in the past 2 decades. The first school was based on engagement with its smaller neighbors on the basis of nonreciprocity, also referred to as the Gujral Doctrine.

The second school of thought seeks a dominant posture and assertive policy towards neighbors, as enunciated in the Gandhi Doctrine. India followed both tracks at various times, eventually favouring the hegemonic model. Had India pursued a broad approach of accommodation with its neighbors, it would not only facilitate better regional integration, but the prospects of fostering sustained peace and conflict resolution would be greater as well. A self-confident neighbourhood that has a stake in, rather than a fear of, India's rise is a harbinger for stronger structures of peace.

India enjoys an edge in geophysical as well as qualitative and quantitative superiority over Pakistan. India can choose the time and place for an offensive, and it "is the conventional imbalance that could bring both sides to the nuclear brink." Zawar Haider Abidi explains the Pakistani nuclear posture, which rejects the concept of no first use primarily due to its perceived vulnerability to Indian conventional advantage. A RAND Corporation study endorses the unlikelihood of a change in Pakistan's nuclear posture "without shifts in the conventional balance of forces, requiring CBMs [confidence-building measures] to demonstrate non-hostile intent" (e.g., halting training along the LOC in Kashmir or the prenotification of major military exercises). As argued elsewhere in this chapter, the best pathway to assured nonuse of nuclear weapons is to undertake conventional arms control measures.

India and Pakistan go back a long way in negotiating treaties and elaborate CBMs. Unfortunately, the record of implementation is rather unimpressive. CBMs are no panacea for peace and security, but they are a useful foundation for potential structural arms control agreements. The basic reasons for the failure of CBMs is continuing distrust, aggressive force postures, forward deployment of military units, and continuing violence in the region. As one Indian author says,

> India has significant and identical CBMs with both China (stronger) and Pakistan (weaker) neighbors, the implementation of Sino-India and Indo-Pakistani CBMs have been different. With China, India has had positive experiences, with forces pulled back and tensions eased. India believes this is so because there is greater political will and common desire to normalize relations in the case of China, but not so in the case with Pakistan.

The reasons go beyond the political will: India's and China's force deployments against each other are neither threatening in real time nor accompanied by active violence.

There is also a fundamental disagreement over the approach to peace and CBMs. India insists on transparency of doctrines as an important ingredient to tension reduction, particularly emphasizing a no first-use policy. Since Pakistan refuses to agree to such a step in the face of a superior conventional force, its diplomats concentrate on bilateral conventional and nuclear force reduction steps and India's offensive doctrines and force postures. Subsequently, the process of agreement is extremely slow. Regardless, there are unilateral and bilateral measures the two countries can take to reign in the nuclear risks.

Unilateral Anti-Escalation Measures

Even though bilateral measures have the greater potential to reduce the likelihood of conventional escalation, there are steps each country can take without reciprocity, which could also mitigate escalation. On Pakistan's side, they can go beyond their ill-defined deterrence doctrine by specifically defining (and announcing) specific policies on key issues with appropriate parliamentary backing.

Strategic Weapons (warheads and missiles). Pakistan could make an official strategic doctrine that encompasses its concerns, doctrinal approach, and security obligations. Four main ingredients around which its doctrinal pronouncements could revolve are:

1. Minimum credible deterrence and eschewing of an arms race with India;
2. No first use of force—conventional or nuclear;
3. No transfer of nuclear technology to any state or nonstate entity or provision of extended deterrence to any other country; and,
4. No use or threat of use of force against a non-nuclear state.

Strategic force postures. Pakistan can formally announce that unless the security situation dramatically deteriorates, its nuclear weapons will remain dealerted, its missiles and nuclear warheads will not be kept mated with delivery vehicles (aircraft or missiles), strategic weapons will remain operationally nondeployed, and Pakistan will provide notification of all missile tests. Islamabad should consider broadening its notification policy by including all neighbors of its tests, particularly Iran, Afghanistan, and China.

Conventional forces. Pakistan can formally announce it will not engage in a conventional arms race and will only maintain an acceptable ratio commensurate with its threats; and will not engage in dangerous hot pursuits, surgical strikes, or limited war with any neighbors across recognized borders or agreed lines of deployment (i.e., no more Kargils.)

Low-intensity conflicts. Pakistan should explicitly renounce the asymmetric strategies of using noncombatants in any shape or form as part of its security policy. It should explicitly announce that it will not allow its state territory or territory under its control to be used for training, organizing, preparing, and executing any form of cross-border violence (i.e., no more Operation GIBRALTAR or other forward policy as an extension of strategic depth). Pakistan should offer a joint regional terrorism cooperative centre and open it to all neighbors and likeminded countries.

India, too, has some nonreciprocity steps it can take to mitigate conventional escalation. The South Asian hegemon can unilaterally announce that it will neither cross borders or the LOC (i.e., no more Siachins), mobilize mechanized forces (i.e., no more Exercise Brass Tacks), or undertake coercive operations (i.e., no more Operation PARAKARMs) against South Asian Association for Regional Cooperation (SAARC) members, and that it will only maintain defensive formations within its border areas. This would preclude Brass Tacks-like developments and allow its smaller neighbors, Pakistan in particular, to focus their domestic military operations on counterinsurgency efforts. Furthermore and most importantly, India does have room to renounce its offensive military doctrines such as Cold Start and unlink future doctrines from the concept of limited war under a nuclear umbrella. Also, India's offensive military exercises can be reshaped not to portray Pakistan obtusely as the sole opposition force. Brazen Chariots, an exercise conducted in April 2008, is one such example that continues to harden Pakistan's belief that India's war preparations are Pakistan-specific. Lastly, India has the capacity to take the lead in coordinating joint military and naval exercises that support regional objectives, such as piracy reduction, expansion of search and rescue networks, and support of disaster relief contingencies. Such exercises not only expand the capabilities and skill sets of each country's militaries and actually improve the safety and security of the region, but they expand the breadth of relationships between rival countries, thereby lessening the chances of a conventional or escalating war.

Bilateral or Reciprocal Anti-escalation Measures

On the heels of the unilateral measures hard-to-attain bilateral agreements will not be so daunting. And as far as reducing the risk of nuclear war on the subcontinent, bilateral and reciprocal measures will have exponentially greater success, making them essential ingredients to long-term nuclear stability. Since nuclear war will most likely be a result of conventional escalation, preventing military crises is the optimum goal of bilateral agreements and can be achieved through systematic steps.

First, India and Pakistan must agree to pull back forces that are identified as offensive and threatening to the other. This is not an untenable goal and, even if not entirely successful at first, can have a stabilizing effect. Merely getting together and pointing out what force postures are threatening will create an awareness of issues and attenuate the risk of inadvertently sending the wrong strategic message. After that could come the mutual creation of a "Low Force Zone" in which force deployments will be mutually negotiated and a "No Offensive Forces Zone" as appropriate.

The next series of bilateral steps would focus on the nuclear weapons themselves. However, such achievements are unlikely without outside support for such moves, particularly from the United States and China.

TACTICS WARFARE

Tactics, in warfare, the art and science of fighting battles on land, on sea, and in the air. It is concerned with the approach to combat; the disposition of troops and other personalities; the use made of various arms, ships, or aircraft; and the execution of movements for attack or defense.

Evolution of the term

The word tactics originates in the Greek taxis, meaning order, arrangement, or disposition—including the kind of disposition in which armed formations used to enter and fight battles. From this, the Greek historian Xenophon derived the term tactica, the art of drawing up soldiers in array. Likewise, the Tactica, an early 10th-century handbook said to have been written under the supervision of the Byzantine emperor Leo VI the Wise, dealt with formations as well as weapons and the ways of fighting with them.

The term tactics fell into disuse during the European Middle Ages. It reappeared only toward the end of the 17th century, when "Tacticks" was used by the English encyclopaedist John Harris to mean "the Art of Disposing any Number of Men into a proposed form of Battle." Further development took place toward the end of the 18th century. Until then, authors had considered fighting to be almost the sum total of war; now, however, it began to be regarded as merely one part of war. The art of fighting itself continued to carry the name tactics, whereas that of making the fight take place under the most favourable circumstances, as well as utilizing it after it had taken place, was given a new name: strategy.

Since then, the terms tactics and strategy have usually marched together, but over time each has acquired both a prescriptive and a descriptive meaning.

There have also been attempts to distinguish between minor tactics, the art of fighting individuals or small units, and grand tactics, a term coined about 1780 by the French military author Jacques-Antoine-Hippolyte de Guibert to describe the conduct of major battles. However, this distinction seems to have been lost recently, and the concept of grand tactics has been replaced by the concept of the so-called operational level of war.

Victory through Force and Guile

The tactics adopted by each separate army on each separate occasion depend on such circumstances as terrain, weather, organization, weaponry, and the enemy in addition to the purpose at hand.

Nevertheless, while circumstances and purposes vary, the fundamental principles of tactics, like those of strategy, are eternal. At bottom they derive from the fact that, in war, two forces, each of which is free to exercise its independent will, meet in an attempt to destroy each other while at the same time attempting to avoid being destroyed. To achieve this double aim, they can rely on either force or guile. Assuming the two sides to be approximately equal—in other words, that neither is so strong as to be able to ride roughshod over the other (in which case tactics are hardly required)—a combination of both force and guile is necessary. To employ force, it is necessary to concentrate in time and place. To employ guile, it is necessary to disperse, hide, and feint. Force is best generated by taking the shortest route toward the objective and focusing all available resources on one and the same action, whereas guile implies dispersion, the use of circuitous paths, and never doing the same thing twice.

These two factors, most conducive to victory in battle, are not complementary; on the contrary, they can normally be employed only at each other's expense. In this way tactics (as well as strategy) are subject to a peculiar logic—one similar to that of competitive games such as football or chess but radically different from that governing technological activities such as construction or engineering, where there is no living, thinking opponent capable of reacting to one's moves. To describe this kind of logic, the American military writer Edward Luttwak has used the term paradoxical. The title is apt, but the idea is as old as warfare itself.

The single most effective means available to the tactician consists of putting his enemy on the horns of a dilemma—deliberately creating a situation in which he is "damned if he does and damned if he does not." For example, commanders have always attempted to outflank or encircle the enemy, thus dividing his forces and compelling him to face in two directions at once. Another example, well known to the early modern age, consisted of confronting the enemy with coordinated attacks by cavalry and cannon—the former to force him to close ranks, the latter to compel him to open them. A good 20th-century example was the World War I practice—revived by the Iraqis in their war against Iran in the 1980s—of shelling the enemy's front with a combination of high explosive and gas. The former was designed to compel him to seek cover, the latter, being heavier than air, to abandon it on pain of suffocation.

The need for Flexibility

Thus considered, the principles of tactics look simple enough. However, it is one thing to analyse tactics in the abstract but entirely another thing to put theory into practice under different circumstances, on different kinds of terrain, against different kinds of enemy, with the aid of troops who may be tired or confused or recalcitrant, and amid every kind of mortal danger. As the great Prussian general Carl von Clausewitz said, "In war everything is simple, but even the simplest thing is difficult." Sophisticated tactics require well-trained, articulated forces consisting of different units that are armed with different weapons and possess different capabilities. Next, these units must be subordinated to a single directing brain and must be employed in a coordinated manner following a single, well-considered plan: hence the principle of unity of command.

Even then, tactics are not just a question of executing a plan, however clever and well conceived. In tactics, even more than elsewhere, a commander who can only make a plan and carry it out avails nothing; inasmuch as he is confronting a living enemy, what matters is his ability to adapt the plan to that enemy's reactions rapidly, smoothly, and without losing his grip. Flexibility is thus a cardinal principle of tactics. But flexibility will prevail only if it can be bound by a firm disciplinary framework. Moreover, flexibility and discipline are not easy to combine and can often be achieved only at each other's expense. Other things being equal, the larger and more powerful a given force, the less flexible it will be.

As an armed force exchanges blows with an enemy, adapting to his moves and forcing him to adapt in return, opportunities to take him by surprise should present themselves. Surprise presupposes secrecy, but secrecy may be hard to combine with the rapid action that is often necessary for implementing surprise. Like everything else in tactics, overcoming this paradox is a matter of striking a balance, first in general and then against a specific enemy, under specific circumstances and with a specific objective in mind.

The importance of terrain

Finally, in tactics (as in strategy) there is the topographical element to consider. Land warfare is fought neither in a vacuum nor on a uniformly checkered board. Instead, it unfolds over concrete terrain, including roads, passages, elevated ground, cover, and obstacles of every kind. Victory goes to him who best understands and utilizes the terrain; this may be done by, for example, occupying dominant ground, utilizing cover, compelling the enemy to fight on terrain for which his forces are not suitable, cornering him, outflanking him, or surrounding him. All these methods are as old as warfare, yet at the same time they remain relevant to the present age. On their correct application the outcome of battle depends.

Bibliography

Ajey Lele: *Strategic Technologies for the Military : Breaking New Frontiers*, Sage, Delhi, 2009.

Alam, Aftab : *US Policy Towards South Asia: Special Reference to Indo-Pak Relations*, Raj, Delhi, 1998.

Anderson, J.: *Transnational Democracy: Political Spaces and Border Crossings*, Routledge: London and New York, 2002.

Anil, K.C.: *Military and Democracy in South Asia : Challenges, Politics and Power*, Sumit Enterprises, Delhi, 2009.

Arend, A.: *International Law and the Use of Military*, London, Routledge, 1993.

Asha Gupta: *Military Rule and Democratization : Changing Perspectives*, Deep & Deep, Delhi, 2003.

Ashton, S.R.: *British Policy Towards the Indian States, 1905-1939*, London, Curzon, 1982.

Bajpai, G.S. : *On Cyber Crime and Cyber Law*, Serials Publications, Delhi, 2011.

Bamzai, P. N. K.: A *History of Kashmir*, Delhi: Metropolitan, 1962.

Barber B.R.: *Strong Democracy. Participatory Politics for a New Age*. Berkeley, University of California Press, 1984.

Barmé, Geremie R. *Shades of Mao: The Posthumous Cult of the Great Leader.* Armonk, N.Y.: M. E. Sharpe, 1996.

Barua, Pradeep: *Gentlemen of the Raj: The Indian Army Officer Corps, 1817–1949,* 2003.

Bernauer, Thomas: *Genes, Trade, and Regulation: The Seeds of Conflict in Food Biotechnology*, Princeton, Princeton University. 2003.

Bhargava, G.S., *Crush India or Pakistan's Death Wish*, ISSD, New Delhi, 1972.

Bhattacharyya, S. K., *Genocide in East Pakistan/Bangladesh: A Horror Story*, A. Ghosh Publishers, 1988.

Bort, E.: *Boundaries and Identities: The Eastern Frontier of the Asia*, Edinburgh: International Social Sciences Institute, University of Edinburgh, 1996.

Bradley, John. *Learning to Glow: A Nuclear Reader*. Tucson: University of Arizona Press, 2000.

Brenner, Susan W. : *Cybercrime : Criminal Threats from Cyberspace*, Pentagon Press, Delhi, 2012.

Brownmiller, Susan: *Against Our Will: Men, Women, and Rape*, Ballantine Books, 1993.

Budge I: *The New Challenge of Direct Democracy*, Oxford, Polity Press, 1996.

Buzan, Barry & Eric Herring: *The Arms Dynamic in World Politics,* London: Lynne Rienner Publishers, 1998.

Chalmers, Johnson. *Autopsy on Peoples War*. Berkeley: University of California Press, 1973.

Chandler, David G: *The Campaigns of Napoleon,* Macmillan, New York, 1966.

Chandra, R.: *Judicial System in Mechanical Warfare,* Lucknow, Print House (India), 1992.

Clausewitz, Carl: *On War,* Michael Howard and Peter Paret (trans and ed), Princeton University Press, Princeton, 1989.

Coakley, J.: *The Territorial Management of Ethnic Conflict,* London: Frank Cass, 2003.

Conway, G. 1992. *Sustainable Rural Livelihoods: Practical Concepts for 21st Century*. Sussex: Institute of Development Studies.

Damrosch, L.F.: *Law and Force in the New International Order,* Boulder, Westview Press, 1991.

David Post : *The Rise of Law in Cyberspace,* 48 Stan, L. Rev. 1367, 1996.

David S: *Understanding Information Drone Warfare,* CCRP Publications, Washington DC, 2001.

Debray, Regis. *Revolution in the Revolution*. New York: Grove Press, Inc., 1993.

Dery, Mark. *Escape Velocity: Cyberculture at the End of the Century* . Grove Press, 1997.

Duffy, Christopher: *The Military Life of Frederick the Great, Atheneum,* New York, 1986.

Ellen Herman, *The Romance of American Psychology: Political Culture in the Age of Experts,* Berkeley: University of California Press, 1995.

Friedman, G.: *The Future of War: Power, Technology and American World Dominance in the 21st Century,* N.Y., Random House, 1996.

Gao, Mobo: *The Battle for China's Past: Mao and the Cultural Revolution,* London, Pluto Press, 2008.

Garrelick, Renee. M.I.T. Beginnings: The Legacy of Nuclear Metals. Concord, MA: Nuclear Metals, Inc., 1995.

Garstka, J J and F P Stein: *Drone Warfare: Developing and Leveraging Information Superiority,* CCRP Publications, Washington DC, 1999.

Gast, A. P. : *The impact of Restricting Information Access on Science and Technology* Retrieved October 1, 2008.

Ghosh, Ajoy : *Indo-Pak Conflict : Threat to South Asian Security,* Reference Press, Delhi, 2003.

Gupta, Asha: *Military Rule and Democratization : Changing Perspectives,* Deep & Deep, Delhi, 2003.

Gupta, S.: *Disrupted Borders: An Intervention in Definitions of Boundaries,* London: River Oram Press, 1993.

Hasan-Askari Rizvi, *Chemical Terrorism and South Asia,* Albuquerque, NM: Sandia National Laboratories, February 2003.

Heathcote, T. A.: *The Indian Army – The Garrison of British Imperial India, 1822–1922.* David & Charles. Newton Abbot, Devon. 1974.

Hoffman, Bruce: *Inside Terrorism and Internet Crime,* New York: Columbia University Press, 1998.

Huntington, S.P.: *The China Modernisation Military and the State,* N.Y., Vintage Books, 1964.

Ikram, S. M.: *Indian Muslims and Partition of India*. Delhi: Atlantic, 1995.

Imtiaz, A.: *State and Foreign Policy: India's Role in South Asia*, New Delhi, Vikas, 1993.

Jagannath P. Panda: *China's Path to Power : Party, Military and the Politics of State Transition*, Pentagon, Delhi, 2010.

James Campbell: *Excursions, Adventures and Field-Sports in Ceylon : Its Commercial and Military Importance*, AES, Delhi, 2006.

Joel Moses: *The Computer Age, A Twenty-Year View*.Cambridge, MA, The MIT Press, 1979.

Jones, W.H.: *Government and Politics of India Military*, London, Hutchinson, 1971.

Juvale, R.P. : *Military Strategy and Diplomacy*, Cyber Tech Publications, Delhi, 2010.

Kanjilal, Kalidas, *The Perishing Humanity*, Sahitya Loke, Calcutta, 1976

Kapur, C.K. : *Chinese Military Modernisation*, Manas, Delhi, 2003.

Keane J.: *Democracy and Civil Liberty*, London, Verso, 1988.

Kumar, Raj : *Weapons and Military Technology*, Sumit Enterprises, Delhi, 2009.

Kunju, N. : *Indo-Pak : Nuclear Cold War*, Reliance, Delhi, 2002.

Laliberte, S. : *Security by Example Defend I.T.* New York, Addison Wesley, 2004.

Leena Parmar: *Military Sociology : Global Perspectives*, Rawat, Delhi, 1999.

Li, Zhisui. *The Private Life of Chairman Mao: The Memoirs of Mao's Personal Physician*. Translated by Tai Hung-chao. New York: Random, 1994.

Madan, Nath: *Family and Kinship: A Study of the Pandits of Rural Kashmir*, Bombay, Asia Publishing House, 1965.

Mary, W.: *Military Space Force: the Cultural Dimensions of Authority*, Cambridge, Belknap Press, 1985.

Mascarenhas, Anthony, *The Rape of Bangla Desh*, Vikas Publications, 1972.

Matinuddin, General Kamal, *Tragedy of Errors: East Pakistan Crisis, 1968–1971*, Wajidalis, Lahore, Pakistan, 1994.

Miller, Richard L. *The U.S. Atlas of Nuclear Fallout, 1951-1962*, Woodlands, TX: Legis Books, 2001.

Montgomery, Bernard Law: *A History of Warfare*, World Publishing Company, New York, 1968.

Mookherjee, Nayanika, *A Lot of History: Sexual Violence, Public Memories and the Bangladesh Liberation War of 1971*, D. Phil thesis in Social Anthropology, SOAS, University of London, 2002.

Moon, P.: *The British Conquest and Dominion of India*. London: Duckworth, 1989.

Nair, A. M.: *An Indian Freedom Fighter in Japan*, Bombay, Orient Longman, 1983.

Nevile, P.: *Lahore: A Sentimental Journey*. New Delhi: Penguin, 1993.

Norris, James A.: *The First Afghan War 1838-1842*, Cambridge, University Press, 1967.

Paul Buis : *Internet Security: Professional Reference*. New Riders: Indianapolis, 1996.

Paul T Augastine: *Combating Cyber Crime*, Crescent Pub, Delhi, 2007.

Peter G. Tsouras: *Dictionary of Military Quotations*, Manas, Delhi, 2006.

Pomeroy, William J.: *Guerrilla Warfare and Marxism*. New York: International Publishers, 1996.

Posen, B.R.: *The Sources of Cyber Crime*, Ithaca, 1984, Cornell Univ. Press.

Quereshi, Major General Hakeem Arshad, *The 1971 Indo-Pak War, A Soldiers Narrative*, Oxford University Press, 2002.

Radhakrishna: *Military Ethics: Guidelines for Peace and War*, Sumit Enterprises, Delhi, 2009.

Randall Forsberg: *The Arms Production Dilemma: Contraction and Restraint in the World Combat Aircraft Industry*, Cambridge, Massachusetts: MIT Press, 1994.

Rhodes, Richard, *The Making of the Atomic Bomb*, New York: Simon and Schuster, 1988.

Robert M Cassidy: *Counterinsurgency and the Global War on Terror : Military Culture and Irregular War*, Pentagon Press, Delhi, 2008.

Rosen, P.: *Societies and Military Power: India and its Armies*, Ithaca, Cornell University Press, 1996.

Rothenberg, Gunther Eric: *The Art of Warfare in the Age of Napoleon*, Indiana University Press, Bloomington, 1978.

Salik, Siddiq, *Witness to Surrender*, Oxford University Press, Karachi, Pakistan, 1977.

Samuel P. Huntington: *The Soldier and the State : The Theory and Politics of Civil-Military Relations*, Natraj Pub, Delhi, 2005.

Shaun Narine, *Explaining ASEAN: Regionalism in Southeast Asia*, Boulder, CO: Lynne Rienner Publishers, 2002.

Sidney Fox: *Klaus Dose, Molecular Evolution and The Origin of Life*, New York: Marcel Dekker, 1977.

Snow, Edgar. *The Long Revolution*. New York: Random House, 1972.

Spear, Thomas: *The Oxford History of Modern India*. Delhi: Oxford University Press, 1978.

Spector, Leonard S., *Going Nuclear*, Cambridge, MA: Ballinger Publishing Company, 1987.

Stern, Philip M. The Oppenheimer Case: Security on Trial. New York: Harper & Row Publishers, 1969.

Totten, Samuel et al., eds., *Century of Genocide: Eyewitness Accounts and Critical Views*, Garland Reference Library, 1997

Van Creveld, Martin: *The Art of War: War and Military Thought*, Smithsonian Books/ Collins, Washington DC, 2005.

Verton, D. : *Black Ice: The invisible Threat of Cyber-terrorism*, New York: McGraw-Hill/ Osborne, 2003.

Wheatcroft, Andrew. *The World Atlas of Revolution*. New York: Simon and Schuster, 1983.

William Aspray: *Computer, A History of the Information Machine*, New York, Basic Books, 1996.

Winkler, Allan M. *Life Under A Cloud: American Anxiety About the Atom*. New York: Oxford University Press, 1993.

Zaheer, Hasan: *The separation of East Pakistan: The rise and realisation of Bengali Muslim nationalism*, Oxford University Press, 1994.

Index

❑❑❑